MY ANCESTOR LAWYER

by Brian Brooks & Mark Herber

SOCIETY OF GENEALOGISTS ENTERPRISES LTD

Published by
Society of Genealogists Enterprises Limited
14 Charterhouse Buildings
Goswell Road
London EC1M 7BA

First edition 2006
Reprinted 2008

© Brian Brooks & Mark Herber 2006

ISBN 10: 1-903462-94-0
ISBN 13: 978-1-903462-94-2

British Library Cataloguing in Publication Data
A CIP Catalogue record for this book is available from the British Library

The Society of Genealogists Enterprises Limited is a wholly owned subsidiary
of the Society of Genealogists, a registered charity, no 233701

Cover Image - Foreground: Sir John Charles Frederic Sigismund Day,
(1826 - 1908). He was called to the bar in 1849 and was a judge of the Queen's
Bench Division from 1882 to 1901. He was known as a stern judge,
particularly when conducting trials at the Central Criminal Court in Old Bailey.
Background: An engraving of Lincoln's Inn hall, chapel and Chancery Court
(T.H. Shepherd, *1830).*

CONTENTS

LIST OF ILLUSTRATIONS

THE AUTHORS

Brian Brooks

Brian Brooks is a notary public of the City of London who qualified in 1952, having been educated in England, Australia and France. He retired from full-time notarial practice in 1961 and established a business as a professional genealogist. He was the author, with Cecil Humphery-Smith, of *A history of the Worshipful Company of Scriveners of London, volume II* (Phillimore, 2001), having been Master of that company in 1963. He has lectured on family history in this country, Australia and the United States and is particularly interested in the history of notaries, attorneys and solicitors. He is a Fellow of the Society of Genealogists.

Mark Herber

Mark Herber is a lawyer who specialises in fraud and insolvency investigations. He is currently working for the Serious Fraud Office and for Nardello Schwartz & Co. He is a member of the Society of Genealogists and has been researching his family tree since 1979. He is also the author of *Ancestral trails: the complete guide to British genealogy and family history* (2nd edn. Sutton Publishing, 2004) which was awarded the 1997 Library Association McColvin Medal for an outstanding work of reference.

Mark is also the author of *Legal London; a pictorial history*, and *Criminal London; a pictorial history from medieval times to 1939*, both published by Phillimore, and of three volumes of transcripts of the 18th-century marriage registers of the Fleet Prison and Rules of the Fleet (Francis Boutle Publishers).

ACKNOWLEDGEMENTS

During the years since 1995, when I was originally asked by the Society of Genealogists to produce this work, I have made many visits to the Public Record Office, now The National Archives. I have been most grateful for much help and co-operation from members of the staff there who produced large numbers of records for me.

In addition, all the law librarians and archivists whom I consulted in preparing this work were most helpful and interested in the project. I have to thank Guy Holborn, Librarian of Lincoln's Inn; Stuart Adams, the Reader Services Librarian at the Middle Temple; Ian Murray, former Archivist to the Inner Temple; Mark Jones, Deputy Librarian of Gray's Inn; Christopher Holland, the Librarian of the Law Society; Lynn Quiney, former Librarian of the Law Society; Nigel Ready, former Secretary of the Society of Scrivener Notaries, Melanie Barber, former Deputy Librarian and Archivist of Lambeth Palace Library and Audrey Walker, Librarian of the Signet Library in Edinburgh.

The librarians of the four Inns of Court and of the Law Society have asked me to explain to family historians that their libraries are private institutions serving the needs of the practising bar and solicitors. All requests for information should therefore be made in writing to the relevant librarian whose addresses are listed in appendix I.

I must acknowledge also the assistance I received from Ian Hilder in obtaining some of the information and copy documents from The National Archives, and from Judith Burns who typed early drafts of the manuscript.

Mark Herber made helpful suggestions for amendments to the text, for additional material (for example about the Inns of Chancery and some of the courts) and for illustrations. He then worked with me in the preparation of the final drafts of this work. I am most grateful for his co-operation and the care he has taken throughout.

Above all, I must express my tremendous gratitude to my late partner Michael Davies who spent many hours with me working on drafts of this narrative. Without his encouragement and support I would never have been able to undertake this task at a time when I was running a busy genealogical practice. I am only sad that he did not live to see the work in print.

BRIAN BROOKS
December 2005

I would like to thank Brian Brooks for inviting me to assist him in the completion of this book, which I hope will be of great interest to family historians (and perhaps to many members of the legal profession). I am also grateful to John Titford who has for many years provided me with a constant stream of documents and information about all aspects of genealogy. I must also thank Else Churchill, the Genealogy Officer of the Society of Genealogists, for her helpful comments on the text of this book, Matthew Gillespie for undertaking the lengthy task of proofing the final draft and Nick Newington-Irving for preparing the index.

MARK HERBER
January 2006

INTRODUCTION

Most people who are interested in genealogy probably agree that the erosion from publications and lectures on family history of the Victorian addiction to inaccurate pedigrees based on snobbery and a desire to connect one's own family with medieval noblemen is both welcome and refreshing. As a consequence, many family historians now research their less fortunate or illustrious ancestors and the documents that record them, for example census returns, parish registers, workhouse records and settlement certificates.

However, there is also a growing interest in middle class occupations and it is therefore a pleasure to write about lawyers and their records for the 'My ancestor' series of books being published by the Society of Genealogists. Although several histories exist of the two main branches of the legal profession – barristers and solicitors – there is no publication written specifically for family historians that reviews the records (particularly the law courts' records) in which a genealogist may obtain information about an ancestor who was a lawyer. This book is intended to fill that gap and to complement Guy Holborn's excellent work *Sources of biographical information on past lawyers* (British and Irish Association of Law Librarians, 1999) referred to below as *'Holborn's sources'*.

Some researchers will know that an ancestor was a lawyer. In other cases, an ancestor's career as a lawyer may be revealed in documents such as civil registration records, census returns, parish registers or wills. The fact that an ancestor was a lawyer may make research much easier. Lawyers tended to come from prosperous families. The proportion of lawyers who left wills was therefore much greater than in the population generally and so you are more likely to find an ancestor's will if he was a lawyer than if he was a shoemaker or miner. Their wills are more likely to have been proved in the Prerogative Court of Canterbury than in the lower courts, and they are easy to find since all registered copies of PCC wills, held at TNA, are available online. Similarly, lawyers were also more likely than most people to marry by licence (rather than banns) and to own a house. Searches in marriage licence and property records are therefore also likely to be more productive than for other ancestors.

Many published works are referred to in this book. Most of them are available at the Society of Genealogists, The National Archives, Guildhall Library or other good reference libraries. Some of the sources noted are available only in the libraries of the four Inns of Court and of the Law Society. As noted above, those libraries are private institutions and all requests for information should therefore be made in writing to the relevant librarian.

A researcher whose ancestor was a lawyer also has the advantage of many records that are peculiar to the legal profession. For example, there are published lists of lawyers dating from the late eighteenth century to the present day. The Inns of Court and the Inns of Chancery (the institutions in which many lawyers were trained) maintained records of their members. There are also records of lawyers being admitted to practise the law (some of these surviving with records of the law courts and some having been maintained by the Law Society).

Some law firms have deposited their records (evidencing their work and their clients' affairs) at local archives. Many lawyers also had other roles in the community, as local politicians or administrators, as trustees of charities or as stewards for landowners. In such cases, a diligent researcher may be able to locate substantial records of a legal ancestor's life and work.

No book on a specialised genealogical subject would be complete without reference to the basic records used by family historians. These include civil registration records of births, marriages and deaths, census returns, parish registers, probate records, marriage licence records and the extensive collections in the library of the Society of Genealogists in London and the Family history library in Salt Lake City. They are described in general guides such as M. Herber, *Ancestral trails: the complete guide to British genealogy and family history* (2nd edn. Sutton Publishing, 2004), referred to below as *'Herber's Ancestral trails'* and in J. Cole and J. Titford, *Tracing your family tree* (4th edn. Countryside Books, 2002).

A genealogist learns the importance of checking any references that he finds. It is worth mentioning two instances where checking basic records against particular records of lawyers produced interesting results. The first concerns the baptism registers for 1813-18 of St James, Clerkenwell, when the occupation of the father is shown in every entry. The father is described as an attorney in 11 entries and as a solicitor in seven entries. Only five of those 18 lawyers can be found in contemporaneous law lists. Perhaps those who do not figure in law lists were in reality only lawyers' clerks rather than qualified lawyers. A second instance where cross-referencing produces interesting results is the tendency, which is not infrequent, for certificates issued by the General Register Office to render the occupation 'sawyer' as 'lawyer'. A capital L and a capital S in nineteenth century writing are easy to confuse.

This volume describes the records of lawyers in England, Wales, Ireland and Scotland (and of English lawyers in India). The writers hope that it will help its readers to discover more about the lives of their ancestors who were in the legal profession.

GLOSSARY AND ABBREVIATIONS

Advocate A person entitled to plead for another before a court. Until the nineteenth century used particularly for those appearing before the ecclesiastical courts.

Affidavit A statement in writing and on oath, sworn before someone who has authority to administer an oath.

Appeal A complaint to a superior court about an injustice done by an inferior court. The party complaining is known as the appellant; the other party is the respondent.

Articled clerk A person bound by a written agreement, known as an indenture or deed of articles, to serve as an apprentice with a practising attorney or solicitor, prior to being admitted himself. Articled clerks are now known as trainee solicitors.

Attorney A person entitled to act for another. Professional attorneys acted for others in legal proceedings before the common law courts.

Bar The place where advocates stand in court to speak for their clients, thus the terms 'barrister' and being 'called to the bar'.

Barrister A person called to the bar by the Inns of Court, giving rights of audience in all courts of England and Wales.

Common law The ancient unwritten law of the kingdom as embodied in judicial decisions.

Conveyance The transfer of ownership of land from one party to another, or the written document by which the transfer is effected.

Counsel A barrister or (in Scotland) an advocate.

Easter term See 'law terms'; for example 4 May to 30 May in 1808 and from 15 April to 8 May from 1831 until 1875.

Equity Rules of justice and fairness that were intended to ameliorate the harshness of certain aspects of the common law.

Fiat An order, usually of a judge.

Hilary term See 'law terms'; for example 23 January to 12 February in 1808 and from 11 to 31 January from 1831 until 1875.

Justice of the peace A person entrusted with the commission of the peace in a county, city or other jurisdiction; also now called a magistrate.

Justices Officers deputed by the Crown to administer justice and do right by way of judgment; for example justices of the High Court and justices of the peace.

Law terms	The four periods, the Easter term, Hilary term, Michaelmas term and Trinity term when the courts sat each year until 1875. The dates of each term varied as did the feast or holy days by which they were calculated.[1] From 1831, the dates of terms were fixed and in 1875, the law terms were replaced by law sittings with the dates governed by rules of court.
Magistrate	A person entrusted with the commission of the peace in a county, city or other jurisdiction; sometimes still known as a justice of the peace.
Michaelmas term	See 'law terms'; for example 6 to 28 November in 1808 and from 2 to 25 November from 1831 until 1875.
Protonotaries	Senior court clerks (sometimes noted as prothonotaries).
Recorder	The principal legal officer of a town or city which has been granted the right to have such an officer. The Crown also appoints recorders to act as part-time judges of the Crown Court (they may also sit as judges of county courts and of the High Court).
Serjeant	The serjeants (sometimes known as serjeants at law) were senior advocates who were members of Serjeant's Inn and who had the exclusive right to appear as advocates before the Court of Common Pleas until the nineteenth century. The Common Serjeant of the City of London was not a serjeant at law but was (and remains) a judicial officer in the City, ranking below the Recorder of the City of London.
Sheriff	The Crown's chief bailiff or officer in a county.
Solicitor	Originally a person who undertook legal work in respect of actions in the Court of Chancery. Since 1875, both attorneys and solicitors have been known as solicitors of the Supreme Court, being admitted by certificate and entitled to provide legal services for reward.
Trinity term	See 'law terms'; for example 17 June to 6 July in 1808 and from 22 May to 12 June from 1831 until 1875.

CUP: Cambridge University Press

FFHS: The Federation of Family History Societies

PRO: The Public Record Office, Kew, now named The National Archives

SoG: The Society of Genealogists

TNA: The National Archives at Kew, formerly named the Public Record Office.

A. THE LEGAL PROFESSION IN ENGLAND AND WALES: A GENERAL HISTORY

Most lawyers in England and Wales are members of the two main branches of the legal profession, that is either barristers or solicitors. There are now 116,000 solicitors (over 93,000 of them practising) and over 11,000 barristers. Solicitors deal with members of the public on a day to day basis. They may be general practitioners dealing for example with conveyancing, wills, civil litigation, divorce and the defence of those charged with criminal offences, or they might specialise in one or more areas of the law. Barristers are trained in the art of advocacy before the courts (and for many years had exclusive rights of audience before the higher English courts). Most barristers also specialise in certain legal subjects. Until recent times, only barristers were eligible to be appointed as judges of most of the courts.

In order to understand the structure and procedure of the English courts (and the history of the legal profession) family historians should be aware of the distinctions between civil law, the common law and equity. The civil law was derived from Roman law and was applied in the ecclesiastical courts, in respect of matters such as probate and matrimonial causes (until those were transferred to the secular courts in the nineteenth century). For centuries, however, most English courts, such as the Court of King's Bench or the Court of Common Pleas, applied the common law of England (that is common to all parts of the realm) which was developed by judges' decisions and supplemented by Acts of Parliament. Both the substance and procedure of the common law resulted in many injustices. For example, the rights of beneficiaries under a trust would not be enforced against trustees. In order to remedy these injustices, certain courts (most importantly the Court of Chancery) began to apply the principles of equity, that is rules of justice and fairness. A litigant might therefore obtain a different result if he started legal proceedings in the Court of Chancery rather than in a common law court. This situation continued until the Judicature Act of 1873 (which took effect in 1875). This act merged the courts of common law and the courts of equity into one, the High Court of Justice, and declared that in the event of a conflict, the rules of equity should apply. The High Court, the Court of Appeal and the Crown Court together constitute the Supreme Court of Judicature.

By the twelfth and thirteenth centuries, the legal profession consisted of a number of groups. The main division was between the civil lawyers and the common lawyers. The civil lawyers studied civil law at Oxford or Cambridge universities and then practised civil law in the ecclesiastical courts. The common lawyers practised the common law and consisted of four groups; judges, serjeants at law, apprentices of the law (also known as apprentices at law) and attorneys. The universities did not teach the common law (the

1

first degree offered was by Oxford University in 1850) and so the common lawyers trained from medieval times at the four Inns of Court in London, that is Lincoln's Inn, the Middle Temple, Inner Temple and Gray's Inn. In addition, the Inns (or Houses) of Chancery were training institutions that were attended by many lawyers before they entered one of the Inns of Court.

The serjeants at law were advocates and had an exclusive right to appear before the Court of Common Pleas (originally the most important of the common law courts) until the late nineteenth century. Apprentices at law were not apprenticed to another person but to the law itself and as the amount of litigation in the courts increased, they began working as advocates and pleaders in certain courts, particularly the Court of King's Bench.

By 1590, the judges accepted that an apprentice's membership of one of the Inns of Court and the 'call' by his Inn of that apprentice to the bar, was sufficient qualification for him to be granted audience before the courts. He could then appear as an advocate in any English court (except, until 1846, in the Court of Common Pleas). In due course, an apprentice at law might be raised to the rank of serjeant at law. The term of apprenticeship was gradually reduced by the judges from 12 years' membership of an Inn to two years (it is now one year for law graduates who pass the Bar examinations). By the end of the sixteenth century, an apprentice at law who had been called to the bar became known as an "utter barrister" or more usually a "barrister" or "barrister at law". Students were also known as "inner barristers".

Attorneys have existed in England and Wales since the twelfth century when it was found necessary for disputes to be settled in ways other than by personal confrontation. By 1181 it was common practice for a litigant to appear in court and to appoint someone, an 'attorney', to conduct his case for him. The word attorney comes from the Norman-French 'attournée', meaning a man who attorns to defend or prosecute a suit. A litigant might choose any man as his attorney, perhaps his neighbour or a local man who could read and write. However, by the late thirteenth century there was a class of men who acted as professional attorneys in exchange for payment. Attorneys worked in the common law courts, such as the Court of Common Pleas and the Court of King's Bench and were officers of those courts.

Whereas barristers had to be near the courts in which they worked (principally in London or other large cities), attorneys were based near their clients and travelled to court when necessary. Attorneys were therefore soon found in most cities and towns across the country.

The introduction into the law of the principles of equity resulted in the rise of a further group of lawyers. Solicitors worked in the courts of equity, particularly in the Court of Chancery, assisting litigants to conduct their cases. The origin of the term 'solicitor' is also Norman-French and comes from the word 'sollicitur' which is derived from the Latin 'solicitare' – to urge or solicit. Solicitors were sometimes employed in the fifteenth century as assistants to substantial landowners or attorneys. However they had no formal status and were not treated as officers of the court. Solicitors were not mentioned in any statute until the Attorneys Act of 1605 that required them merely to be of sufficient and honest disposition. Solicitors soon came to carry out the same functions (in the courts of equity) as those carried out by attorneys in the common law courts. During the seventeenth century, the standing of solicitors improved and some men, particularly in London, practised as both attorneys and solicitors.

Although only the serjeants and barristers had rights of audience before the superior English courts, attorneys and solicitors did engage in advocacy. Attorneys had rights of audience before many courts of local jurisdiction around the country, for example at sessions of the justices of the peace (later named Magistrates' Courts), borough courts and in the county courts established in 1846. Even in the superior courts, many hearings were conducted by court officials rather than by judges. For instance, in the Court of King's Bench and Court of Common Pleas (the two busiest courts), many procedural matters were dealt with on motions argued by attorneys. Solicitors made similar applications in the Court of Chancery.

In the sixteenth century, the barristers began to try to exclude attorneys and solicitors from the Inns of Court and restrict them to the Inns of Chancery. The first attempt was an order made in 1555 by Middle Temple declaring that:

> *no common attorney should be admitted to the Company and in all admissions it should be implied that every gentleman, when he refuseth study [in order] to practice attorneyship, shall be dismissed from this Company and shall have liberty to go and resort to the House of Chancery whence he came.*

Lincoln's Inn and Inner Temple made similar orders. However, they were not strictly enforced (in part because many barristers and attorneys were related to each other) and many attorneys remained members of the Inns of Court. It also became more difficult for attorneys to become barristers. By the end of the eighteenth century the Inns of Court required a gap between a man's cessation of practice as an attorney and his call to the bar. The imposition of this gap, when an attorney could not earn legal fees, made a transfer to the bar less attractive for practitioners. Attorneys and solicitors were finally excluded from the Inns of Court in 1828 but exceptions were still made. For example,

William Gregory was admitted as a solicitor in 1845 and became President of the Law Society. Both he and his brother had kept terms in Lincoln's Inn while they were articled clerks (their period of training).

During the seventeenth century, attorneys became more numerous and complaints were made about excessive numbers of them being in practice. In 1633 the Court of Common Pleas made a rule requiring a person to serve as a clerk to an attorney for six years before he could be admitted to practice. In 1654 the judges prescribed an apprenticeship of five years, followed by an examination. However these examinations were not always insisted upon, as Sir William Dugdale noted in *Origines juridiciales or historical memorials of the English laws, courts of justice, forms of tryall ... also a chronology of the Lord Chancellors, justices [etc]* (1666), because;

> *a judge considers every attorney he admits as a new client who may bring him business, and therefore his lordship is not severe respecting the attorney's knowledge, the want of which tends to increase the business of the judge's chambers.*

By the beginning of the eighteenth century the judges had become anxious about the activities of attorneys. John Evelyn noted in his diary in 1700 that the House of Commons had;

> *voted that the exorbitant number of attorneys be lessened, now indeed swarming and ... eating out of the estates of people, provoking them to go to law.*

In addition there were complaints that unqualified persons were practising as attorneys. The situation was greatly improved by the 'Act for the better regulating of attorneys and solicitors' in 1729. This provided that no person could be admitted as an attorney or solicitor without having served articles of clerkship for five years with a qualified practitioner, who was not to have more than two clerks at any one time. Any infringement of this statute was punishable by a fine of £500. It was also enacted that attorneys should not;

> *admit into their offices any persons to be their clerks whose parents or themselves have not freehold estates in lands, tenements or hereditaments of the value of £40 per annum or are not worth £1000 in money.*

Researchers with Catholic ancestors will find that very few of them practised law between 1673 and 1791. As officers of the court, attorneys had long had to swear an oath before being admitted to practise in a court but the Test Act of 1673 also required persons holding an office 'under his Majesty' and those called to the bar to take the oaths of supremacy and allegiance. This prevented Catholics from acting as attorneys or barristers until the requirement for the oaths was abolished in 1791. Catholics were able to act as solicitors until 1729 (and as conveyances and special pleaders, described below).

From 1785, attorneys and solicitors were required to take out practising certificates each year. The records that relate to the issue of these certificates are considered later. However, this also enabled the production of annual lists - the law lists - of those men entitled to practise.

The four Inns of Court, of which barristers were members (and which remain responsible for the new entrants to the barristers' profession), continued to thrive. Many attorneys continued to train at the Inns of Chancery but those institutions gradually decayed in the eighteenth and nineteenth centuries. Their limited educational role passed to the Law Society (formed in 1825) that also became responsible for the training, conduct and regulation of all attorneys and solicitors practising in England and Wales.

As noted, the Judicature Act of 1873 merged the courts of common law and the courts of equity in 1875. The distinction between solicitors and attorneys came to an end and the term attorney was abolished, being replaced by 'solicitor of the Supreme Court'.

Most barristers are sole practitioners. They are not permitted to form partnerships but most have rooms in shared chambers, dividing expenses (for example the cost of employing clerks) between them. Barristers are permitted to take paid employment, for example in government or commercial organisations, and many are now employed in the public and private sectors.

Historically, most attorneys and solicitors worked as sole practitioners (but could also be employed in government or in commercial organisations). However, they were permitted to form partnerships and by 1800, firms of attorneys or solicitors with two, three or four partners were common, particularly in cities. They might also employ younger attorneys or solicitors and one or more clerks. As years passed, some firms became larger, with perhaps 10 or 20 partners and many employees. More solicitors were also employed in central government, by local authorities and by commercial or other organisations.

A major change occurred in 1919 when the Sex Disqualification (Removal) Act opened the legal profession to women and it was in 1922 that the first women (Ivy Williams and Carrie Morrison respectively) were called to the Bar and admitted as a solicitor in England. Many women now serve as judges and over half of new English solicitors are women.

Many people advocate a merger of the two main branches of the legal profession, principally on the ground of reducing costs for members of the public who need legal services. However, it is generally accepted that the division of the profession between solicitors and barristers results in a higher level of legal expertise being available to the public and so the profession remains divided today. Most lawyers are either solicitors (regulated by the Law Society) or barristers (members of the Inns of Court). However, it is common for a solicitor to re-qualify as a barrister, or vice-versa, and solicitors continue to press for extended rights of advocacy (solicitors with suitable experience may now obtain rights of audience before the High Court).

The legal profession has continued to evolve in order to provide consumers (whether individuals or businesses) with the legal services that they require. In recent years, two further groups of lawyers have developed, known as legal executives and licensed conveyancers, with separate systems of training and their own regulatory bodies. Lawyers have always employed clerks to assist them; whether in copying documents, lodging papers at court or even undertaking certain legal work (for example conveyancing, the formation of companies and some litigation). Many of these 'unadmitted' law clerks may be incorrectly noted in genealogical records as lawyers. Law clerks set up their own societies, for example the National Federation of Law Clerks and (in 1928) the Solicitors Managing Clerks Society which in 1968 became The Institute of Legal Executives. By 1991, the institute had over 21,000 fellows, members and students. The end of the solicitors' monopoly in conveyancing in 1984 resulted in the appearance of licensed conveyancers, regulated by the Council for Licensed Conveyancers. Law clerks, legal executives and licensed conveyancers are not dealt with in this book because of their relatively recent origin and because very few records about them (except for lists in published legal directories) are publicly available.

Another recent development has been the enormous growth of some law firms and the internationalisation of legal services. Two hundred years ago, most English attorneys and solicitors were sole practitioners or in partnership with one, two or three other lawyers. Thousands of British lawyers are still sole practitioners or partners in small firms. However, many British law firms have offices in two, three or more cities and a firm of 100 lawyers is not unusual. The largest London firms of lawyers, such as Clifford Chance, Linklaters & Paines and Allen & Overy, each have over 2,000 lawyers and many offices around the world. The lawyers in those firms include many who are qualified in jurisdictions as diverse as the United States, Germany, Russia and China. Other British law firms have formed international alliances with foreign law firms and many foreign law firms, particularly American firms, have established offices in London and have British partners and employees.

B. LAWYERS: THEIR SOCIETIES, INSTITUTIONS AND RECORDS

B1. JUDGES

Judges of the English and Welsh courts are appointed by the Lord Chancellor. Historically, judges were chosen from the ranks of barristers, and so information about them can be found in the records of barristers, considered below. However, in recent years solicitors have also become eligible for appointment.

Judges who sat from 1272 to 1900 in the superior courts, such as the Court of Common Pleas, the Court of Chancery, the Court of King's Bench, the High Court of Justice and the Court of Appeal, are listed in J. Sainty, *The judges of England 1272-1900: a list of judges of the superior courts* (Selden Society, 1993). Judges are also listed in published law lists, described below, that date from the late eighteenth century.

Detailed biographies of judges up to the mid-nineteenth century appear in E. Foss, *The judges of England; with sketches of their lives* (9 vols. John Murray, 1848-64) or in the abridged version, E. Foss, *Biographia juridica, a biographical dictionary of the judges of England 1066-1870* (John Murray, 1870). Biographies of later judges are contained in A.B. Schofield, *Dictionary of legal biography 1845-1945* (Barry Rose, 1998). Biographical dictionaries of Welsh and Irish judges are noted below.

Many senior judges have also been the subject of more detailed works. Biographies of those men appointed as Lord Chancellor are contained in four works:

- J. Campbell, *The lives of the Lord Chancellors and Keepers of the Great Seal of England from the earliest times to the reign of [King George IV] Queen Victoria* (John Murray, 1845-68), the various editions are described in *Holborn's sources*
- J.B. Atlay, *The Victorian Chancellors* (Smith Elder, 1906-08),
- R.F.V. Heuston, *Lives of the Lord Chancellors 1885-1940* (Clarendon Press, 1964), and
- R.F.V. Heuston, *Lives of the Lord Chancellors 1940-1970* (Clarendon Press, 1987).

Biographies of the men who have held the office of Lord Chief Justice are contained in the various editions of J. Campbell, *The lives of the Chief Justices of England from the Norman conquest till the death of Lord Tenterden* (John Murray, 1849-74).

Most judges are also included in biographical dictionaries (described in section C.2), such as *The Dictionary of National Biography* and the various editions of *Who's who* and

Who was who. Biographies of many judges have also been published and they can be located through the lists noted in *Holborn's sources* or, by the name of the judge, in catalogues of reference libraries.

Most cities and boroughs had the right to have their own quarter sessions (the equivalent of the counties' quarter sessions before justices of the peace) and courts of record (mainly for small debt claims). They also had the right to appoint judges of those courts, usually known as recorders. Many recorders (whose duties were only part-time) were barristers. The published law lists include lists of recorders; for example the *Law list 1856* noted William Henry Bodkin, a barrister of King's Bench Walk in the Temple, as the Recorder of Dover.

County courts were also established throughout England and Wales by statute in 1846. Lists of county court judges are also included in the law lists. County court judges from 1846 to 1888 are also listed in J. Haydn, *The book of dignities, containing lists of the official personages of the British Empire* (3rd edn. W.H. Allen, 1894). Later sections of this book deal with the ecclesiastical courts and with the records of lawyers and the courts in Scotland, Ireland and India. Haydn's work also includes lists up to the 1880s of judges who sat in Irish courts, in some church courts (the Court of Arches, the Prerogative Court of Canterbury and the Consistory Court of London) and in the Supreme Courts (later the High Courts) of Bengal, Madras and Bombay in India.

Published law reports (described in section E.5 below), that is reports of many cases decided by the courts since medieval times, usually record the names of the judges who heard a particular case and record the text of their judgments.

B2. BARRISTERS

Historically, the bar was a small group of men; there were only about 230 barristers in 1780. However, the bar expanded rapidly in later years (as did the legal profession generally) so that there are now over 11,000 barristers.

Barristers (often referred to as 'counsel') have to be members of one of the four Inns of Court (each also referred to as an 'Honourable Society'); that is Lincoln's Inn, the Middle Temple, the Inner Temple and Gray's Inn. They are independent, self-governing bodies and were all founded in the fourteenth century. The Inns of Court have the exclusive right, authorised by the judiciary, of calling persons to the bar, that is granting them rights of audience in most (and now all) English courts. The Inns also had the right to discipline and control the educational requirements of members of the bar.

The Inns of Court probably came into existence to regulate and protect barristers but also to provide education in English common law (which was not then taught at the two universities of Oxford and Cambridge). Legal education at the Inns originally extended for up to seven or eight years (and included obligations of dining in the Inns) and ended with the student being admitted to practise as a barrister before the courts of England and Wales by being 'called to the bar' by his Inn. The qualification period was reduced, for university graduates, to three years by the 1840s and to two years by 1964. The education provided at an Inn of Court consisted of lectures (by senior members of the bar known as 'readers') and 'moots', that were exercises in arguing cases in a mock court. In 1852 the Inns of Court jointly set up the Council of Legal Education which instituted lectures and examinations for students. These examinations became compulsory in 1872.

Most barristers now attend university for three years and obtain a law degree. Those with non-law degrees must obtain the Graduate Diploma in Law (also known as the Common Professional Examination) which normally involves one year's study. A student must then obtain admission to one of the Inns of Court and take the Bar Vocational Course (usually over one year) and he is then called to the bar. He must then spend one year as a 'pupil' of a more senior barrister (a formal system of 'pupillage' was instituted in 1958).

In late medieval times, it was not unusual for a man to join an Inn but never be called to the bar. However, by the eighteenth century most of those who entered the Inns of Court did go on to practise law. Barristers are not permitted to enter into partnerships but they share offices, known as chambers. A barrister, after he had been called to the bar, would purchase a life interest in chambers in his Inn or rent them. Prior to entering one of the Inns of Court, a barrister may also have been a member of one of the Inns of Chancery, described below.

Each of the Inns of Court had three ranks of members; 'Benchers', barristers and students. Each Inn was (and still is) governed by a body of its senior members, known as Benchers or 'Masters of the Bench'. Their business meetings are known as 'Parliaments' (in Middle Temple and Inner Temple), 'Councils' (in Lincoln's Inn) and 'Pensions' (in Gray's Inn). They dealt with admissions to each society, training, calls to the bar, barristers' chambers in the Inn (and other property matters), finance and disciplinary matters.

The Bar Council (originally named the Bar Committee) was established in 1883 and the Senate of the Four Inns of Court (of which the Council of Legal Education is a committee) was set up in 1966. Together, they are the governing body of the profession and responsible, *inter alia*, for professional standards and the education and discipline of barristers.

There are some detailed studies of barristers. W.R. Prest, *The rise of the barristers, a social history of the English Bar 1590-1640* (Clarendon Press, 1986) contains references to hundreds of barristers from that period, extracted from court documents and published material, and includes biographies of 385 Benchers of the Inns. Some other studies, which include references to many barristers, are noted in *Holborn's sources*.

Detailed information about a barrister can be found in the records of the four Inns of Court. These are kept by the libraries of each Inn and described in the following sections. There is an online database of the barristers of Inner Temple and published admission registers of the other Inns of Court but most of these sources extend only up to the late nineteenth century. Fortunately, barristers are also included in the published law lists that date from the late eighteenth century (*see* section C.1 below). These are therefore a convenient source in which to trace the careers of barristers, particularly since the late nineteenth century. Useful information about barristers in the nineteenth and twentieth centuries can also be found in published biographical dictionaries (reviewed in section C.2 below), in two published works by A. May and D. Lynch (section D.18 below) and in the journal *The weekly notes* (section E.1).

B3. LINCOLN'S INN

General information about this Inn can be found in G. Hurst, *A short history of Lincoln's Inn* (Constable, 1946). The admission registers up to 1896 have been published in two volumes of *The records of the Honourable Society of Lincoln's Inn*:

- *volume I: admissions 1420-1799* (Lincoln's Inn, 1896).
- *volume II: admissions 1800-1893, chapel registers; baptisms 1716-1806, marriages 1695-1754, burials 1695-1852* (Lincoln's Inn, 1896).

Illustration 1 is a typical page from the first volume, showing those admitted between 10 May and 19 October 1637. From 28 June 1805, the admission registers also give the student's address and age and his father's name, address and occupation, as in this example:

1818 Jan 5, Frederick Augustus Carrington, of Berkeley, co. Glouc., Esq (aged 16), only son of Rev. Caleb Carrington, Vicar of Berkeley aforesaid.

The marriage or burial of a barrister of Lincoln's Inn (and a few from the other Inns), or the baptism of a barrister's children may also be found in the register of Lincoln's Inn

folio 125.

1637   May   10   RICHARD BEALE, son and heir app. of John B., of City of London, gen.   [Northants, gen.

          ,,   11   JOHN ADAMS, son and heir app. of William A., of Charwelton,

folio 125b.

          ,,   16   HUMPHREY HARRIS, 6th son of Sir Thomas H., late of Town of Shewsbury, bart., decd.

folio 126.

          ,,   16   NICHOLAS GRICE, son of Thomas G., late of Littleton, Middx., clericus, decd., special admission.

          ,,   16   FRANCIS WALTHAM, son and heir of Richard W., late of City of London, gen., decd.

folio 126b.

          ,,   18   EDMUND PETTIE, son and heir app. of Maximilian P., of Thame, Oxon, arm.   [Norfolk, gen., decd.

          ,,   22   WILLIAM COCKE, son and heir of Nicholas C., late of Twyford,

folio 127.

        June   5   EDMUND BUTLER, son and heir app. of Sir Thomas B., of Clogrennan, Ireland, knt. and bart.   [and bart.

          ,,   5   PEIRCE BUTLER, 2nd son of Sir Thomas B., of Clogrennan, knt.

folio 127b.

          ,,   8   THOMAS ABBISSE, 2nd son of William A., late of Statfold, Beds, gen., decd.   [Linc., arm.

          ,,   12   HENRY OSNEY, son and heir app. of Robert O., of Louth, co.

folio 128.

          ,,   28   THOMAS MILWARD, son and heir app. of Thos. M., of Allchurch, co. Worc., arm.   [Devon, arm.

        Oct.   2   THEOPHILUS GARLAND, son and heir app. of John G., of Marwood,

folio 128b.

          ,,   14   THOMAS TROSSE, son and heir app. of George T., of Newton Abbot, Devon, gen.   [co. Durham, arm., bencher.

          ,,   16   JOHN TEMPEST, son and heir app. of Thomas T., of Swainston,

folio 129.

          ,,   18   ROBERT HERNE, son and heir app. of Robt. H., of Tibbenham,

Illustration 1: A page from the published register of admissions of Lincoln's Inn.

chapel. For example, the register includes the marriage in March 1695/6 of Francis Gregor of the Middle Temple and the marriage in July 1696 of John Lymbury of Gray's Inn. However, many of the entries do not relate to barristers but to other Londoners such as tradesmen and servants.

Lincoln's Inn library holds typescript continuations of the admissions registers for 1894-1956 and 1957-73, the latter including baptisms and marriages in the Inn chapel 1905-73. The SoG holds typescript extracts of baptisms 1807-52.

Six volumes of *The records of the Honourable Society of Lincoln's Inn: the Black Books* (minutes of the council meetings of Lincoln's Inn) have been published: volume I 1422-1586, II 1586-1660, III 1660-1775, IV 1776-1845, V 1845-1914 and VI 1914-1965 (Lincoln's Inn, 1897-2001). These minutes deal with the appointments of the Inn's officials and with the Inn's accounts and property as well as the education, calls to the bar and disciplining of barristers. The minutes therefore provide information about many members of the Inn. Other records of the Inn include the Red Book, in seven volumes, from 1614 (dealing with finance and buildings) and Treasurers' accounts of 1672-81 and 1713-22.

Lincoln's Inn library also holds transcripts made in 1741 and 1927 of the memorial inscriptions in the undercroft of Lincoln's Inn chapel. Members of Lincoln's Inn who died in the Second World War are commemorated on the war memorial in the Inn and members who died (and those who served) in the First World War are listed in a manuscript book held in the library. The library also holds a typescript index, by P.C. Beddingham, of the coats of arms depicted at various points in the Inn's premises, and a manuscript work, by M.S. Thorpe and C. Thorpe, entititled *Biographical sketches of Lincoln's Inn men (readers, treasurers and benefactors) 1600-1919, whose arms are emblazoned in the windows of the chapel.*

Lincoln's Inn library has one of the largest collections of legal manuscripts in the country. The original catalogue of manuscripts, by J. Hunter was printed in 1838 but there is a typescript addendum to it. The collection includes the Inn's own records, summarised above, but also some notebooks and opinions of judges who were members of the Inn.

Illustration 2 is an engraving of Lincoln's Inn hall and chapel in about 1830. Similar engravings (or photographs) of other parts of Lincoln's Inn, the other Inns of Court, the Inns of Chancery and the law courts will be important to your family history if your ancestor was a lawyer. M. Herber, *Legal London; a pictorial history* (Phillimore, 1999) includes a selection of illustrations. Others can be found in many of the published works noted in this book or in collections held at archives. Good starting points for research are the collections at Guildhall Library and the London Metropolitan Archives.

Many other records of Middle Temple have been published. The most volumes are:

- *A catalogue of notable Middle Templars with brief biographic...* Temple, 1902) by J. Hutchinson. This contains useful biogra... men who trained at Middle Temple.
- *Minutes of Parliament of the Middle Temple...* 1904-1905) by C.T. **Martin**, in four volumes, includin... Latin or repeating the English wording where the orig...
- *The Middle Temple bench book*, being a register of... from the earliest records to the present time, fr... Temple, 1912), second edition by J.B. Willia... editions contain **biographies of the Inn's** P... fathers' names, addresses, occupations, car... bearings. There is also a further volume...
- *A calendar of the Middle Temple recor...* This volume includes extracts from... the accounts of 1637-1800,...
- *Roll of honour*, including the na... the hall of the Honourable Soc... Temple, 1925). This includes brie... or badges appear in the hall's window.

Members of both Middle and Inner Temple used ... church in about 1900. The surviving registers of bap... from 1628 and include many lawyers but also people wit... law. They have been published in G.D. **Squibb, *The register of*** ... 1629-1853, **marriages** 1628-1760 (**Harleian Society**, 1979) and in... of **burials** *at the Temple Church 1628-1853* (**H. Southeran**, 1905)... burial entries are:

Wm Dolbyn, Kt, one of the judges of the King's Bench, buried in the south isle, January... the 29th 1693-4,
Richard Curst of the Inner Temple, gent, buried in the round the 9th of August 1673.

The registers include many entries for the **baptism or burial of lawyers' children** (and a large **number of foundlings**). The monuments in Temple church and its churchyard commemorate many lawyers and members of their families. They have been transcribed and published in A. Esdaile, *Temple church monuments* (G. Barber, 1933), for example:

Illustration 3: Temple church: a postcard from about 1900.

Knights T...
Hospitaller, who leas...
of the Inns of Court: M...

The surviving records of Middle...
commence in 1501. These are:

1) Admission registers from 1658 to date (wh...
found in the Minutes of Parliament.

2) Calls to the bar from 1748.

3) Minutes of Parliament since 1501. Parliament was res...
the Inn, the library, the chambers and Temple church. Its m...
matters such as the occupancy of chambers and donations by...
to about 1657 they record admissions to the Inn (some entries noting...
membership of an Inn of Chancery). After that date these details are in...
admission registers.

4) Indexes to minutes 1501-1775, 1776-1840 and also for later years.

5) Examinations: candidates and results, 1877-1914.

6) Applications for chambers, rents, etc. from 1747.

7) Accounts of the Treasurer from 1658.

8) Deeds and leases, some from 1606.

9) Account books since 1637.

The records of admissions to Middle Temple up to 1944 have been published in H.A.C. Sturgess, *Register of admissions to the Honourable Society of Middle Temple 1501-1944* (Butterworth, 1949) in three volumes. There are also two supplementary volumes, covering admissions of 1944-75, published by Middle Temple in 1978. A typical seventeenth century entry from the published registers notes the student's date of admission and his father's name:

1647 May 15 Roger Charnocke son & heir of George C of Harwoden, Northants decd

Some entries also note the date upon which a student was called to the bar. By the nineteenth century, most entries record a student's age and his father's occupation and address:

1890 Jan 21. William Henry Whadcoat, of Trinity College, Cambridge, (18), eldest son of John Henry W.. of 18 Highbury Crescent, Middx, banker. Called 17 Nov. 1892.

Here lyeth the body of John Ruce, gent, late member of the Inner Temple who departed this life the 25th of November 1720 in the 59th year of his age and of Elizabeth his wife, daughter of Sir Robert Wright, Lord Chief Justice of the King's Bench who died the 21st of October 1753 in the 83rd year of her age.

The manuscript collection in Middle Temple library includes call papers since the late nineteenth century, some containing character references for students and barristers and details of their academic attainments. There are also financial records since 1637 that include members' payments to the Inn and records of students and barristers dining there. The Inn also has an extensive collection of coats of arms borne by Readers and Treasurers of the Inn and displayed in Middle Temple Hall.

Published histories of the Middle Temple and Inner Temple include J.B. Williamson, *The history of the Temple, London, from the institution of the order of the Knights of the Temple to the close of the Stuart period* (John Murray, 1924), G. Noel, *A portrait of the Inner Temple* (Michael Russell, 2002) and H.H.L. Bellot, *The Inner and Middle Temple: legal, literary and historic associations* (Methuen, 1902).

B5. THE INNER TEMPLE

Research of an ancestor who was a member of Inner Temple has recently become much easier by reason of the Inn's production of a database of its records of admission. The database can be accessed on the Inn's web site. The database presently covers the period 1660-1850 (with about 10,000 entries) but will be expanded during 2006 to include admissions back to 1547. In some cases, only limited information is available. For example, John Charnocke, gentleman of London is noted as having been admitted on 8 June 1675. In contrast, Pynsent Chernocke is noted as having been admitted on 6 November 1684 but also recorded as the son and heir apparent of Sir Villiers Chernocke, Baronet of Holcott, Bedfordshire.

Until the database is complete, earlier admissions can be found in two published works. W.H. Cooke, *Students admitted to the Inner Temple 1571-1625* (printed in 1868) lists those admitted to the Inn during this period, with dates of admission and varying amounts of information about each student (in many cases the name of his father). Another version by W.H. Cooke, *Students admitted to the Inner Temple 1547-1660* (printed in 1877) contains similar information but some biographical information in this version is omitted from that noted above (and vice-versa). Typical entries from the latter version, for admissions in November 1656, are:

Thomas Robinson. Prothonotary of King's Bench. Called to the Bench, 1677. Purchased Kentwell Hall, Suffolk. Created a Baronet, 1682. Killed during the fire of this Inn, 1683.
Samuel Gilbert, [of] Bridgerevill, Cornwall.
John Price, [of] Esher, Surrey. Son of George Price.

The Inner Temple web site points out that it is unlikely that further biographical details, about a barrister who is included in the database, will be found in the Inn's archives. However, these archives do include information about admissions of barristers after 1850 as well as information about a barrister's life in the Inn. The most important records of the Inner Temple, described on the Inn's web site, are:

1) The admission books from 1547 to the present day.
2) The admission stamp duty books 1683-1947. They duplicate the admission registers to some extent but sometimes contain more information.
3) Certificates of admissions from other Inns 1668-1818.
4) Acts of the Inner Temple Parliament from 1505.
5) Records of calls to the bar from 1642 and call papers 1840-1959 (proposal papers and certificates of standing).
6) Records of chambers and rents, including chambers admittances 1554-1667, account books 1759-1836, bonds 1753-1863, books 1709-60 and index.
7) Bar bonds 1672-1873 and bar books from 1788.

Although for the most part superseded by the online database, the library of Inner Temple holds five volumes of typescript lists of students' names and dates of admission (the first four prepared by R.L. Lloyd) as follows:

• 1505-1659 (chronological entries)
• 1660-1750 (chronological entries)
• Index for 1505-1750
• 1751-1850 (alphabetical entries)
• 1851-1929 (alphabetical entries)

Many admissions are also recorded in *A calendar of the Inner Temple records*. This has been published in five volumes: volume I 1505-1603 (Inner Temple, 1896), volume II 1603-1660 (Inner Temple, 1898) and volume III 1660-1714 (Inner Temple, 1901), each edited by F.A. Inderwick and volumes IV 1714-1750 (Inner Temple, 1933), and V 1750-1800 (Inner Temple, 1936), edited by R.A. Roberts. Inner Temple library also holds a typescript continuation of this calendar, covering 1800-33, edited by B. Given. All these volumes include many extracts from the proceedings and orders of the Benchers of Inner Temple "in Parliament" and from surviving account books. They include the appointments of Readers and officers of the Inn, lists of those called to the bar, disciplinary matters and the lettings of chambers. An appendix to the first volume contains the roll of a subsidy levied on senior members of the Inns of Court and Inns of Chancery in 1523.

Members who served in the First World War are listed in C. Darling, *Inner Templars who volunteered and served in the Great War, with additional names and corrections to Dec 31, 1923*, published in 1924.

The Inner Temple library holds disciplinary records that may be consulted for occurrences more than 70 years old such as the bankruptcy of a member. In addition, the manuscript records held in the library contain much information about members of the Inn and there is a detailed, indexed, published catalogue (in three volumes) to the manuscripts: J. Conway-Davies, *Catalogue of manuscripts in the library of the Honourable Society of Inner Temple* (Oxford University Press, 1972).

B6. GRAY'S INN

Gray's Inn library holds extensive records of the Inn, its members and students. There is a typescript list of the archives, *Gray's Inn library guide to additional manuscripts acquired since, or included in, the Catalogue of Ancient MSS 1869*, compiled in 1971 by A.K.R. Kiralfy and R.A. Routledge, revised by Miss Routledge to include accessions up to 1976.

Some of these records have been published, most importantly its registers of admissions, in Joseph Foster, *The register of admissions to Gray's Inn, 1521-1889, together with the register of marriages in Gray's Inn chapel 1695-1754* (Hansard Publishing Union, 1889). The early admissions usually give only the name of the student admitted but, by the early seventeenth century, most entries also named the student's father. More recent entries give the ages of those admitted. Illustration 4 is a typical page from this volume, listing the admissions from 19 May 1609 to 2 February 1609/10, for example that of Henry Swinnerton, son and heir of John Swinnerton, Knight, on 8 November. For the admissions of those men whose surnames commenced with A, B or C, more extensive biographical entries were published in Joseph Foster, *Collectanea genealogica* (Hazell, Watson & Viney, 1882-85).

Manuscript minute books listing calls to the bar and manuscript or typescript registers of admissions since 1890 are held in Gray's Inn library. The name and address of the student's father is omitted from the registers nowadays. The Gray's Inn magazine *Graya*, which has been published since 1927, contains lists of those persons admitted to the Inn,

1609. **folio 629—(continued).**

May 19. FRANCIS JERMY, son and heir of William J., of Workingworth, Suffolk, Esq.

" " JOHN STEEDE, son and heir of William S., of Harrietsham, Kent, gent.

" " JOHN JAY, of London, gent.

" 26. THOMAS WHARTON, son and heir of Humphrey W., of Scales, co. York, gent.

folio 640.

" " JOHN BLENCOWE, son and heir of Henry B., of Blencowe, Cumberland, Esq.

" " WILLIAM GLEGGE, son and heir of William G., of Le Grange, co. Chester, gent.

June 30. THOMAS HAMPSON, of Oriel College, Oxon, gent.

" " THOMAS GILBIE, of Bolle, Notts, Esq.

" " JOHN HODGES, of Lufton, co. Somerset, gent.

" " JOHN BUNNINGTON, of Barcotte, co. Derby, gent.

" " FRANCIS PETYTT, of Boughton-under-Blean, Kent, Esq.

" " WILLIAM GLOVER, of London, gent.

folio 641.

Aug. 7. FRANCIS LOVELACE, son of Lancelot L., now reader.

" 8. JOHN ELLIOT, son of Thomas E., Esq., and Katharine his wife, daughter and [heir of Nowell Sotherton, one of the Barons of the Exchequer.

" 10. ROBERT GOODRIGE, of Ipswich, Suffolk, now of Barnard's Inn (erased).

" " RICHARD KEBLE, of Newton, Suffolk, gent.

" 11. JOHN DRURY, of Furnivals (sic), gent.

" " EDWARD AMHERST, of Lewes, Sussex, of Clifford's Inn, gent.

" " ROBERT BOWES, son of Ralph B., of Barnes, in Bishoprick of Durham.

" " JOHN HALES, of Kersley, co. Warwick, gent.

" " JAMES LAWSON, son of Ralph L., of Brough, co. York, Knight.

" " NATHANIEL GULSTON, Fellow of Trinity College, Oxon.

" " ROBERT BARON, of Worcester, now of Barnard's Inn, gent. (erased).

Nov. 3. HENRY FELTON, son and heir of Anthony F., of Playford, Suffolk, Knight.

" 8. JOHN SHADWELL, of Lynedon, co. Stafford, gent.

folio 642.

" " EDWARD CARDINALL, of Furnival's Inn, and East Bergholt, Suffolk, gent.

" " HENRY SWINNERTON, son and heir of John S., Knight.

" " THOMAS MYNOT, gent.

" 27. VINCENT LOWE, son and heir of Patrick L., of Denby, co. Derby.

" " GEORGE SCOTT, son and heir of William S., of Conghurst, Kent.

" " JOHN COOKE, son and heir of Paul C., of North Somercoates, co. Lincoln, gent.

1609-10.

Jan. 24. JOHN CONIERS, of West Brompton, co. Northampton.

" " EDMUND ANDERSON, of Manton, co. Lincoln, gent.

" " JOHN CHOMLEY, gent., son of Henry C., of Burton Coggles, co. Lincoln, Knight.

Feb. 2. THOMAS HOLLAND, S.T.P., Oxford.

NATHANIEL HYDE, gent., son of John H., late of London...

Illustration 4: A page from the published admissions register of Gray's Inn.

20

calls to the Bar, obituaries of members and articles concerning the history of Gray's Inn. A card index to *Graya* is held in Gray's Inn library.

The register of marriages in Gray's Inn chapel from 1695 to 1754, contained in Foster's work, includes many barristers of Gray's Inn but also many people with no connection to the law (as in the cases of Temple church and Lincoln's Inn chapel). Manuscript extracts from the chapel's register of baptisms 1704-1862 are held at the SoG.

Records of Pensions (meetings of the ruling body of Gray's Inn), have been published in R.J. Fletcher, *The pension book of Gray's Inn volume I 1569-1669* and *volume II, 1669-1800* (Gray's Inn, 1901-09). These record the proceedings of, and orders made by, the Benchers 'in Pension'. It includes the appointment of Readers, lists of those called to the bar, disciplinary matters, the appointments of the Inn's officers (and employees such as porters) and the lettings of chambers. Appendices to the first volume contain accounts and a list of Treasurers of Gray's Inn from 1532 to 1669. The appendices to the second volume contain accounts and lists of the occupants of chambers in 1668 and of the Treasurers up to 1909.

Another published work is *The war book of Gray's Inn, containing names of members who served, with biographical notices of those who fell ... and ... the activities of the society during the war* (Gray's Inn, 1921). A sample entry is that for Lieutenant Philip Leo Beard. He was called to the bar in 1909 and practised in Birmingham until 1914 when he received a commission in the Royal Warwickshire Regiment. He died of wounds in France on 9 September 1916, aged 34.

Gray's Inn library holds certain private papers of deceased members of the Inn and a *List of persons practising as country conveyancers, not being barristers or attornies.* The manuscripts include a book of orders, volume 18 (covering May 1888 to March 1894), lists of the members of Gray's Inn, Staple Inn and Barnard's Inn in 1585, lists of officials of the Inn (as well as a cook, butler and laundress) from 1564 to 1800 and a list of 18 duels that took place between 1599 and 1815.

The published histories of Gray's Inn include W.R. Douthwaite, *Gray's Inn, its history & associations* (Reeves & Turner, 1886), which lists eminent members of the Inn, and F. Cowper, *A prospect of Gray's Inn* (2nd edn. Gray's Inn, 1985).

B7. SERJEANTS' INN

Serjeants' Inn was not concerned with the education of lawyers but was more of a club. Its members were judges and those advocates, known as serjeants at law, who were considered to be the leading men in their profession. They were also members of the Order of the Coif, which took its name from the coif or cap that its members were required to wear.

The origin of the serjeants at law can be traced back to the 'narratores' or 'counters of the bench' of the thirteenth century who were authorised by the judges to act as advocates before the busiest royal court, the Court of Common Bench (later named the Court of Common Pleas). Indeed, until 1846, the serjeants had the exclusive right to appear as advocates before that court. Furthermore, the appointment of a barrister to the rank of serjeant was a necessary precursor to his appointment as a common law judge (that is a judge of the Court of Common Pleas and the Court of King's Bench). From the fourteenth until the nineteenth century, a number of serjeants at law were also appointed as King's Serjeants, to act as counsel for the Crown (fulfilling some of the duties of the modern Attorney General and Solicitor General).

By the late fourteenth century, the counters had become known as 'servientes ad legem' or serjeants at law (although exactly why is unclear). From this period until 1875, serjeants at law were created by the monarch's writ, but the judges of the Common Pleas played a major part in deciding which 'apprentices-at-law' (later barristers) should be chosen for the honour. Serjeants also practised in other courts, such the Court of King's Bench and appeared in many famous criminal trials in the nineteenth century, particularly at the Central Criminal Court.

However, the serjeants lost their pre-eminence. From the sixteenth century, the increasing importance of the Court of King's Bench and the Court of Chancery (in which many of the most important cases came to be heard), reduced the amount of business for the serjeants in the Common Pleas. In 1671, King's Counsel were declared to have precedence over the serjeants at law and the best barristers thereafter tended to prefer advancement to the rank of King's Counsel over that of the Order of the Coif. In 1846, parliament removed the serjeants' monopoly in the Common Pleas by giving all barristers equal rights of audience. From that date, most barristers only accepted elevation to the rank of serjeant because it was a necessary pre-requisite to appointment as a judge of the common law courts. However, this requirement was abolished in 1875 and no more serjeants were created. The last of them, Lord Lindley, Master of the Rolls, died in 1921.

The serjeants occupied three inns. The first, Scroope's Inn in Holborn, was vacated in the fifteenth century. By the late fifteenth century, the serjeants were occupying two inns, one in Chancery Lane and one in Fleet Street. Serjeants' Inn in Chancery Lane (originally known as Farringdon Inn) was first leased to the judges and serjeants in 1416.

It was sold in 1877. The inn of the serjeants in Fleet Street was occupied from / vacated in 1758.

J. H. Baker, *The order of serjeants at law* (Selden Society, 1984) is a detailed history of the serjeants, with transcripts of many documents and a list, with some biographical details, of the approximately 1,000 men known to have been serjeants. Two examples of entries are:

> *Marshall, Samuel, created 1787, Serjeants' Inn Chancery Lane, Deputy Steward of the Marshalsea 1800-10, Deputy Justice Chester 1815, Justice Chester 1818-23, died 10 September 1823 (Gentleman's Magazine).*

> *Rokeby, Thomas, created 1689, Serjeants' Inn Fleet Street, Justice of the Common Pleas 1689-95, knight 1689, Justice of the King's Bench 1695-99, died 26 November 1699 (MI, Kirk Sandall, Yorks).*

The surviving records of Serjeants' Inn in Chancery Lane are at TNA (ref: PRO 30/23) and those of Serjeants' Inn in Fleet Street have been published in H.C. King, *Records and documents concerning Serjeants' Inn Fleet Street* (Richard Flint, 1922). Information about the serjeants is also included in A. Pulling, *The Order of the Coif* (William Clowes, 1884). Information about individual serjeants can be found in the records of the Inn of Court of which the serjeant had been a member. Many of the writs by which serjeants were appointed were enrolled on the Close and Patent Rolls and are described in Baker's work.

B8. QUEEN'S (OR KING'S) COUNSEL AND THE LAW OFFICERS

The title of Queen's Counsel (Q.C.) or King's Counsel (K.C.) when the sovereign is male, has been conferred on senior members of the Bar since 1604 when the first such appointment, of Sir Francis Bacon, was made. All those barristers appointed as K.C. or Q.C. since then are listed in J. Sainty, *A list of law officers, King's Counsel and holders of patents of precedence* (Selden Society, 1987), with notes of their judicial appointments.

Sainty's work also lists those barristers who were appointed as the senior law officers of the Crown, that is as the King's Serjeants (from 1278 to 1866), the Attorney General (since 1315), the Solicitor General (since 1461) and the Advocate General (since 1604). These officers advised the Crown on legal matters and also acted for the Crown in the law courts. Information about the men holding these offices is included in the sources for barristers noted above.

B9. ATTORNEYS AND SOLICITORS

The origin and development of the 'lower branch' of the legal profession is the subject of H. Kirk, *Portrait of a profession: a history of the solicitors' profession 1100 to the present day* (Oyez, 1976) and M. Birks, *Gentlemen of the law* (Stevens, 1960). There are also two studies of specific periods: C. W. Brooks, *Pettyfoggers and vipers of the Commonwealth: the 'lower branch' of the legal profession in early modern England* (CUP, 1986) and R. Robson, *The attorney in eighteenth century England* (CUP, 1959). These are recommended reading for any family historian interested in learning about the life of an ancestor who was an attorney or solicitor. In particular, Robson's work provides much information about the life and work of provincial attorneys and articled clerks in the eighteenth century, with many references to diaries, accounts and other lawyers' papers that survive in archives.

An Act of Parliament of 1402 required attorneys to be admitted to practice in a court by being examined by the judges and sworn as an officer of that court. Records of admissions do not survive from this period - most such records only commencing in the early eighteenth century – but names of lawyers were included in this period on the plea rolls of the courts (described in section D). The number of attorneys admitted to the courts gradually increased. There were about 180 attorneys in 1480 but over 1,000 in 1606. By 1697/8, there were 1,096 attorneys on the roll of the Court of Common Pleas and 544 on the roll of the Court of King's Bench. In other courts, the clerks and officials tried to keep the attorneys' lucrative work to themselves and limit the number of attorneys admitted. Only four attorneys were permitted to practice in the Court of Exchequer in 1697/8, as the court officials themselves advised litigants (and pocketed the fees). No attorneys were admitted in the Court of Chancery, where the clerks acted as officials of the courts but also as advisors to the litigants.

This resulted in the rise of solicitors. As noted above, solicitors were intermediaries who assisted litigants to conduct their cases in the courts of equity. They did not need any qualifications and were not officers of the court. Many of the attorneys who were admitted in a common law court also acted as solicitors in the courts of Chancery or Exchequer. These men might describe themselves as an attorney on one occasion and as a solicitor on another, or even as an 'attorney and solicitor'. The authorities gradually prevented court officials acting for the parties to litigation and solicitors were soon carrying out the same functions (in the courts of equity) as those carried out by attorneys in the common law courts.

Although originally permitted to become members of the Inns of Court, attorneys and solicitors were gradually excluded. Many were students at the Inns of Chancery (considered below) but it was not until the nineteenth century that the Law Society took responsibility for the training of attorneys and solicitors (and for admissions and discipline).

The 'Act for the better regulation of attorneys and solicitors' in 1729 confirmed that an attorney had to be formally admitted to each court in which he was to practice (they were examined by a judge, took the prescribed oath and their names were entered on a roll) but the Act also required solicitors to be admitted in this manner.. There were special provisions for attorneys and solicitors who were already practising. The Act specified the oath to be taken:

> *I AB do swear that I will truly and honestly demean myself in the practice of an attorney/solicitor, according to the best of my ability.*

The Act also permitted attorneys, who had been admitted to a common law court, to be admitted as solicitors of the Court of Chancery. The work of attorneys and solicitors became more similar and the terms 'attorney' and 'solicitor' interchangeable. Importantly, the 1729 Act also provided that no person could be admitted as an attorney or solicitor without having served articles of clerkship (the equivalent of an apprenticeship) for five years with a qualified practitioner. Records of articles survive in the courts' archives, reviewed below, and in archives held by the Law Society.

Lists of attorneys and solicitors admitted pursuant to the 1729 Act were printed in 1729 and 1731 for the House of Commons. The 1731 list included 2,236 attorneys of the Common Pleas, 893 attorneys of the King's Bench and 1,700 solicitors in Chancery (some names appear on more than one list but there are probably over 3,000 names). Copies are held at TNA, the British Library and the SoG and they have been reprinted in S. Lambert, *House of Commons sessional papers of the eighteenth century. Vol 13: George III, legal profession 1730-32* (Scholarly Resources, 1975). These lists are arranged by court, then by the first letter of the lawyer's surname, then chronologically. Illustration 5 is the first page of the list of solicitors admitted in the Court of Exchequer, commencing with John Battie of Sheffield who was admitted on 1 July 1729. Illustration 6 is a page from the list of solicitors admitted in the Court of Chancery.

Articles of clerkship were subject to the stamp duty levied on apprenticeship indentures and so many articled clerks appear in the apprenticeship registers of 1710-1811 in series IR 1 at TNA. These name the attorney or solicitor to whom a clerk was articled and usually the clerk's father. A major part of these apprenticeship registers have been indexed and the indexes can be seen on microfiche at the SoG or accessed on the web site of British Origins. Extracts from the registers have also been published, for

LISTS

OF

ATTORNIES and SOLICITORS,

Admitted in Pursuance of the late A C T

For the better Regulation of Attornies and Solicitors.

A LIST of all such Persons who, in pursuance of the late Act for the better Regulation of Attornies and Solicitors, have been Admitted by the Barons of the *Exchequer* Solicitors in His Majesty's Court of *Exchequer*, with the Places of their usual Abode, when and where Admitted, and by whom.

Solicitors Names.	Places of Abode.	When admitted.	Where.	By whom.
Battie John	Of Sheffield *in the County* of York	1729. July 1.		
Burnell James	Of Lofthouse *in the County of* York	5.		
Bragg Henry	Of Hudderfield *in the* County of York	Oct. 30.		
Calcutt James	Of Daventry *in the County* of Northampton	July 3.		
Chandler Samuel	Of Portsmouth *in the* County of Southampton, *and of* New-Inn, London.	9.		
Donne John	Of Crewkerne *in the Coun-*			

Illustration 5: Extract from the list of solicitors admitted in the Court of Exchequer pursuant to the Act for the better regulation of attornies and solicitors, 1729.

Perfons admitted.	Their Places of Abode.		By whom admitted.	And when
				1729
Alfop William	Weft Littleton	Gloucefter. ⎫		
Algood Lancelot	Hexham	Northumberland. ⎬ Mafters Holford, Bennett.		8 December
Andrews William	Worcefter.			
Alfop John	Afhborne	Derby. ⎫	Holford, Bennett.	20 February
Applewaite Henry	Wickham	Suffolk. ⎭		
Audley Ralph	Newcaftle under Lyne.		Lightboun, Kinafton.	18 December
Auftin John	Northampton.		Elde, Thurfton.	4
Aland Charles	Trowbridge	Wilts. ⎫		
Adams John	Swanzey	Glamorgan. ⎬	Mafham, Burroughs.	11
Akehurft Alexander	Leatherhead	Surrey. ⎭		
A Court Richard	Auxbridge	Somerfet. ⎫		
Adey Jofeph, jun.	Litchfield.			
Afhton Thomas	Eaft Markham	Nottingham. ⎬	Tothill, Allen.	7
Awbery Harwood	Reading.			
Afhfield Thomas	Parfhore	Worcefter. ⎭		
Agas Henry	Kelvedon	Effex. ⎫		
Amyat John	Totnefs.	⎬	Tothill, Allen.	12
Adams James	Briftol.	⎭		
Buck John	Rotheram	York.	Elde, Burroughs.	6 March 1729
Bulman Robert	Morpeth		Thurfton, Burroughs.	16 May 1730
Brown John	Newcaftle upon Tyne.		Mafham, Burroughs.	3 June
Browell Mark	Of the fame Place.		Elde, Burroughs.	8
Bawden Hugh	Truro.		Bennett, Mafham. ⎫	
Butler Thomas	Wells.		Tothill, Allen. ⎬ 19	
Batty John	Sheffield.		Burroughs, Allen. ⎭	
Barnard Chriftopher	Leeds.		Mafham, Burroughs.	16
Booth Richard	York.		Tothill, Allen. ⎫	
Brockett Lawrence	Hilton	Durham. ⎭	Tothill, Allen.	
Batty William	Sheffield.		Burroughs, Allen. ⎬ 20	
Bean William	York.			
Bean Henry	Beverley.		Thurfton, Allen. ⎭	
Barftow Thomas	Leeds.		Holford, Burroughs.	22
Blennerhaffett William	Flemby	Cumberland. ⎫	Holford, Mafham.	23
Beatniffe Richard	Kingfton upon Hull.			
Brown John	Woodbridge	Suffolk. ⎫		
Butler Robert	Bradford	York. ⎬	Holford, Mafham.	25
Brierton William	Brinton.	Norfolk. ⎭		
Barnham James	Norwich.			
Burnell James	Lofthoufe	York. ⎫	Bennett, Burroughs. ⎫	
Buck Samuel	Rotheram	York. ⎭		
Brownfword John	Wigton	Cumberland.	Holford, Bennett. ⎬ 26	
Buxton Jof.	York.		Holford, Burroughs. ⎭	
Bowes William	York.			
Brownfword Charles	Kendall	Weftmorland. ⎬	Holford, Bennett. ⎫	
Burden Richard	Doncafter.		⎬ 27	
Brewer William	Stroude.	Gloucefter.	Holford, Burroughs. ⎭	
Bridges James	Keynfham.	Somerfet.	Bennett, Kinafton. ⎫	
Buckworth Thomas	Spalding.	Lincoln.	Bennett, Thurfton. ⎬ 29	
Barnes Thomas	Shrewfbury.			
Beresford Edward	Holme.	Lincoln. ⎬	Bennett, Allen. ⎫	
Blackenbury Car.	Spilfby.	Lincoln. ⎭	⎬ 30	
Brook George	Halfted.	Effex. ⎭		

Illustration 6: Extract from the list of solicitors admitted in the Court of Exchequer pursuant to the Act for the better regulation of attornies and solicitors, 1729.

27

example in *Surrey apprenticeships from the registers in the Public Record Office 1711-1731* (Surrey Record Society, 1929). Most entries note the names of the apprentice, his father and master; the date and term of the articles and the premium paid. Thus William Richardson (son of William, of the parish of St George the Martyr) was articled to Charles Barnard, a London attorney, on 15 November 1725 for five years. A premium of £304 and 10 shillings was paid to the attorney.

Robson noted, in his work noted above, that in the period around 1712, the premiums paid to attorneys for taking an articled clerk varied from £20 up to £268. By 1754, a premium could be as high as £400 although it might be lower than £50. Entry to the profession was impossible for the poorer sections of society but it was open to the middle and upper classes.

An Act of 1749 required that, within three months of the admission of an attorney or solicitor, an affidavit should be filed with the court attesting to the due execution of his articles. This was to prevent the forgery of deeds of articles and ensure that clerks really did serve five years in articles. An affidavit certifying that the clerk had completed his articles also had to be filed. Many of the deeds of articles and affidavits survive in court records but sometimes there are registers of these affidavits and articles, noting their dates and main terms, and identifying the clerk (and often one of his parents), his master and the person swearing the affidavit.

In 1785 an Act was passed by which attorneys and solicitors were required each year to take out practising certificates. The courts were required to register these certificates. Certificates were at first issued by officials in the courts of Common Pleas, King's Bench and Exchequer, later by the Commissioner of Stamps and subsequently by the Law Society. At first, the fee payable for a certificate was £5 for Town attorneys and solicitors (those practising in London) or £3 if they practised in the country. An attorney or solicitor was also required to deliver the certificate to the court or courts in which he practised and the court officials were required to keep registers of those certificates. As we shall see below, this Act resulted in the production of some useful records of attorneys and solicitors (both in the records of the law courts and those held by the Law Society).

Illustrations 7 and 8 are examples of practising certificates issued to the attorney Alfred Simpson of New Malton, Yorkshire. Illustration 7 is a certificate issued by the Stamp Office on 16 November 1837. Illustration 8 is a certificate issued by the Law Society (then known as the Incorporated Law Society) on 16 November 1860. Similar certificates may be found in collections of personal or business papers in archives.

CERTIFICATE for an Attorney, Solicitor, Proctor, or Notary Public, admitted or enrolled Three Years or upwards, and resident in the Country beyond the Limits of the Two-penny Post.

£8.

No. *5983*

Office for Stamps & Taxes, Somerset Place.

I *Teesdale Cockell*, duly appointed by the Commissioners of Stamps and Taxes, Do hereby certify, That *Alfred Simpson*

of New Malton, Yorkshire, Gent

hath delivered into my Office a Note in Writing, containing his Name, and Place of Residence as herein set forth, pursuant to the Acts of Parliament relating to the Stamp Duties on Certificates to be taken out by Attornies, Solicitors, and others, and that he hath paid the Duty for this Certificate, by virtue whereof he is at liberty to practise as an Attorney, Solicitor, Proctor, or Notary Public, (if duly admitted or enrolled,) from the day of the Date hereof, until the Fifteenth day of November, One Thousand Eight Hundred and Thirty-eight, both inclusive, and no longer.

Given under my Hand, this Sixteenth day of November, in the Year of our Lord One Thousand Eight Hundred and Thirty-seven.

Teesdale Cockell,

Registrar.

Entered at ——————— ~~my Office,~~ *the Masters Office,*
this *third* day of *January 1838*

Note.—This Certificate must be entered at the proper Office of the Court in which you were admitted or enrolled.

Illustration 7: Practising certificate issued to the attorney Alfred Simpson of New Malton, Yorkshire by the Stamp Office on 16 November 1837.

No. *7888*   REGISTRAR'S CERTIFICATE   1860-61

c

𝕻𝖚𝖗𝖘𝖚𝖆𝖓𝖙 to an Act passed in the Session of Parliament holden in the 23rd and 24th Years of the Reign of Queen Victoria, intituled "An Act to amend the Laws relating to Attorneys, Solicitors, Proctors, and Certificated Conveyancers," the INCORPORATED LAW SOCIETY, the Registrar of Attorneys and Solicitors appointed under the Act of the Session holden in the 6th and 7th Years of Queen Victoria, "for consolidating and amending several of the Laws relating to Attorneys and Solicitors practising in England and Wales," 𝕳𝖊𝖗𝖊𝖇𝖞 𝕮𝖊𝖗𝖙𝖎𝖋𝖎𝖊𝖘 That

Alfred Simpson

Attorney-at-Law, whose place of business *is* at *New Malton*

hath this Day delivered and left with the Secretary of the said Society, a Declaration in Writing, signed by the said Attorney's London Agent, on his behalf, containing his Name and Place or Places of Business, and the Court or one of the Courts of which he is admitted an Attorney, together with the Term and Year in or as of which he was so admitted: and the said Society hereby further certifies, That the said Attorney is duly enrolled in the Court of QUEEN'S BENCH _____ at Westminster, and is entitled to practise as such Attorney, *upon this Certificate being duly stamped as required by Law.* Given under the hand of the Secretary of the INCORPORATED LAW SOCIETY, this 16th Day of November, 1860.

B. Maughan
Secretary.

Illustration 8: Practising certificate issued to Alfred Simpson by the Law Society on 16 November 1860.

The number of attorneys and solicitors continued to increase (by 1802, there were about 5,400 practitioners). Societies of attorneys and solicitors were also formed in the eighteenth century to regulate and protect the profession. The 'Society of Gentlemen Practisers in the Several Courts of Law and Equity' was founded in 1739 and (confusingly) often referred to as 'The Law Society'. The present-day Law Society holds manuscript records of the Society of Gentlemen Practisers for 1740-1819 and those up to 1810 have been published in E. Freshfield, *The records of the Society of Gentlemen Practisers in the courts of law and equity called the Law Society* (The Law Society, 1897).

The society made proposals for law reform and also took action against attorneys who were guilty of unprofessional or illegal conduct. For example, Landon Jones was convicted of conspiracy in 1744, put in the pillory and then imprisoned. His name was struck off the roll of attorneys of the Court of Common Pleas. However, Jones continued to act as a solicitor. The Society of Gentleman Practisers was successful in getting Jones struck off the roll of the Court of Chancery in 1746 (the record of this is noted in section D.3 below). An attorney named William Wreathock became a highwayman and was convicted and transported. However, he returned to England and again practised as an attorney. The society succeeded in having Wreathock struck off the rolls of the Court of Common Pleas in 1758. It also successfully opposed an attempt by the Scriveners' Company in the mid-eighteenth century to secure a monopoly over conveyancing business in the City of London. Some charitable gifts were also made by the society to members or to the dependants of deceased members. For example, Mrs Colston, widow of John Colston, petitioned the society for relief and was granted £20 in view of the great services that Colston had rendered to the society.

However, this 'Law Society' was dissolved following the foundation of the present-day Law Society. This was founded in 1825 as the 'Law Institution' but was granted a Royal Charter in 1831 and renamed as 'The Society of Attorneys, Solicitors, Proctors and others not being barristers practising in the Courts of Law and Equity of the United Kingdom'. Thankfully, its name was changed to 'The Law Society of the United Kingdom' and again, in 1903, to 'The Law Society'. The Law Society soon began to be involved in the education of lawyers, initially by providing lectures at its Chancery Lane premises.

In the eighteenth century, a number of provincial law societies were also formed. The first was in Bristol in 1770, followed by those in Yorkshire in 1786 and Somerset in 1796. In the next 25 years, provincial law societies were also formed in Sunderland, Leeds, Devon, Manchester, Plymouth, Gloucester, Birmingham, Hull and Kent. Many societies started as social clubs (most originally met in hotels or taverns) and then became involved in creating libraries and discussing legal reform or other matters affecting the profession. Some societies made charitable gifts. For example, the Yorkshire Law Society agreed in 1789 to pay two shillings and six pence a week to support John Moxen, an attorney in the Leeds workhouse.

Lists of these societies are included, with the names of their secretaries, in the law lists and some law lists also note a solicitor's membership of a local law society. Some records of these societies survive. Bristol Record Office, for example, holds a register of members of Bristol Law Society for 1871-75. Minutes survive for the Bristol Law Society (1774-80), the Birmingham Law Society (1818-30) and the Yorkshire Law Society (1786-1834). Minutes, registers of members and other records may be in local archives or still held by the societies. Some lists of members and other records are included in published histories of these societies, many of which are listed in *Holborn's sources*.

Efforts were made to improve the education of attorneys. The five-year period of articles was reduced in 1821, for those graduating with a law degree, to three years. The requirement that judges should examine attorneys and solicitors being admitted to practise had rarely been taken very seriously. The eighteenth-century attorney, William Hickey described how his 'examination' by a judge, Mr Justice Yates of the Court of King's Bench (a friend of his father), consisted of four or five questions, such as 'how I liked the law' over breakfast. The judges saw the need for standards to be improved and delegated their powers of examination to the Law Society in 1835. The first Law Society examination for those wishing to be admitted as attorneys or solicitors took place in 1836.

The Solicitors Act of 1839 created the office of Registrar of Attorneys and Solicitors, to keep an alphabetical roll of attorneys and solicitors and issue certificates to those who had been duly admitted and enrolled (although the courts continued to keep their own records of admissions). In 1843, the Law Society was made the Registrar of Attorneys and Solicitors.

The Judicature Act of 1873 merged the courts of common law and the courts of equity. The distinction between solicitors and attorneys was abolished and 'solicitors of the Supreme Court' were admitted to practise in all courts by the issue of their practising certificates by the Law Society. Articles of clerkship were also lodged with the society (as well as at court). By Acts of 1888, 1910 and 1919, a committee of the Law Society was also given the right to determine complaints against solicitors, to suspend them or even to remove their names from the roll of solicitors. The Law Society, based at Chancery Lane in London and at Redditch in Worcestershire remains the professional body for all solicitors practising in England and Wales and responsible for the issue, each year, of a solicitor's practising certificate. Consequently, the Law Society holds useful information about lawyers including:

1) the roll of solicitors (those presently holding a practising certificate),
2) a register of the admissions of attorneys and solicitors to practice since 1845,
3) registers of articles of clerkship since 1860, and
4) disciplinary records

The information available therefore includes an attorney or solicitor's date of birth, the date of his articles, the name of the lawyer to whom he was articled, the name and occupation of his father, and any findings by a disciplinary tribunal. Enquiries are dealt with for a fee (£100 per hour plus VAT) and should be directed to the Registration department of the Law Society at its offices in Redditch.

The education and training of solicitors was gradually improved during the twentieth century. From 1922, attendance of students for one year at an approved law school was made compulsory. Similarly to barristers, most solicitors now attend university for three years and obtain a law degree. Those with non-law degrees must obtain the Graduate Diploma in Law (also known as the Common Professional Examination) normally involving one year's study. A student must then attend the Legal Practice Course (at the College of Law or a university) usually over one year. Finally, the student must obtain a training contract with a practising solicitor (formerly called articles of clerkship) for two years, after which the student is admitted as a solicitor of the Supreme Court of Judicature.

One further major change from the eighteenth century is that premiums, payable to solicitors by articled clerks or their parents for the benfit of training, have now disappeared. Trainee solicitors are now generally well-paid, thus opening the profession to all those who achieve the required academic standards.

The best method of starting research for an ancestor who was a solicitor or attorney since the late eighteenth century is to consult the published law lists and the Brooks index at the SoG (described in section C.1). Many of the records of attorneys and solicitors being admitted to the courts in which they practised (and records of an attorney's articles of clerkship) survive, principally for the period up to 1875, with the other records of each court at TNA (described in section D below). You may also locate your ancestor in biographical dictionaries, directories, school or university registers, and in the records of the Inns of Chancery.

B10. THE INNS OF CHANCERY

The Inns of Chancery no longer exist but they were originally preparatory schools for students intending to enter one of the Inns of Court. They also rented chambers to practising lawyers. However, they later became little more than social clubs for their members (mostly attorneys and solicitors). H.H.L. Bellot, *The Inner and Middle Temple; legal, literary and historic associations* (Methuen, 1902) includes brief histories of these Inns.

The Inns of Chancery were first described by Chief Justice Fortescue in about 1468. He stated that there were 10 Inns of Chancery (but did not give their names) and noted the number of students at each of them as not less than 100. Fortescue explained that:

> *the most part of them are young men learning or studying ... the elements of the law who, profiting therein as they grow to ripeness, so are they admitted into the greater Inns of the same study called the Inns of Court.*

However, as the Inns of Court began to oppose the admission of attorneys and solicitors, those practitioners increasingly remained members of the Inns of Chancery.

Of the 10 Inns of Chancery that existed in 1468, two soon disappeared. Strand Inn (sometimes called Chester Inn) was demolished in 1549 to make way for the construction of a palace for the Protector Somerset. The identity of the other Inn is uncertain, it may have been Symond's Inn on Chancery Lane or St George's Inn, near Newgate (which was demolished in the sixteenth century). The surviving eight Inns of Chancery were all affiliated to one of the Inns of Court. Furnival's Inn and Thavies (or Davy's) Inn were affiliated to Lincoln's Inn. Clement's Inn, Clifford's Inn and Lyon's Inn were affiliated to Inner Temple. New Inn was affiliated to Middle Temple. Staple Inn and Barnard's Inn were affiliated to Gray's Inn.

Each of the Inns of Chancery, also styled 'Honourable Societies', were organised in similar manner to the Inns of Court. The members and students were governed by a 'Principal' and 'Ancients' who sat in a council (at most of the Inns known as the 'Pension' or 'Pention'). Each Inn had a hall and sets of chambers which were rented to practising lawyers (who might be members of the Inn) but none had a chapel, the Inn members using nearby churches (for example, pews were reserved for members of Clement's Inn at St Clement Danes). The Inns of Court were landlords of some of the Inns of Chancery but also appointed senior barristers as Readers to deliver lectures to the students at the Inns of Chancery.

Membership of an Inn of Chancery for a year or two was originally necessary before a student entered an Inn of Court. Students often progressed to the Inn of Court to which their Inn of Chancery was affiliated but they might enter one of the other Inns. For example, Thomas More was a student of New Inn but was then admitted to Lincoln's Inn. As the divisions between barristers and attorneys increased, fewer entrants to the Inns of Court attended an Inn of Chancery beforehand. For example, after 1660, only a handful of students at Barnards Inn went on to an Inn of Court. Most of the decreasing number of students who did attend the Inns of Chancery subsequently became attorneys or solicitors.

Many practising attorneys and solicitors were members of the Inns of Chancery and some (whether members or not) rented chambers within the Inns. As the Inns of Court took steps to exclude attorneys and solicitors, they made the Inns of Chancery their own dining and social clubs. Those wishing to become attorneys or solicitors obtained most of their legal education from articles rather than lectures or 'moots' at the Inns of Chancery. The number of students at the Inns of Chancery therefore declined and the practising lawyers became an increasing proportion of the membership of each Inn.

The 1729 Act noted above not only made provision for the admission of attorneys and solicitors in the courts but, importantly, ended the requirement that they should be members of one of the Inns (although this requirement had commonly been ignored). The Inns of Chancery also gradually ceased to provide legal education for students (this function was undertaken by the Law Society from the nineteenth century). They became little more than members' clubs, with buildings rented out as chambers to practising lawyers, court officials and even members of other professions. One by one, the Inns closed; many of their buildings were demolished and their surviving records (very few for some of the Inns) were deposited in archives or with other institutions.

Furnival's Inn

Furnival's Inn was established in about 1383 on the north side of Holborn. It had 80 members and students in 1586. However, it had been reduced to a small concern (six ancients and 16 juniors) by 1817 and Lincoln's Inn, which owned the freehold of Furnival's Inn's premises, refused to renew its lease. The Prudential Assurance Company building was subsequently built on the site. No membership records of the Inn have survived. There are some deeds of the Inn's premises and a manuscript held in Middle Temple Library, dating from 1636, has been transcribed in D.S. Bland, *Early records of Furnival's Inn, edited from a Middle Temple manuscript* (King's College Department of Extra-Mural Studies, 1957). It includes the names of some of the Principals and of a few members of the Inn.

Thavies Inn

Thavies Inn, also in Holborn, dated from about 1348. It had 40 members and students in 1586. The society failed to secure a renewal of its lease, in the 1760s, from Lincoln's Inn (that had owned the freehold since 1549). The society was therefore dissolved and its buildings were subsequently destroyed by fire. No records of members appear to have survived.

Clement's Inn

Clement's Inn, which dated from about 1480, stood on land near St Clement Danes. It had 100 members and students in 1586 but, like all the Inns of Chancery, declined. Part of Clement's Inn was sold in 1868 and the remainder of it in 1884.

TNA holds a collection of documents from Clement's Inn (ref: PRO 30/26/74/1-11). This includes two admission books covering 1656-1790 and 1790-1883, constitutions and orders (late fifteenth to seventeenth centuries), Pension orders 1683-1781, various deeds, papers and accounts from 1631-1763 and oaths taken by members on their admission, with signatures, from 1815-66. Inner Temple Library holds a Pension book of the Inn for 1714-49/50.[2]

The entries in the admission books are chronological, with the name, address and occupation of the person admitted and his date of admission. They also give the name, address and occupation of the person (sometimes two or three persons) acting as 'pledge' for the new member, that is as a surety for the new member's good behaviour and his payment of dues to the Inn. Many of those acting as pledge were other members of the Inn. Most of the entries before 1733 are in Latin. Illustration 9 is a page from the second admission book, with four entries from 1791, including that of William Gale of Houghton Street, St Clement Danes, Middlesex. His pledge was John Buxton of Broad Street in the parish of St James.

A transcript of the admission books is included in C. Carr, *The Pension book of Clement's Inn* (Selden Society, 1960), with some biographical information about certain members. For example, it is noted that Simon Urlin, from Ampthill, Bedfordshire (admitted to Clement's Inn in 1669) had been admitted as an attorney of the Bedford Court of Pleas in 1667 and was also practising in the Court of Common Pleas in 1678. John Penny of St Clement Danes was admitted in 1701. He was Principal of the Inn from 1728 to 1739 and murdered in his chambers (by his servant John Hall) in 1741.

Carr's work also includes a transcript of the Pension book for 1714-49/50 held by Inner Temple Library and the constitutions and pension orders of 1683-1781 held at TNA. Most of the entries in the Pension book are concerned with the arrears owed by

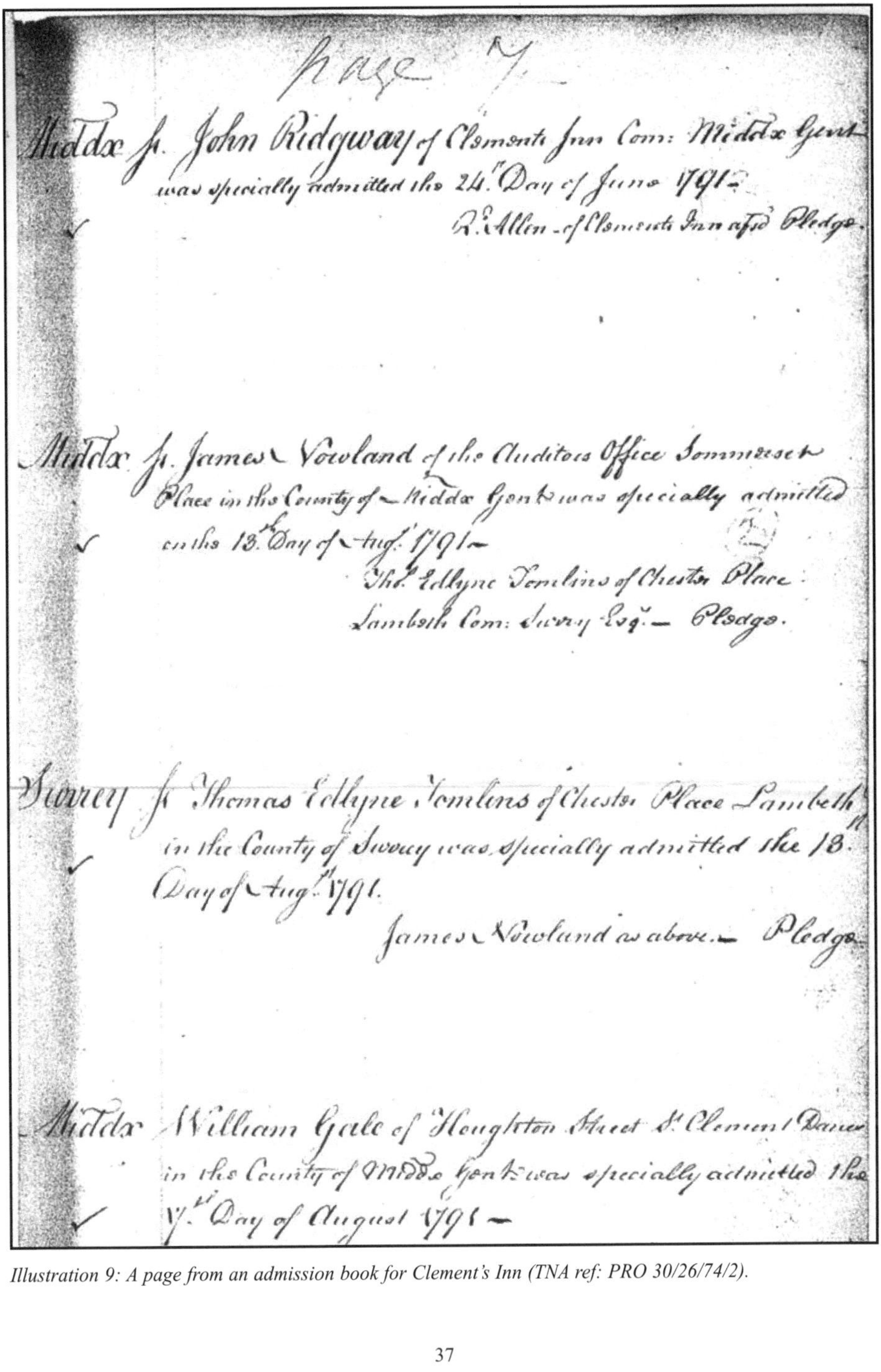

page 7

Middx ʃ. John Ridgway of Clements Inn Com: Middx Gent was specially admitted the 24th Day of June 1791 —
R.d Allen – of Clements Inn afsd Pledge.

Middx ʃ. James Nowland of the Auditors Office Sommerset Place in the County of Middx Gent was specially admitted on the 13th Day of Aug.t 1791 —
Thos. Edlyne Tomlins of Chester Place Lambeth Com: Surry Esq.r — Pledge.

Surrey ʃ. Thomas Edlyne Tomlins of Chester Place Lambeth in the County of Surrey was specially admitted the 13th Day of Aug.t 1791.
James Nowland as above — Pledge.

Middx William Gale of Houghton Street St. Clement Danes in the County of Middx Gent was specially admitted the 17th Day of August 1791 —

Illustration 9: A page from an admission book for Clement's Inn (TNA ref: PRO 30/26/74/2).

members to the Inn, the lease of chambers and the audit of the Principal's accounts. On 28 November 1734, it was noted that 11 members, including Thomas Colly, Leonard Cotton and Morgan Gwyn, were 'greatly in arrears to this society and their debts looked upon as desparate'. It was ordered that their names be struck out of the rolls. In 1721, the Pension book lists the names of the 62 members of the Inn and their contributions to the repair of the church of St Clement Danes.

As at the other Inns of Chancery, many men who were not lawyers joined Clement's Inn during the eighteenth century. They included merchants, surgeons, clergymen, a stockbroker, a Bank of England employee and even actors, musicians, authors, plumbers and a shoemaker. Benjamin Disraeli's father, Isaac D'Israeli, a City of London merchant, became a member of the Inn on 15 October 1793. The admission book also lists one woman as a member: a widow named Jane Frith, of Sloane Street, Chelsea, who was admitted on 7 May 1795.

Clifford's Inn
Clifford's Inn was founded in about 1345. It stood near Fleet Street, behind St Dunstan in the West and is described in C.M. Hay-Edwards, *A history of Clifford's Inn* (T. W. Laurie, 1912). It was administered by a Principal and 12 'rules' or governors. Membership of the Inn declined in the nineteenth century. No new members were admitted after 1877 and the Inn's membership had sunk to only 16 by 1899. Its premises were sold in 1903 and the site is now covered by modern offices.

TNA holds an account book of the Principal of Clifford's Inn for 1738-54 (ref: LC 9/344). The location of other records of the Inn was unknown (three minute-books dating back to 1609 were lost when Inner Temple library was bombed in the Second World War) until some administrative records of the Principal or his clerk came to light in 1998. They are now in Inner Temple library and described in an article on the Inner Temple website by C. Rider, *Lost in the past: the rediscovered archives of Clifford's Inn*. They do not include membership or admission registers but do include title deeds for the Inn's premises, chambers' admissions books and draft minute and account books that refer to many members of the Inn.

Lyon's Inn
Lyon's Inn dated from about 1420. It had 80 members and students in 1586. Its buildings had become very neglected by 1800 and the property was sold and demolished in 1863. The site is now covered by Australia House and Bush House. The Inn's records have disappeared.

New Inn

New Inn dated back to about 1460 and was situated to the west of the site on which the Law Courts now stand. The Inn had 80 members and students in 1586 but the number of admissions declined in the eighteenth and nineteenth centuries and, in 1899, the London County Council compulsorily acquired the Inn for the Kingsway improvement scheme.

Many records of the Inn were located and deposited in Middle Temple library in 1990. They include admission books for 1743 to 1852 and minute and order books of the Pension from 1674/5 to 1791.

Staple Inn

Staple Inn was originally a customs house for the wool trade. It became an Inn of Chancery by 1413 and by 1586 it was the largest of those Inns, accommodating 145 members and students. It fell into decline in the nineteenth century. Its buildings were sold in 1884 but many of them survive on the south side of Holborn, near Chancery Lane underground station. Most of the surviving records of the Inn are held in Gray's Inn library. Illustration 10 is a postcard, dating from about 1900, of the Inn's courtyard. It is still a quiet and beautiful place.

There are two illustrated histories of Staple Inn: T.C. Worsfold, *Staple Inn and its story* (Bumpus, 1903) and E. Williams, *Staple Inn, customs house, wool court and Inn of Chancery: its mediaeval surroundings and associations* (Constable, 1906). The latter work describes the coats of arms in the windows of Staple Inn Hall, lists the members of the Inn in 1585, the Principals from 1580 to 1884 and the admissions of members from 1716 to 1881 (from the admissions book for this period held at Gray's Inn). The admissions give the name of the member, the date of admission and in some cases the name and address of the surety.

The Law Society holds the registers of admissions to chambers in Staple Inn for 1728-76, 1777-1808 and 1810-80 as well as a minute book of the Pension covering the period 1751-90.

Barnard's Inn

Barnard's Inn is thought to have been an Inn of Chancery since 1435. It accommodated 112 members and students in 1586 but it declined during the eighteenth and nineteenth centuries, there being no admissions after 1870. In *Great Expectations* Dickens described the Inn as 'the dingiest collection of shabby buildings ever squeezed together in a rank corner as a club for Tom-cats'. The premises were purchased by the Mercers' Company in 1892.

Illustration 10: The courtyard of Staple Inn: a postcard from about 1900.

Gray's Inn library holds the surviving records of Barnard's Inn, including admission registers for 1620-1756 and 1799-1869 (most entries until 1733 being in Latin), accounts for 1620-41 and 'Pention' books of orders (including some admissions) for 1722-40, 1743-71 and 1773-1913. The admission registers note a member's place of origin, the date of admission and the admission fee. Some admissions were 'general' and some were 'special'. General admission cost 6s 8d. Special admission was either free (for example for sons of the 'Antients' of the Inn) or cost 16s (possibly for those of higher social status). A few entries are annotated, for example with the word 'mort' (dead).

The records of the Inn have been published, with a list from 1586 of the Inn's 112 members and students, and some illustrations of the Inn, in C.W. Brooks, *The admissions registers of Barnard's Inn 1620-1869* (Selden Society, 1995). Some biographical information is also provided for some members. These are two of the entries:

> *3 Nov 1624. Samuel Bradstreete, Cambridge, Cambs. general [admission] 6s 8d.*
> *'Mort'. Attorney of the Common Pleas 1630 (TNA ref: CP 40/2257).*

> *8 July 1716. John Batty, St Dunstan in the West, London. general [admission] 6s 8d*
> *Elected antient 1728. Principal 1738-43. Noted dead in 1759 (Pention book). Attorney of*
> *the Common Pleas 1730 [lists pursuant to 1729 Act].*

B11. DOCTORS OF LAW AND ADVOCATES

Until the nineteenth century, the ecclesiastical courts (described in section D) dealt with many matters of importance, for example probate, matrimonial disputes and claims of slander. The lawyers who practised in these courts (and the Court of Admiralty) were advocates (or Doctors of Law) and proctors. The advocates were the equivalent of barristers in the secular courts. They had to take the degree of Doctor of Civil Law at university (indicated by the letters 'LL.D' after their names). The proctors were the equivalent of attorneys and solicitors. Barristers, attorneys and solicitors were only entitled to act in the ecclesiastical courts (unless dispensation was obtained) following legislation of 1857 to 1877.

Many advocates obtained positions as judges of the Court of Admiralty and as masters in the Court of Chancery. They were also appointed to important positions in the church courts, particularly as judges of the High Court of Delegates and as Chancellors of English and Welsh dioceses or as archdeacons' officials (presiding over bishops' or archdeacons' courts).

The name Doctors' Commons was applied to the group of buildings near St Paul's Cathedral in London that housed many of the ecclesiastical courts and in which many advocates and proctors had their chambers and offices. Much information about the courts, buildings and institutions in Doctors' Commons appears in volume 15 of *London topographical record* (London Topographical Society, 1931)

The Society of Doctors' Commons (also known as the College of Advocates and Doctors of Law) was founded shortly before 1494. Membership was not compulsory for advocates and, until 1569, some proctors were members. The society's surviving records are in Lambeth Palace Library (LPL) and at TNA. The oldest record, the subscription book (LPL ref: DC1), begins in 1511. It lists 767 of the members of the College alive in that year or who joined between 1511 and 1855, noting the payment of their entrance fees or promises to pay annual contributions (and the members' signatures). G. D. Squibb, *Doctors' Commons: a history of the College of Advocates and Doctors of Law* (Clarendon Press, 1977) describes the College and lists the College's Presidents and its known members with biographical details. It also lists those advocates (who may have been members) who are not mentioned in the College records. Two biographies from Squibb's work, for advocates with contrasting careers, are:

> *Richard Zouche, B.C.L., New College, Oxford from Winchester College; son of Francis Zouche of Anstey, co. Wilts; admitted to Doctors' Commons, 30 Jan 1618, D.C.L. 8 Apr 1619; admitted Court of Arches 30 Apr 1619; Treasurer 1627-8; Judge of the Court of Admiralty 1641-3; President 1660; married Sarah, dau of John Hart of London, proctor; died 1 Mar 1661.*

> *William Beaw, D.C.L., Magdalen College, Oxford; admitted Court of Arches, 2 Nov 1696; admitted to Doctors' Commons, 3 Nov 1696; son of William Beaw, Bishop of Llandaff; imprisoned for debt in the Fleet Prison for 35 years; died there 6 Jan 1738.*

The other surviving records of the College are described in Squibb's work. They include:

1) The 'Long book' (TNA ref: PRO 30/26/8); various accounts and (for 1679-1828) minutes of members' meetings,
2) The minute book (LPL ref: DC2); minutes of members' meetings, 1828-1865,
3) Leases to members, 1675-1819 (LPL ref: DC9) and rent book 1787-1830 (LPL ref: DC22), and
4) Commons book, 1738-79 (LPL ref: DC25), listing the names of the members in commons (and the quantities of wine drunk).

More detailed biographies of about 200 advocates who practised between 1603 and 1641 are contained in B.P. Levack, *The civil lawyers in England 1603-1641, a political study* (Clarendon Press, 1973). For example, a shortened version of the entry for Robert Mason is:

> *Born 1590, son of George Mason of New Windsor, gent by Barbara, daughter of John Perkins of Flints. Scholar of St John's College, Cambridge, 1606; B.A. 1610; M.A. 1613; senior proctor 1619-20; LL.D. 1628; admission Doctors' Commons 1629. Chancellor of the Diocese of Winchester, 1630. Judge of Vice-Admiralty Court of Hants and the Isle of Wight 1637. Advocate in High Court of Admiralty 1638. Chancellor of the Diocese of Rochester 1661-2. Purchased manor of Itchell in Crondal, Hants, 1629. Married Judith, daughter of Charles Buckle 1633.*

The law lists contain the names of the advocates with the dates of their admission to the College and the positions that they occupied, mainly in the church courts. For example, the *Law list 1853* shows that John Haggard, LL.D, admitted to the College on 3 November 1818, was Chancellor of the dioceses of Winchester, Lincoln and Manchester and also Official of the Archdeacons of Surrey, Essex, Colchester and St Albans and the Commissary of Surrey.

Admissions of advocates to practice in the Court of Arches are recorded in the Archbishop of Canterbury's Act Books, some of which are indexed in E. Dunkin and C. Jenkins: *Index to the Act Books of the Archbishops of Canterbury 1663-1859 vols I & II* (British Record Society: 1929 & 1938). This includes, for example, the admission of Matthew Tyndall in 1685 (he became a member of Doctors' Commons the same year) but also includes some advocates who were admitted to the Court of Arches but never joined the College of Advocates. Some advocates practised in the courts at York and so references to them may be found in the records of the Archbishops of York (held at the Borthwick Institute of Historical Research).

The advocates lost the monopoly over their work in the nineteenth century. Matrimonial and probate matters were transferred from the church courts to new (secular) courts of Divorce and Matrimonial Causes and of Probate in 1857. Serjeants and barristers could appear in those courts. Barristers were also permitted to appear in the Court of Arches in 1857 and the Court of Admiralty in 1859. Advocates were given the right to practise in any English court but the justification of the existence of the advocates had disappeared. The last admission of an advocate to Doctors' Commons took place in 1855 and the last advocate died in 1912.

B12. PROCTORS

Proctors practised in the High Court of Admiralty and in the church courts, described in section D.20, such as the Consistory Court of London, the Prerogative Court of Canterbury and the Court of Arches. In chapter 24 of *David Copperfield*, Dickens gives a vivid picture of a visit to a proctor's office in Doctors' Commons, followed by an appearance in court there.

Most proctors were also notaries and until 1569, some proctors were members of Doctors' Commons. By the early nineteenth century, those entering the profession had to serve articles (of seven years) with a senior proctor. Many proctors had law degrees. Proctors lost much of their work when probate and matrimonial matters were transferred from the church courts to the new secular courts. An Act of 1877 permitted solicitors to practice in the church courts and no more proctors were appointed after this.

Proctors in London are listed in the law lists both separately and in the lists of attorneys and solicitors. From 1861 the law lists give the dates of their admissions.

It was usual for proctors to be admitted to the courts in which they practised at the start of their careers. These admissions were recorded in act books. Lambeth Palace Library holds a card index of advocates and proctors who practised in the Court of Arches from 1700 to 1862, compiled from the following records that are held in the library:

1) Commissions for the admission of advocates and proctors   1700 – 1859
2) Fiats for the admission of advocates   1703 – 1855
3) Fiats for the admission of proctors   1668 – 1859
4) Testimonials of proctors   1834 – 1862

This index does not list all the advocates and proctors practising in the Court of Arches. Details of others are to be found in the muniment books and act books of the Archbishop of Canterbury and in the 'Proctors' term fees books'.

The faculties by which proctors are appointed are contained in the muniment books of the Faculty Office of the Archbishop of Canterbury, dating from 1534, at Lambeth Palace Library (ref: FI). The admissions of many proctors to the Court of Arches are noted in E. Dunkin and C. Jenkins, *Index to the Act Books of the Archbishops of Canterbury 1663-1859* (2 vols, British Record Society, 1929-38). For example, there are references to five men named Toller; that is Edward Toller in 1790, his sons Edward (in 1815) and Charles (in 1827) and also Edward William Toller in 1850 and Charles George Toller in 1859.

The Proctors' term fees books are held at Lambeth Palace Library and cover the periods 1761-1838 (ref: DC20) and 1839-58 (ref: DC21). They contain the names of all proctors practising in the Court of Arches during these periods, recording their contributions to repairs and other expenses of the courtroom.

Cases heard in the Court of Arches (and conducted by proctors) are listed in J. Houston, *An index of cases in the records of the Court of Arches at Lambeth Palace Library* (British Record Society, 1972). Proctors were also parties in many of these cases. For example, Peter Barrett, a proctor in the Court of Arches, sued a number of people for non-payment of his fees and also brought proceedings against the Churchwardens of Colebrook, Buckinghamshire in 1670 for allowing unlicensed preaching.

The records of the High Court of Admiralty and the Prerogative Court of Canterbury, held at TNA (*see* sections D.5 and D.20 below), also include material about proctors who practised in those courts. An article 'The proctor' by J. Titford in *Family Tree Magazine* in January 1991 provides useful information about proctors and refers to a list of proctors (with some biographical information) held by Mr Titford in which searches can be made for a small fee.

Provincial proctors practised in cathedral cities such as Canterbury, York, Chichester, Chester, Lichfield, Hereford and Gloucester. Information about the admission and work of these proctors may be found in diocesan records and the publications of local history societies. Diocesan records are generally held in county record offices or city archives. Those records that relate to proctors can be found in the catalogues at each archive or in the online catalogues available through the web site of Access to Archives ('A2A'), which by October 2005 contained 8.6 million catalogue entries from 390 archives and libraries. For example, London Metropolitan Archives holds records of the Consistory Court of London that include appointments of proctors in that court in the period 1556-78/9. Worcestershire Record Office holds records of the appointment of 201 proctors in the Consistory Court of the Diocese of Worcester in the period 1785-89. The Borthwick Institute of Historical Research in York holds many records of the Archbishop of York. The catalogue includes the following entries:

Files of papers, generally comprising a petition, letters testimonial, the archbishop's fiat and a declaration, relating to the admission of proctors and advocates of the ecclesiastical courts of York 1622-1864 [Ref Proct/Adm]
Register of proctors' certificates 1785-1910 [Ref Proct/Reg]
Resignations 1758-1853 [Ref Proct/Res]

One example of the published material about proctors that is available is volume 46 of *The Transactions of the Bristol & Gloucestershire Archaeological Society* (1924). This contains an article, entitled 'The Consistory Court of the Diocese of Gloucester', by F.S. Hockaday, which explains the procedure of this court and describes the duties of proctors.

B13. CONVEYANCERS AND SPECIAL PLEADERS

Conveyancers were lawyers who specialised in the conveyancing of property. This work is now undertaken by solicitors and licensed conveyancers. Most conveyancers were members of the Inns of Court (and some had chambers in the Inns) but until 1828 they were permitted to undertake their work without being called to the bar (and taking the necessary oaths of supremacy and allegiance). They were said to practise 'under the bar'. Many Catholics therefore worked as conveyancers.

As noted above, an Act of 1785 required attorneys and solicitors to take out annual practising certificates (at a fee of £3 or £5). The attorneys and solicitors petitioned the House of Commons protesting against this requirement, complaining that the Act did not extend to;

> *persons who called themselves Conveyancers ... and that for want of a positive Law restrictive of the practice of conveyancing, many illiterate and unqualified Men have intruded themselves into that Branch of the Profession to the great Prejudice of the Public by the Promoting of Litigation and the Disgrace of the Profession of the Law.*

The requirement to take out annual practising certificates was extended to conveyancers in 1804. Conveyancers are included in the law lists but there are not many of them. The earliest law lists do not mention them at all but the *Law list 1790* included their names in two separate lists. The first was the 'List of counsel', including the names and addresses of barristers. Some of these barristers were shown also to be conveyancers. The second list is headed 'Conveyancers'. Of the 59 individuals named in this list, 29 were also barristers.

The list of provincial attorneys in the *Law list 1790* does not include any conveyancers but some appear in the law lists a few years later. In the *Law list 1808* there were 111 conveyancers in England and Wales, 65 of them in London. In the case of the provincial conveyancers, it is noticeable that some of them practised in small country places, such as Appleton-le-Moors (Yorkshire) and Horningsham (Wiltshire). Others practised in country towns such as Redruth (Cornwall) and St Neots (Huntingdonshire).

A conveyancer named James Robinson Walsh is noted in the *Law list 1819* as practising at Halstead, Essex and in that of 1835 as having an office at Sudbury, Suffolk. There is no reference to him in any other years and so it may be that he had only a brief practice in each place, perhaps because of opposition from local attorneys. His son Francis Eldridge Walsh is recorded at Sudbury in the *Law list 1836*. He had been admitted as a solicitor in 1835 so presumably he took over whatever practice his father might have had.

Three conveyancers named Cuddon practised in Norwich in the mid-nineteenth century. James Cuddon is described as a certificated conveyancer in G. K. Blyth, *The Norwich guide & directory 1842*. He practised in partnership with his son James Cuddon, junior. The practice was presumably successful for in 1845 he was Lord of the Manor of Gooderstone, Norfolk. James Cuddon, junior, and Francis Thomas Cuddon last appear as conveyancers in the *Law list 1856*.

By 1835, the number of conveyancers in England and Wales had risen to 134 but by 1861 there had been a steep decline in their numbers to 53 (18 in London and 35 in the provinces). Conveyancers had almost disappeared by 1900. The last of them, Samuel Whitty Chandler, who practised at Sherborne in Dorset and later at Bournemouth, died in 1927. The amount of his estate (£81,432 11s. 5d) indicates that, although the profession of conveyancers had come to an end, the members of that profession had been prosperous. Charles Bailey, who practised as a conveyancer from his home (5 Stratford Place, Oxford Street, London) is shown in the census return in 1851 as employing a butler, a page, a cook and two housemaids.

Special pleaders were lawyers (usually barristers) who specialised in drafting written pleadings for actions in the common law courts. Pleadings set out the allegations and answers of the parties. By the eighteenth century, the rules and art of pleading in the common law courts had acquired a 'Byzantine complexity' (the rules of pleading are now much more straightforward) and so some lawyers concentrated on this area of practice. Similarly to conveyancers, special pleaders were members of the Inns of Court and most practised from chambers in the Inns of Court. However, prior to 1828, many were not called to the bar (and so Catholics were able to undertake this work).

Special pleaders are included in the law lists. The *Law list 1790* included their names in the 'List of counsel', in which some barristers were shown also to be special pleaders. It also contained lists of special pleaders, draftsmen in equity and draftsmen in common law. All of them were practising in London and most of them were also members of the bar. The list of draftsmen in common law named only five men, four of whom had been called to the bar.

B14. NOTARIES AND SCRIVENERS

Notaries translate and prepare documents in foreign languages and forms. Their certificates have international authority. The duties of a notary public in England and Wales are described in an article in *Halsbury's laws of England* by W.E. Harrison and A.C. Comerford:

> *A notary public is a duly appointed officer whose public office it is, among other matters, to draw, attest or certify, usually under his official seal, deeds and other documents, including conveyances of real and personal property and powers of attorney relating to real and personal property ... to note or certify transactions relating to negotiable instruments, to prepare wills or other testamentary documents, to draw up protests or other formal papers relating to occurrences on the voyages of ships and their navigation as well as the carriage of cargo in ships.*

The origins of the notarial profession go back to Roman days when the 'notarius' was a slave or freedman who took notes – notae – of judicial proceedings. However, the modern notary really corresponds to the 'tabellio' who copied and authenticated legal documents. Medieval notaries were public officials, appointed either by the Pope or the Holy Roman Emperor. In England, up to the end of the thirteenth century, there was no notarial profession as such although there were some notaries in practice (most, if not all, ecclesiastics), deriving their authority from the Pope or from the Archbishop of Canterbury as Papal Delegate. Laymen were appointed as notaries from the late fourteenth century and they included a number of scriveners (described below). English notaries soon became established independently of foreign control and foreign notaries seem to have been excluded from England. During the Reformation, the monarch, as head of the church, assumed the right to grant notarial faculties by an Act of 1534 (revoked during Queen Mary's reign but revived by Queen Elizabeth). Ever since, notaries have received their faculties from the Archbishop of Canterbury, acting through the Court of Faculties, on behalf of the monarch as head of the Church.

A scrivener was a writer of charters, deeds and other important documents, particularly those relating to the conveyance of property. Many craftsmen founded fraternities to protect themselves against competition and protect the populace against bad workmanship. The fraternities in London developed into the City livery companies. The Scriveners' Company was established as a guild in the late fourteenth century and received a charter in 1617. It is often said that London notaries have an unbroken connection with this company. This is not quite correct. In the early days of the Scriveners' Company most, if not all, London notaries belonged to it (and most Scriveners were also notaries), but the relationship gradually came to an end and by 1748, no notaries appear to have been members of the company.

In 1748, the Scriveners' Company produced a report about continuing encroachments on their rights by notaries and attorneys. A petition was presented to the Court of Common Council of the City of London asking it to require all persons practising the art of a scrivener in London, Westminster and the borough of Southwark to become free of the company. The report noted that until 1665 attorneys and solicitors did not practise as scriveners, that is undertake conveyancing, but after that date they began to do so (and paid quarterage to the company for the privilege). However, from around 1700, when commerce and conveyancing increased considerably, attorneys, solicitors and notaries all practised the art of a scrivener in the City. The report added that in 1700 there had been only six attorneys in the City but their numbers had grown enormously, whereas the numbers of scriveners had declined. The report added that before 1729, scriveners had acted as attorneys but that the 1729 Act, for regulating attorneys, prevented scriveners practising as attorneys 'for want of the qualifications required by that Act, serving a five years clerkship to some attorney'. The Court of Common Council took notice of the Scriveners' plea and in 1752 enacted that:

persons not being free of the City of London who ... exercise the trade, occupation, art, mystery, or science of Scrivener in [or within three miles[3] of] the City of London, should take upon themselves the freedom ... of the Company of Scriveners.

Sixteen London notaries promptly joined the company. Despite this, scriveners declined as a profession because attorneys undertook most conveyancing and then an 1804 Act prohibited conveyancing by persons other than barristers, attorneys, solicitors, proctors or notaries.

The notarial profession continued to flourish due to the importance of translated documents. The Public Notaries Act of 1801 provided that nobody should be admitted as a notary unless he had served seven years' articles to a public notary.[4]

Records of the Scriveners' Company, including rolls of members from 1732, are held at Guildhall Library. Many earlier members and apprentices are listed in F.W. Steer, *Scriveners' Company common paper 1357-1628 with a continuation to 1678* (London Record Society, 1968). The history of the company has been published; the first volume by F.W. Steer (Phillimore, 1973) and a second by B. Brooks and C. Humphery-Smith (Phillimore, 2001).

The notarial profession in London has always been a small one. The *Law list 1793* contains the names of 43 notaries in London. The *Law list 1853* shows 31 notaries in London, all of them members of the Scriveners' Company. Two particular facets of the notarial profession in London may be of interest to family historians. First, it has always included many foreigners or individuals of foreign extraction because of the need for skills in foreign languages and the translation of legal documents. For example, wills left by foreign testators who had property in England or Wales had to be proved not only in their own country but also in the Prerogative Court of Canterbury until 1858, then in the Court of Probate and later in the High Court of Justice. Before the probate could be re-sealed here translations certified by a notary had to be produced. Candidates for the notarial examination have to take not only papers in law (such as real and personal property) and notarial practice, but also examinations in two foreign languages, dealing particularly with legal terminology. Many notaries who practised in England were born on the Continent – in Holland, France, Germany, Switzerland, Denmark, Norway, Spain and Portugal. For example, in the seventeenth century, the notaries in London included several foreigners, sometimes referred to as 'notaries strangers'. Joshua Maynet, presumably a Frenchman, was a notary in the City in 1632. In 1655 Mr. Marius and Mr. Daniel, probably Dutch, were described as 'Notaries on the Backside of the Exchange'.

Another interesting facet of the profession is that it has tended, to a remarkable extent, to descend in families. A number of families have produced notaries in each generation and the descent of notarial practices can be clearly established. At present there are 28 notaries public of the City of London (seven of them women) who belong to six firms. Four firms have their origins in the eighteenth century. The firm of de Pinnas derives from three notaries;

1) Joseph Cortissos who was admitted in 1757 and later took in as a partner his cousin Jacob de Pinna, whose faculty dates from 1772,
2) Tobias Atkinson, admitted in 1765, who was subsequently in partnership with John Withers and William Scorer, and
3) John Mitchell, admitted in February 1771, who formed a partnership with John Venn.

The firm of John Venn & Sons also derives from the partnership of Mitchell & Venn. The firm Cheeswrights dates back to William Dunbar, who became a notary in November 1771. John Newton & Sons originates with William Tudman who was admitted in 1738. From his partner William Newton, admitted in 1775, descended in the male line 10 London notaries, the last of whom died in 1979.

The Society of Public Notaries of London (now the Society of Scrivener Notaries), to which London members of the profession belong, was established in or about 1808 but formal meetings of notaries were held in London in earlier years. On 1 July 1797 the 15 leading London notaries met at the George & Vulture Tavern to consider their scale of fees.

Many notaries in the eighteenth and nineteenth centuries engaged in commercial enterprises that were ancillary to their notarial work. For example, William Newton described himself as a banker in his will of 1813 and referred to his sons as being in charge of the notarial side of his business. Andrew Gram, a Norwegian who practised as a notary in the City of London and died in 1806, was also a timber merchant. The notaries Gilson and Cheeswright were also ship and insurance brokers in the City in the late eighteenth and early nineteenth centuries. Judah Uzielli, a Jewish notary who had become a Christian, was Foreign Secretary to the London Society for Promoting Christianity among the Jews from 1809 to 1812.

The notaries who practised in the provinces were often also the principal attorneys or solicitors in market towns, large ports and cathedral cities. Although nowadays a provincial notary is also a solicitor, this has not always been the case. Indexes to wills proved in the Prerogative Court of Canterbury in the period 1605-75 include a number of notaries public outside London. Most lived in cathedral cities like Lincoln, or large towns such as Lewes, but some were in small places, for example Robert Hall of Palgrave in Suffolk, Edward Rhodes of Wilberton in the Isle of Ely and Reginald Pyndar of Breadsall in Derbyshire.

The *Law list 1805* names 128 notaries in practice in places other than London. Most of them were also attorneys although some were proctors. The places where these notaries practised and the number of notaries at each place were: Birmingham (1), Boston (1), Bridgwater (1), Bristol (2), Bury St Edmunds (1), Chester (5), Chichester (1), Cowes (3), Dartmouth (3), Deal (1), Dover (3), Durham (4), Exeter (3), Falmouth (4), Folkestone (1), Gosport (2), Gravesend (1), Halifax (1), Harleston (1), Harwich (2), Ilfracombe (2), Leicester (2), Lincoln (1), Lichfield (5), Liverpool (10), Lymington (1), King's Lynn (2), Manchester (3), Marazion (1), Margate (1), Milford (Pembrokeshire) (1), Newcastle-under-Lyme (1), Newcastle-upon-Tyne (1), Northampton (1), Norwich (1), Oxford (1), Penryn (Cornwall) (1), Plymouth (7), Plymouth Dock (1), Poole (2), Portsmouth (3), Ramsgate (2), Rochester (2), Scilly Islands (2), Sheerness (1), Sheffield (1), North Shields (1), South Shields (1), Southampton (2), Sunderland (2), Weymouth (4), Whitehaven (1), Wimborne (1), Worcester (2), Workington (1), Great Yarmouth (6) and York (10).

Most of these places are cathedral cities, where notaries worked as proctors in the church courts, or ports, where they dealt with shipping matters, in particular making ships' protests. A protest was a declaration, made before a notary by a ship's master, after a voyage during which cargo was damaged. It was signed by the master, witnessed by the notary and recorded in the notary's protest book, as a protection against insurance claims. An interesting book on this subject is G. Hampson, *Southampton notarial protest books 1756-1810* (Southampton University Press, 1973), which deals with the notarial practices in Southampton of Thomas Ridding and his son Thomas Ridding, both of whom were attorneys as well as notaries.

The faculties by which notaries are appointed are in the muniment books, dating from 1534, of the Faculty Office of the Archbishop of Canterbury at Lambeth Palace Library (ref: FI). Faculties usually record the diocese in which the notary was born and sometimes his actual birthplace. This is the faculty of 30 November 1771 of William Dunbar, a London notary:

Frederick by Divine Providence Archbishop of Canterbury ... by Authority of Parliament lawfully empowered for the purpose herein written to our beloved in Christ William Dunbar a literate person born in the parish of Dyke in the Shire of Elgin and Forres North Britain Health and Grace We being willing by reason of your Merits to confer on you a suitable title or promotion do create you a Publick Notary previous Examination and the other Requisites to be herein observed having been had and do out of our Favour towards you admit you into the number and Society of Notaries to the end that you may henceforward in all places exercise such office of Notary Hereby decreeing that full Faith ought to be given as well in our Judgment as thereout to the Instruments to be from this time made by you the Oaths hereunder written having been by us or our Master of the Faculties first required of you and by you taken.

I William Dunbar do sincerely promise and swear that I will be faithful and bear true Allegiance to his Majesty King George So help me God.

I William Dunbar do swear that I abhor detest and abjure as Impious and Heretical that Damnable Doctrine and Position that Princes excommunicated or deprived by the Pope or any Authority of the See of Rome may be deposed or murthered by their subjects or any other whatsoever; And I do declare that no Foreign Prince, Person, Prelate, State or Potentate hath or might have any Power, Jurisdiction, Superiority, Preeminence or Authority Ecclesiastical or Spiritual within this Realm, So help me God.

I William Dunbar do swear that I will faithfully exercise the Office of a Notary Publick. I will faithfully make Contracts wherein the Consent of Parties is required by adding or diminishing nothing without the Will of such Parties that may alter the substance of the Fact But if in making any Instrument wherein the Will of one Party alone is required this I will also do to wit I will add or diminish nothing that may alter the substance of the Fact against the Will of the Party himself I will not make Instruments of any Contract in which I shall know there is Violence or Fraud I will reduce Contracts into an Instrument or Register, and after I shall have so reduced the same I will not maliciously delay to make a Publick Instrument therefrom against the Will of him or them on whose behalf such Contract is to be drawn; saving to myself my just and accustomed Fee So help me God.'

Lambeth Palace library also holds (ref: FII) fiats, which are orders to proceed with the application for admission as a notary public. The library also holds the following papers relating to public notaries, with reference FIII:

1) Papers relating to notaries struck off since 1860,
2) A list of notaries granted faculties 1775-1802,
3) Registers of annual certificates, affidavits of annual certificates since 1813,
4) Lists of foreign notaries (English notaries practising overseas) 1800-1922,
5) Papers relating to readmissions 1800-59,
6) Registers of articled clerks 1801-1955,
7) Affidavits of contracts of articled clerks since 1801, and
8) Calendars of foreign notaries since 1801.

English notaries were appointed by the Archbishop of Canterbury but there were Roman Catholic notaries in England before 1829. The records of their admissions are also at Lambeth Palace Library. One Roman Catholic notary was Thomas McKiernan, an Irishman, who obtained his notarial faculty on 27 July 1801, swearing the special oath provided by the Faculty Office for Catholics. He became a freeman of the Scriveners' Company by redemption (payment) on 27 June 1805, a freeman of the City of London by redemption on 11 July 1805 and a liveryman of the Scriveners' Company on 30 July 1806. Another was Hugh Bourke, also Irish, who became a freeman of the Scriveners' Company by redemption on 29 July 1807 and obtained his notarial faculty on 8 August of the same year. Both Thomas McKiernan and Hugh Bourke practised as notaries in the City of London.

Family historians with ancestors who were notaries may like to read C.W. Brooks, R.H. Hemholz and P.G. Stein, *Notaries Public in England since the Reformation* (Erskine Press, 1991).

B15. COURT OFFICIALS

Each court was staffed by clerks and officials with various functions, for example filing records, issuing court documents or collecting fees. Many of these officials were lawyers.

The published law lists included sections on each of the superior courts (and many of the lesser courts around the country), with lists of the senior officials serving in each.

The lists do not indicate whether those officers were lawyers but their names sometimes appear in the lists of barristers and attorneys. For example, the entry for the Court of Common Pleas in the *Law list 1826* listed 47 officials (in addition to the four judges and their eight clerks). The officials included George Watlington, one of the three 'Prothonotaries', who also appeared in the list of barristers and Richard Bremridge, the 'Clerk of the Judgments and Reversals' who also appeared in the list of London attorneys as practising from 41 Chancery Lane.

Similar lists of court officials are also included in some directories and almanacs, for example in *The court and city register compleat for the year 1744* and in *The British Imperial calendar 1823*. The latter included 16 pages of such lists for the courts, with about 200 officials of the Court of Chancery (including officials of the Commissioners of Lunacy and Commissioners of Bankruptcy). In contrast, only a judge, a Prothonotary and one barrister were listed for the Whitechapel Court, a small court for the recovery of debts that only sat on Thursdays.

Court officials are recorded in the archives of each court, most of which are held at TNA and at county or city record offices. However, those records are not always easy to find or use. They may include lists of officers but more commonly they are records of appointment, or merely passing reference to a clerk or official in a document that was prepared for another purpose. Consequently, the best place to start research is in the published works available about each court since these include many references to the court officials, compiled from the court records. These works are noted in section D below.

B16. LAWYERS EMPLOYED BY GOVERNMENT, COMMERCIAL AND OTHER ORGANISATIONS

Barristers, attorneys and solicitors could be employed by central government, local authorities and commercial or other bodies, such as a railway company or a charity. These lawyers will be included in the sources noted above and in the law lists. These lawyers should also be referred to in the archives of their employers. These archives may be held at TNA or in county or city record offices or they may have been retained by the employer.

Some important published records include references to employed lawyers. The best way of locating these works is through library catalogues. For example, government departments have employed many lawyers and there are some published lists of government employees, such as the series 'Office-holders in Modern Britain'. For example, J.C. Sainty, *Admiralty officials 1660-1870* (University of London Institute of

Historical Research, 1975) includes 28 men who held the position of 'Admiralty Counsel' over this period, 12 men who were employed as 'Admiralty Solicitor', 26 appointed as the 'Admiralty Advocate' and 12 appointed as the 'Admiralty Proctor'.

B17. MEMBERS OF PARLIAMENT

Many lawyers also had careers as Members of Parliament. In the period 1754 to 1790, about 120 barristers, 10 attorneys and eight advocates from Doctors' Commons were members of the House of Commons. There are detailed biographical dictionaries of MPs, in particular the volumes of *The history of Parliament*, such as that by Sir Lewis Namier and J. Brooke, *The House of Commons 1754-1790* (HMSO, 1964), and M. Stenton, *Who's who of British Members of Parliament* (Harvester Press, 1976-81).

B18. CLERKS OF THE PEACE

Clerks of the peace, also known as clerks to the justices and later magistrates' clerks, were appointed to assist the justices of the peace in entering their judgments, other procedural matters and keeping their records. From 1888, the clerks also acted as clerks to county councils. The origins and duties of the office are described in Sir Edgar Stephen, *The clerks of the counties 1360-1960* (The Society of Clerks of the Peace of Counties and of Clerks of County Councils, 1961). This work also contains lists of the men known to have held this office (and in some counties the office of deputy clerk) in each county of England and Wales, with some biographical notes about them. Clerks were required to have some knowledge of the law and so most were attorneys, solicitors or barristers.

For example, the entries in Stephen's work for Oxfordshire record that Paul Elers was clerk of the peace from 1777 to 1781. He was a barrister of Middle Temple and had been a justice of the peace from 1746 to 1777 but became impoverished and so was offered the post of clerk of the peace. The clerk of the peace for Oxfordshire from 1831 to 1881 was John Marriott Davenport. He was admitted as a solicitor in 1830 and held various offices in the church courts, including that of registrar of the Court of Probate for Oxfordshire, Berkshire and Buckinghamshire.

The entries in Stephen's work also reveal the family links between lawyers. The list of clerks for Buckinghamshire includes an entry for Acton Chaplin, an attorney who practised at Aylesbury and was town clerk of that place. He died in 1815, having been clerk of the peace for Buckinghamshire 1787-1813 and from 1793 to 1805 joint clerk of the Grand Junction Canal Company. His son-in-law Thomas Tindal was clerk of the peace for Buckinghamshire 1813-38. Born in 1783, he was also an attorney at Aylesbury and was the brother of Sir Nicholas Conyngham Tindal, Chief Justice of the Court of Common Pleas. His son Acton Tindal, born in 1811, practised at Aylesbury as an attorney and succeeded his father as clerk of the peace. He was also Under Sheriff and lord of the manor of Aylesbury. His other offices included those of clerk to the justices, Aylesbury division, a registrar of the Archdeaconry of Buckinghamshire and clerk of the Aylesbury guardians 1835-38. He died in 1880.

The law lists record many attorneys as also being Clerks of the Peace. For example, the *Law list 1833* included Robert Whincop of Lynn, Norfolk, William Oakes Hunt of Stratford-upon-Avon and Charles Markham of Northampton.

B19. CLERKS OF LIVERY COMPANIES OF THE CITY OF LONDON

Many attorneys and solicitors have acted as clerks of livery companies in the City of London in addition to running their own legal practices. Park Nelson, of 11 Essex Street, Strand, for example, was clerk of the Scriveners' Company 1828-76. He was also President of the Law Society in 1872. Beaumont Charles Luttly, of Wandsworth, Surrey, and Dyers' Hall, College Street, Dowgate Hill, was clerk to the Dyers' Company and also clerk to the Commissioners of Taxes for West Brixton and the Surrey Iron Railway Company in 1846.

The law lists refer to many of these lawyers. For example, the *Law list 1833* recorded Daniel Ferard of 22 Austin Friars, London, as clerk of the Woolmen's Company (and as steward of a number of manors) and William Harry Sadgrove of 26 Nicholas Lane, Lombard Street, as clerk of the Poulterers' Company. Thomas Glover Kensit was recorded as clerk of the Skinners' Company. .

Most livery companies have deposited their records at Guildhall Library, which also holds a large collection of published histories of the companies (many of which include lists of those men who have acted as clerks).

B20. VESTRY CLERKS

Every parish was governed by a vestry. Most surviving vestry minutes and other records are in county record offices. Lawyers often acted as clerks to vestries and were so described in law lists. Archibald Campbell Russell, for instance, a solicitor with offices at 1 Lant Street, Southwark, was vestry clerk of St George's Church, Southwark in 1820. The *Law list 1833* recorded William Bartholomew of 50 Red Lion Street, Clerkenwell, as the vestry clerk of St John's Clerkenwell. From 1856, the law lists included separate lists of vestry clerks who were lawyers.

B21. STEWARDS OF MANORS

Solicitors were often appointed as stewards of manors, their duties being to represent the lord of the manor and preside at manorial courts on behalf of the lord. Stewards were sometimes local solicitors such as Charles Gilbert of Lewes, Sussex, who was steward of manors in the South Downs, the Weald and Pevensey Marsh in the late eighteenth and early nineteenth centuries. Some London solicitors were also stewards of manors. Edward Bunce of 72 Gower Street, Bedford Square, for example, was steward of the manors of Hayes, Heston, Norwood, Southall and Northall in Middlesex and of Langley Marsh and Graves in Buckinghamshire in 1818. Thomas Brook Bridges Stevens, of 23 Bolton Street, Piccadilly, Carlton Chambers, Regent Street and Tamworth, Staffordshire was steward of the manor of Hemlingford and Kingsbury in 1851. He was also solicitor to the Military, Naval and County Service Club.

Manorial records can be located through the Manorial Documents Register held by the Royal Commission on Historical Manuscripts, now part of TNA, at Kew. Part of the register can be accessed online.

B22. CORONERS

The office of coroner dates back to 1194. It is the coroner's duty to investigate sudden or suspicious deaths. Coroners are lawyers or medical practitioners.

There are many references to coroners in the law lists. The *Law list 1830*, for example, includes George White, an attorney at Grantham, who was coroner for Lincolnshire. The *Law list 1833* recorded William Baker of 10 Church Row, Limehouse, as coroner for Middlesex (and also vestry clerk of St Anne, Limehouse and clerk to the trustees of the East India Dock Company). Many law lists include lists of all coroners (whether lawyers or medical men).

J. Gibson and C. Rogers, *Coroners' records* (2nd edn. FFHS, 1997) contains detailed information about the location of coroners' records in England and Wales. The records are closed to the public for 75 years. Many older records have not survived but those that have are generally held in county record offices and city archives (and a few have been transcribed and published). Many records of coroners' inquests are also at TNA on the files of the Court of King's Bench. Writs for the election of coroners are in Chancery files at TNA. Coroners' inquests were commonly reported in local newspapers from the nineteenth century and so information about a lawyer who sat as a coroner can be obtained from these reports.

C. SOME OTHER PUBLISHED RECORDS OF LAWYERS

C1. LAW LISTS

The published law lists are the basic source of information about lawyers from 1775 to the present day. The early law lists are simple lists of the names and addresses of lawyers. However, further information was gradually included in these lists. This included the year of admission of a lawyer, the courts in which he practised and (in some lists) a lawyer's official positions and even the names of some of his clients.

Finding an ancestor who was a lawyer in the law lists is quite easy. Each list includes a number of sections, for judges, barristers, London attorneys (including solicitors, they were not listed separately) and country attorneys (and solicitors). In each section, the entries for those lawyers are in alphabetical order. If you find your ancestor in one list, you can then review the lists for earlier and later years in order to extract all the entries for him and all the information that the lists contain.

There is no overall index to the entries in the law lists. However, Brian Brooks has created a card index to the attorneys and solicitors appearing in the law lists for 1780, 1790, 1793, 1800, 1802, 1805, 1808-28, 1830-1840, 1843-49, 1851-55 and 1861, with information from other sources such as the 1851 census. Much of the index (excluding the parts for London, Middlesex, Sussex and Wales) has been deposited at the SoG. The SoG has converted it into a database that can be viewed in book form (SoG ref: PR/LAW/115503). It is in three parts; an alphabetical listing, the lawyers' career details and the lawyers' genealogical details.

The Brooks index refers to about 5,500 attorneys and solicitors. As an example, the entry in the alphabetical listing for John Eagles takes you to the career details section in which it is noted that John was admitted in Easter term 1822 and appears in the law lists for 1823-28, 1830-40, 1843-49 and 1851-55. He is also noted as an attorney of Dunstable Street in Ampthill, Bedfordshire in Pigot's *Directory of Bedfordshire 1839* and as deputy coroner for Bedfordshire in the 1851 census. The section of genealogical details notes that John was the son of Ezra Eagles (for whom there is also an entry in the index). He was baptised on 1 March 1801 at Ampthill, married Frances Arrowsmith at St George the Martyr, Middlesex and had two daughters (Sarah and Elizabeth) who were baptised at Ampthill. The index also contains entries for John's brother Ezra, a solicitor, and his son Ezra (an attorney and solicitor).

There are two other important indexes of attorneys and solicitors. The Law Society holds a manuscript index with biographical information, in 17 volumes and an index volume, of some attorneys and solicitors from about 1200 up to 1906, that was prepared by W.U.S.G. Richards. A card index to about 8,000 attorneys and solicitors from the seventeenth century up to 1900 (mainly country attorneys of the nineteenth century) has been prepared by T. Cockerill (of The Old Mill House, Weston Colville, Cambridge CB1 5NY). Searches are undertaken for a fee (of £2.50 and SAE).

The first law list was published in 1775 by John Browne, who appears to have been an apothecary, not a lawyer. Only one issue of this is known to exist. It is in the possession of the Law Society. After this first edition, the *Law list* was issued in 1777, 1779, 1780, 1782, 1783, 1785, 1787, 1789, 1790 and 1792. The *Law list* then appeared annually until it ceased publication after the 1801 edition. All these editions (and a complete run of later law lists) are in the Law Society library. Some of them (and many of the later published law lists) can also be consulted at the SoG, the Guildhall Library, the library at TNA, the British Library, and at some large reference libraries.

As noted above, an Act of 1785 imposed a duty of £5 or £3 on the practising certificates that attorneys were required to obtain. Collection of this duty was the responsibility of clerks in the Court of King's Bench, the Court of Common Pleas and the Court of Exchequer. The Commissioner of Stamps took over collection of this duty in 1797. John Hughes, of the Stamp Office, who had been appointed to sign the attorneys' certificates, began publication of the annual *New law list* in 1798, on the basis of information collected by the Stamp Office. It is important to note that the law lists from 1798 therefore only included attorneys who had taken out practising certificates for the relevant year. If a lawyer disappears from the law lists after a sequence of entries, you should not assume that he had died or emigrated. The lawyer may have gone into business and not wished to pay for the privilege of a practising certificate that he was not going to use. He might have been too old to practise (or he may even have been refused a certificate for some reason).

In 1803 the *New law list* assumed the name of *Clarke's new law list* (the publishers being W. Clarke & Sons) and was published under this name until 1840. Publication was undertaken from 1841 by V. and R. Stevens and G. S. Norton (later named Stevens and Sons Limited) who issued the publication annually under the name the *Law list* until 1976.

The law lists were published from 1860 by authority of the Commissioners of Inland Revenue and from 1896 by authority of the Law Society. They were the official directory of lawyers and constituted prima facie evidence that every attorney or solicitor included had taken out his practising certificate for that year. It is important to note that most law lists have listed those attorneys and solicitors who obtained their annual practising certificates. A man may therefore disappear from the law lists because he ceased to practise rather than because he died or emigrated. Entries for him may recommence a few years later (if he returned to practise after a period).

There have been a number of other published directories, particularly in recent years. *The solicitors' diary, almanac and legal directory* was published from about 1843 under various titles. It was published by Waterlows from 1875. After the *Law list* ceased publication in 1976, Waterlow's publication became the directory that was authorised by the Law Society. The Law Society now publishes its own annual directory, *The Law Society's directory of solicitors and barristers*. Other recent directories of barristers and solicitors include *Butterworth's law directory* (1985 to date), *The bar list of the United Kingdom* (1977-84) and *Hazell's guide to the judiciary and the courts with ... bar list* (1985-99).

Illustration 11 is an extract, listing London attorneys, from the *Law list 1780*. The entries are limited to an attorney's name and address, sometimes exact as in the case of John Lind of 8 Old Buildings, Lincoln's Inn but sometimes vague as in the case of Samuel Lister of 'Little Chelsea'. The early editions of the law lists contain a considerable amount of information in addition to the names and addresses of lawyers. For example, the *Law list 1780* notes:

All the Judges, Serjeants, Counsellors, Attornies, Officers of all the different Courts, Commissioners of Bankrupts, Doctors [of Law], Proctors, the Lord Mayor, Aldermen, Common Council and their several Committees, Bankers, Public Notaries, Surveyors, City Brokers, Auctioneers etc [and] A Complete List of the Common and Civil Law Offices, Hours of Attendance and Business done at each, the English and Welsh Circuits with the Names and Residence of the Judges, Serjeants and Counsel, pointing out the different circuits they go:- A Term and other useful Tables etc, ... The Attornies in the Country have their Names, Places of Abode and Distances from London inserted. Also a correct List of Stage-Coaches, with the Fares, Times and Places from whence they set out.

Most of the information in the *Law list 1780* is correct but there are mistakes such as 'Andrew Gran' for Andrew Gram, a notary who practised in Leadenhall Street. When attorneys were in partnership only the surnames of the partners appear at this time, for example Wilson & Peele, attorneys, 3 Symond's Inn. The entries for country attorneys are sometimes less informative than for London ones. The *Law list 1780* gives the surnames of six attorneys at Peterborough but the Christian names of only five of them.

The law lists published from 1785 to 1801 noted the court in which the London attorneys (but not for those in the provinces) practised by a code; (k) for King's Bench, (c) for Common Pleas or (kc) for both.

Lewis Henry, Holborn court, Grey's inn 6
Lewis Thomas, Mount row, Lambeth
Lewis Thomas, Old Boswell court, Carey ft. 20
Lewis and Bennett, Old Broad street 58
Lickbarrow Rowland, (Common Pleas office,) Tanfield court, Middle Temple
Lightfoot Christoper, King Edward ft. Bridewell
Lind John, Lincoln's inn Old buildings 8
Lindsay John, Holborn court, Grey's inn 13
Lindsay Hugh, Bartlett's buildings 1
Lister Samuel, Little Chelsea
Little James, Blackman street, Southwark
Littlehales Joseph, Lincoln's inn Old build. 26
Lloyd John, Furnival's inn 3
Lloyd, James street, Bedford row 15
Lloyd Benjamin, Symond's Inn 9
Lloyd John, Mincing lane 2
Lodge Samuel, Furnival's inn 10
Loggen Thomas, Basinghall street 83
Long George, Bond's court, Walbrook 7
Longworth Richard, Bell savage yard, Ludgate hill 7
Loveridge William, Union court, Broad street 11
Lowe Samuel, Chapel fair cafe, Lincoln's inn. Old buildings
Lowe James, (Office,) Fleet Prison
Lowe Thomas, Lincoln's inn Old buildings 19
Lowden George, Elm court, Middle Temple 4

Lowndes

Lowndes Richard, Coney court, Grey's inn
Lowndes and Kilvington, Bell yard, Temple bar
Lowter Thomas, Lambs buildings, Mid. Temp. 4
Lucas Charles, New inn, Wych street 7
Lucas Josiah, Brook street, Holborn 10
Ludley Thomas, Jermyn street
Lyon and Brograve, Coney court, Grey's inn 3

MABERLEY and Eyres, Christ Hospital
Macbean Wm. Castle court, Birchin lane 4
Machon William, Clifford's inn 6
Macquillin James Richard, Lyon's inn 2
Maddock Henry, Carey street, Lincoln's inn 10
Maddock John, Duke street, Lincoln's Inn fields
Maddox Illidge, Staple inn Coffee house
Mainstone James, Essex street, Strand
Mainwaring Thomas, Bartlett's build. Holb. 14
Maire Robert, Lincoln's inn Old Buildings 21

F 2   Mal-

Illustration 11: List of London attorneys from the Law list 1780.

The *Law list 1790* contained the full name of each partner in a firm as well as addresses. Illustration 12 is an extract, listing London attorneys. At that time, most attorneys were sole practitioners but there were firms with two, three or even four partners. One example is the partnership of Townly Ward (admitted in the Court of Common Pleas), Jonathan Dennett (admitted in both the King's Bench and Common Pleas) and William Graves and Robert Dennett (both admitted in the King's Bench) practising from 13 Sherborne Lane. Unlike today, the name of a firm of more than one attorney was then always that of all the partners.

An early example of a firm which continued to use the name of one of the partners after he had died or retired was Dyneley, Coverdale & Lee, of 1 Field Court, Gray's Inn. John Dyneley, a partner in this firm, last appears in the *Law list 1839* but his name continued to appear in law lists as part of the partnership name until 1845. The firm became Coverdale, Lee & Collyer-Bristow by 1861 and Coverdale, Lee, Collyer-Bristow & Withers by 1863.

The *New law list 1798* (later editions of this are referred to below as the *Law list*) did not record the courts in which attorneys practised. Some later editions did note those attorneys admitted to practise in the Court for Insolvent Debtors. For example, the attorneys of that court included in the *Law list 1833* included James Chilton of 1 Freeman's Court, Cornhill, London and James Crump of Birmingham.

Later editions also gave additional information about many attorneys. For example, Anthony Highmore, junior, of Bury Court, St Mary Axe, was described in the *Law list 1800* as clerk of the Glasssellers' Company, Secretary to the London Lying-in Hospital in City Road and the Smallpox and Inoculation Hospitals at St Pancras. John Poynder, of Bridewell Hospital, New Bridge Street, was Clerk of Bridewell and Bethlem Hospitals. The *Law list 1830* also described him as Secretary to the New Rupture Society. The *Law list 1833* described Thomas Ridding of Southampton as the town clerk, John Pexall Kidson of Sunderland as solicitor to the Ship Owners' Society and Robert Tibbits of Warwick as clerk to the magistrates. The *Law list 1854* included a solicitor named William Henry Hart, of 1 Albert Terrace, New Cross, Deptford, who informed readers that he was also a record agent, legal antiquarian and genealogist.

From 1798, the law lists contained a surname index of the country attorneys. In addition, they noted the London agents of country attorneys. Sometimes a country attorney and his London agent were related to one another. The identity of the London agent can sometimes help to identify an attorney who moved from one provincial town to another but retained the same agent.

and Liberty of Weftminfter, at the Office, Suffolk ftreet, Cavendifh fquare, 16

Venables Lazarus, (kc) Buggin George (k) and Blefdale Giles (c) Hatton court, Threadneedle ftreet, 3

Vernon John, jun. (c) Vines Sam, (k) & Fry Charles (k) Lincoln's innr New fquare, 10

Vicray Henry (k) Little St. Martin's lane, 7

Vincent Francis (k), and Ware George (k) Corner of Lant ftreet, Borough, Southwark

Vines Samuel, (k) Fry Charles (k) and Vernon John, jun. (kc) Lincoln's Inn New-fquare, 10

Vyfe Charles (k) Effex Court, Temple, 2

WADDINGTON William (k) & Kell Chrift. (k) Red Lion court, Fleet ftreet, 4

Wade Charles (k) and Sandys Hannibal (k) Crane court, Fleet ftreet

Wadefon Weyman Sam. (k) and Hardy Tickner Geo. (k) London ftreet, Fenchurch ftreet, 18, and Auftin friars

Walford Thomas (k) at Mr. Foulkes's, Covent garden Church yard, and at Brompton

Walford Theophilus (e) and Meyrick William (k) Red lion fquare, Holborn, 17

Walker James (k) near King's Bench Prifon, St. Georg's fields

Walker William (k) Adam ftreet, Adelphi, 10

Walker Edmund (k) Serjeant's inn, Chancery lane, 2, and (Exchequer Office of Pleas) Linc. inn Old fq. 9

Walker Charles (k) Chapter-houfe-court, St. Paul's Church yard

Wall Hawkins, (k) Paper building, Inner temple, 13 and 3

Wall William (c) Weft Smithfield, 36

Wall William (k) Red lion fquare, Holborn

Wallis John (k) King's Road, Gray's inn lane

Wallis Albany (kc) and Troward Richard (k) Norf.lk ftreet, Strand, 20

Walter Edw. (k) Heathcote Robert (kc) and Heathcote Charles (k) Upper Shadwell, 185

Walter Rob. (k) Kirton John (k) and Gray William (c) Holborn court, Gray's inn, 4

Walton John (k) and Walton William (k) (Girdlers hall)

Walton Robert (kc) Inner Temple lane, 3,

Ward Edward (k) Chancery lane

Ward Henry (k) Walham green, near Folham

Ward Townly (c) Dennett Robert (kc) Graves Wil-liam (k) and Dennett Robert (k) Sherbone lane, 13

Ward Jofeph (k) New Store ftreet, Bedford fquare, 21

Wardell Chriftopher (c) Mount ftr. Grofvenor fquare, 21

Ware George (k) and Vincent Francis (k) Corner of Lant ftreet, Borough, Southwark

Warry John (c) New inn, 3

Warry Richarc (k) Barnard's inn 1, and New inn 3

Waterfield David (k) near King's arms ftairs, Lambeth

Watkinfon William (k) Garden court, Gray's inn

Watfon William (k) Canterbury place, Lambeth

Watfon Tho. (k) Bankfide, Surry fide, Black Friars bridge

Watfon John (c) near the French Ch. Threadneedle ftr. 52

Watts William (k) Staple inn, 6

Watts John (k) Catherine fquare, St. Catherine's

Webb William (k) (King's Bench Office) Inner temple

Webb William (c) Layton's build. High ftr. Borough, 5

Webfter Thomas (k) & Son (k) Queen ftr. Cheapfide, 25

Wedd Rob. (kc) Dufour's place, Golden fquare

Wegener Samuel (c) Red Lion ftr. Wapping, and Brown's Coffee houfe, Mitre court, Fleet ftreet

Weight-

Illustration 12: List of London attorneys from the Law list 1790.

Some law lists gave a lawyer's private address as well as a business one. Stafford Spurr, for example, a London solicitor, is listed in the *Law list 1833* as practising at Copthall Court and living at 21 Woburn Place. Certain entries in law lists give some indication of the type of building in which the lawyer practised. The *Law list 1790* gives the address for John Edwards and his partner Roger Mellor, both attorneys of the Court of King's Bench, as 'New Bridge Street, Blackfriars – office door behind the house in Water-lane'.

The term and year in which every attorney or solicitor was admitted appears for the first time in the *Law list 1861*. The dates in this volume are occasionally incorrect as can be seen from comparing entries for two London solicitors, Robert George Augustus Hilleary and Gustavus Edward Hilleary. The *Law list 1861* gives their respective dates of admission as Hilary term of 1835 and Michaelmas term of 1828. However, the *Law list 1854* and later editions give the dates in reverse order, suggesting that the dates published in 1861 were incorrect.

The law lists of the nineteenth century sometimes show attorneys or solicitors having offices that were at a considerable distance from one another. William Fraser, for example, who was town clerk of Grimsby, also had premises at 5 Holborn Court, Gray's Inn in 1815. In the law lists of 1856 to 1859, Ambrose Parsons was noted as a solicitor and notary of Brighton and Hong Kong. By the *Law list 1860*, he was of Gray's Inn and Burton-on-Trent. In the 1860s, 1870s and 1880s he had an office in the City of London and acted as a Chinese agent, that is to say he acted on behalf of colleagues in China. In his will, made in 1889, he mentions his 'late friend and partner in Hong Kong William Gaskell'.

The nineteenth century law lists also have numerous entries for attorneys and solicitors that give the names of corporate clients (although in some cases it is unclear whether the noted company was the lawyer's client or employer). For example, William Batty, Joseph Lowless and Thomas Crosse of 3 Hatton Court, Threadneedle Street were identified in the *Law list 1833* as solicitors to the London Assurance, Hudson's Bay and English Copper companies. The *Law list 1851* recorded the same firm, as 'Messrs Crosse' (still at 3 Hatton Court, Threadneedle Street but also with an office in Gravesend) as solicitors to the Hudson's Bay Company. George Fry of 62 Mark Lane and Greenwich was solicitor to the Old Woolwich Steam Packet Company and the Continental Cattle Steamship Conveyance Company. Henry Martin Harvey of 11 Fenchurch Buildings was solicitor to the London Hospital. Solicitors also sometimes had duties other than commercial ones that are mentioned in law lists for this period. The *Law list 1851* notes that William Jones of 2 St Mildred's Court, Poultry, was librarian to the Royal Cambrian Institution and a parliamentary agent. William Mark Fladgate of 43 Craven Street, Strand, was 'solicitor to the Hungerford Market Company and to

Marlborough College'. William Tooke, of 3 Holborn Court, Gray's Inn and later of 39 Bedford Row, was for many years solicitor to the St Katharine Dock Company and to Middlesex Hospital. In the *Law list 1819* he had also been noted as solicitor to the Society for the Suppression of Mendicity.

Publication in law lists of references to lawyers' clients was discontinued in the 1860s. The *Law list 1854* included this notice:

> *The Compiler ... has received directions to omit after the names of Attorneys, as unnecessary and cumbrous to the work, all offices and employments not of a public character; such only as are retained have received the sanction of authority.*

The law lists also included lists of barristers. This is important because the published admission registers of barristers of Inner Temple, Gray's Inn and Lincoln's Inn extend only up to 1850, 1889 and 1893 respectively. The law lists are therefore a convenient source for tracing the careers of many barristers and also note the addresses of the chambers from which barristers practised.

Earlier lists noted a barrister's name, address and important offices that he held. For example, the *Law list 1808* included an entry for John Beauclerk of 4 New Square, Lincoln's Inn. He appeared on the Midland assize circuit and at the Nottingham, Leicester and Northampton Quarter Sessions. He was also a Commissioner of Bankrupts. Charles Fanshawe of 1 Essex Court, Temple Inn was also listed. He appeared on the Western assize circuit and at the Exeter and Devon Quarter Sessions, and was also Recorder of Exeter and Tiverton. More information was provided in later law lists. From 1841, they noted the Inn of Court to which a barrister belonged and the date on which he had been called to the bar.

Publication of the law lists continued into the twentieth century in similar format. Illustration 13 is an extract from the list of country solicitors, from the *Law list 1910*, listing the solicitors practising in Hailsham, Sussex; Hale, Cheshire; Halesowen, Worcestershire; Halesworth, Suffolk and Halifax, Yorkshire. Solicitors are listed individually (with the month and year of admission) and a note of the firm in which they worked. In recent years, some law lists have been arranged in a different manner. They retained sections for London solicitors and for country solicitors (divided by place), but each section is arranged by firm, with a firm's entry listing all its partners and the solicitors employed by that firm (with all names indexed).

In addition to entries for law firms, modern law lists include entries for other organisations that employ barristers and solicitors. As noted above, law lists included

HAILSHAM, Sussex.

‡[Coles, Henry Hartland. June 1886, c.o. (Coles, Sons & Tilburn).   *Tippetts.*

*Coles, John Berriman Campion. Aug. 1883, c.o., p.o., cl. to cons. taxes (Pevensey liberty) (Coles, Sons & Tilburn).   *Tippetts.*

*Coles, John Henry Campion. H. 1856, c.o., p.o. (Coles, Sons & Tilburn).   *Tippetts.*

=Kent, Alfred, J.P. E. 1858, c.o., p.c.   *Bridgman, Willcocks & Co.*   *Tippetts.*

*Swann, Oliver Howard. May 1883, c.o.   *Swann, Hardman & Co.*

Tilburn, George Frederic. Aug. 1903 (Coles, Sons & Tilburn).   *Tippetts.*

HALE, Cheshire.

Barlow, Samuel Joseph. Aug. 1896.   *Dangerfield & Blythe.*

*Buckley, Charles Arthur. July 1895, c.o.   *Pritchard, Englefield & Co.*

*Cooper, Charles James. May 1876, sol. and not., c.o., law cl. to dist. counc.   *Ranie, Johnstone & Sanders.*

*Denham, William Henry. Apr. 1909.   *Haslam & Sanders.*

*Galloway, Henry, J.P. T. 1864, c.o. (Payne, Galloway & Payne).   *Ranie, Johnstone & Co.*

*Goulty, William Howard, B.A. Jan. 1885, c.o.   *Davenport, Cunliffe & Co.*

Jonghaus, Thomas Chadwick. Dec. 1904.   *S. G. Skelton.*

Keogh, Alfred. Nov. 1905.   *Austin & Austin.*

Lawton, James Gooblen. Dec. 1876, c.o.   *J. H. Lee & Watts.*

*‡[Payne, John Henry, B.A. cantab. April 1884, c.o. (Payne, Galloway & Payne).   *Busk, Mellor & Co.*

*Shorrocks, Henry. June 1907.   *Hare & Co.*

=Yates, James. Dec. 1906.   *Williamson, Hill & Co.*

HALESOWEN, Worcestershire.

Goodman, Fred Tench. Aug. 1901 (Homfray, Goodman & Mellor).   *Dennison, Horne & Co.*

Goodman, Harold Temple. Nov. 1905.   *Dennison, Horne & Co.*

Green, George. June 1897.   *Dennison, Horne & Co.*

Grove, Ernest Harry. May 1893, cl. to dist. counc.   *Dennison, Horne & Co.*

Hollowell, Alfred. Aug. 1887. (Homfray, Holberton & Mellor).   *Sharpe, Pritchard & Co.*

Homfray, Alfred. Feb. 1881, c.o. (Homfray, Holberton & Mellor).   *Sharpe, Pritchard, Hol-berton & Mellor).*

*Mellor, Percy Bernull de Clegg. Jan. 1888 (Homfray, Holberton & Mellor).   *Sharpe, Pritchard & Co.*

*Parish, Charles Ernest. Sept. 1900.   *T. D. Jones & Co.*

Weston, George Augustus. Dec. 1887.   *G. S. Warmington & Edmonds.*

HALESWORTH, Suffolk. County Ct. No. 38.

Mullens, Harold Arthur. Nov. 1891, c.o., cl. to guards., sup. reg., cl. to vestr. and to cons. taxes Blything div.   *F. A. Graham.*

HALESWORTH—continued. *And London.*

Ram, Francis Robert. Aug. 1873. *And London.*   *Scott-Lawren & Palmer.*

*Palmer, Henry. T. 1873. *And London.*   *Bridges, Sawtell & Co.*

Ram, Francis Robert. Aug. 1900 (Cross, Ram & Sons).   *Bridges, Sawtell & Co.*

*Ram, Willett. M. 1860, c.o., reg. co. ct., cl. to mags. Blything div. (Cross, Ram & Sons).   *Bridges, Sawtell & Co.*

Ram, Willett, jun. Feb. 1897 (Cross, Ram & Sons).   *Bridges, Sawtell & Co.*

HALIFAX, Yorkshire. County Ct. No. 12. [Dist. Reg.]

Ainley, Herbert. Apr. 1891, c.o.   *Fielder & Jones.*

*Aked, James William. May 1896, c.o. (Dickons & Aked).   *Jaques & Co.*

Alexander, Robert Disney Leith. Dec. 1909. *And London.*

Ambler, William Henry Tate. Apr. 1892.

Ashling, Herbert. Feb. 1899, tn. cl.   *Helliwell, Harby & Co.*

Bailey, William. July 1885.   *J. R. Hall.*

Bairstow, John, B.A. Feb. 1894.   *Gibson & Weldon.*

Bastide, Harry. May 1888, c.o. (H. Bastide & Co.).

Bearder, Harold Ingham. Dec. 1908.   *Gibson & Weldon.*

Bentley, Frank. Sept. 1900, c.o.   *Firth & Co.*

*Bocock, Herbert. July 1899, c.o. (W. H. Bocock & Son).   *Jaques & Co.*

*Bocock, William Henry. Feb. 1881, c.o., p.c., p.o. (W. H. Bocock & Son).   *Fielder & Jones.*

*‡[Booth, Edgar. Feb. 1881, p.c. (Tubb, Booth & Helliwell).   *Helliwell, Harby & Co.*

*Buckley, George Dyson. Nov. 1893, c.o.   *Gibson & Weldon.*

Clarkson, Charles. Nov. 1904.   *Williamson, Hill & Co.*

*Clarkson, James. Mar. 1882, c.o.   *Williamson, Hill & Co.*

Crossley, John Wilkinson. Feb. 1889.   *Emmet & Co.*

*Dey, Lewis Irving. Dec. 1895, c.o.   *Walker & Rowe.*

*‡[Dickons, James Norton. E. 1861, c.o. (Dickons & Aked).   *Jaques & Co.*

Dodgson, Joseph. Nov. 1885, c.o.   *Fielder & Jones.*

*‡[@Evans, Richard Watson, B.A., LL.B., J.P. Feb. 1883, sol. and not., c.o., jt. cl. to Southowram dist. counc. (Godfrey Rhodes & Evans).   *Firth & Co.*

*‡[Farrar, John Riley. Aug. 1882, c.o.   *Helliwell, Harby & Co.*

Foster, Ronald Crossfield. Dec. 1894, c.o. (Land & Foster).   *Williamson, Hill & Co.*

Gared, David. Mar. 1896, c.o.   *Fielder & Jones.*

*‡[Helliwell, John Henry. Dec. 1882, c.o. (Tubb, Booth & Helliwell).   *Helliwell, Harby & Co.*

*‡[Hill, Ernest Hatton. Aug. 1889, c.o., cl. Hipper-holme dist. counc. (Hill & Norris).   *Sewell, Edwards & Co.*

*Hinchliffe, Ernest William. June 1901, c.o.   *Graves & Weldon.*

Illustration 13: List of London attorneys from the Law list 1910.

reference to positions held by attorneys and solicitors with organisations such as the London livery companies, or as secretaries and clerks to vestries and hospitals. Some law lists even referred to attorneys' and solicitors' clients. However, the law lists were not so helpful in identifying the employers of attorneys and solicitors; often omitting the names of the employers entirely. The *Law list 1910* included the London solicitor Charles Cochrane Hussey. The name of his employer can be guessed from the address noted for him: 'Great Western Railway station, Paddington'.

Later law lists are more helpful. For example, the *Law list 1953* noted the barrister Francis H.C. Taylor as employed in the Treasury Solicitor's Department in Whitehall and another barrister, Sir Charles Bruce Locker Tennyson C.M.G., as legal assistant in the Colonial Office. Since the law lists have had entries arranged by firm, as noted above, entries have also been included for government and commercial employers of lawyers. For example, the *Law list 1974* includes entries for organisations such as British Airways, British Steel Corporation, the Department of Environment, Canada Life Assurance Company and the Engineering Employers' Federation, with the names of hundreds of solicitors employed by them.

Some law lists noted, by symbols, a solicitor's membership of a local law society. For example, the *Law list 1910* noted solicitors who were members of the Law Society, Kent Law Society, the Berks, Bucks and Oxfordshire Incorporated Law Society, the Incorporated Law Society for Cardiff and District, Gloucestershire and Wiltshire Law Society, Herts Law Society, the Incorporated Law Society of Liverpool, Manchester Law Association, the Monmouthshire Incorporated Law Society, the Stockport Incorporated Law Society and the Worcester and Worcestershire Incorporated Law Society.

The law lists also include information about English lawyers who practised abroad. Some examples are noted below in section G1.

C2. BIOGRAPHICAL DICTIONARIES

L. Stephen and S. Lee, *The Dictionary of National Biography* (66 vols. Smith, Elder & Co, 1885-1901, with supplements to 1990 and also now on CD-ROM) is to be found in many libraries. It contains many articles about judges and other noteworthy lawyers. A new edition, in 60 volumes, was also published in 2004 by Oxford University Press and can be accessed online. The volumes of *Who's who* (published since 1849) and *Who was who* (for those who died after 1897) also contain many biographies of lawyers. For example, *Who was who 1916-1928* (A&C Black, 1929) includes this entry for a solicitor:

JOHNSON, Sir Henry James, Kt., created 1911; Solicitor; born 14 June 1851; son of Manuel John Johnson, Radcliffe Observer, Oxford and Caroline, daughter of Prof. J.A. Ogle, Oxford; married 1884, Pauline, daughter of Julius Hinterhuber, Salzburg; one son; educated: Winchester; Oxford, M.A. President, Law Society 1910-11; firm Waltons and Co, 101 Leadenhall Street, E.C. Address: 55 Sloane Gardens, S.W. Telephone Victoria 3481. Clubs; United University, Savile (Died 1 March 1917).

Another useful series of biographical dictionaries is that published by W.T. Pike in the period 1898 to 1912, subtitled *Contemporary biographies*. These 33 volumes, each covering a British or Irish city or county, included hundreds of biographies (with photographs) of men in the professions. The volume for London includes over 180 judges and barristers and over 150 solicitors and four notaries public. This is a typical entry (next to a photo of Mr Campion):

CAMPION. Harold Gilmour Campion, Streatham and 23, Old Broad Street, E.C.; son of the late Admiral Hubert Campion, C.B.; born in Kent in 1865; educated at Tonbridge School. Articled to the late William Moon, of Lincoln's Inn Fields, and has been in practice as a solicitor since 1887; has with him in partnership his brother, Ivon Hamilton; is a Fellow of the Royal Geographical Society; a Freemason; member of Felicity Lodge, No. 58. Married Ellen Wilton, daughter of the late Thomas Everet, and has issue two children, Hubert Wilton and Marjorie.

J. Whishaw, *A synopsis of the members of the English bar* (Stevens, 1835) is a list of all those called to the bar (and still alive in 1835). More useful is J. Foster, *Men-at-the-bar: a biographical hand-list of the members of the various Inns of Court, including Her Majesty's judges* (2nd edn. Hazell, Watson and Viney, 1885) because it includes short biographies of over 7,000 barristers who were alive in 1885. This entry is typical:

Rae, William Fraser, a student of Lincoln's Inn 2 Nov 1857 (then aged 22), called to the bar 30 April 1861 (eldest son of George Rae, Esq late of Edinburgh, dec.); born 3 March 1835; married 29 Aug 1860, Sara Eliza, 2nd dau. of J. Fordati, Esq of the Isle of Man and of London.
36 Holland Villas Road, Kensington, W; 3 Pump Court, Temple, E.C.

It is unfortunate that most of Foster's work on barristers was never published. He prepared a consolidated list, with biographical information (in five volumes), of all men recorded as admitted to the Inns of Court up to 1800. This 'Inns of Court register' contains over 50,000 entries. He also prepared a consolidated list, with biographical information (in 14 volumes), of all men called to the bar between 1518 and 1887. Foster's work on admissions was continued up to 1887 by R.F. Scott (about 20,000 entries in nine further volumes) and supplemented by marriage and obituary notices from *The Times* of 1901 to 1932. These manuscript works are held at Cambridge University Library.[5]

Brief biographies of noteworthy lawyers are included in A.W.B. Simpson, *Biographical dictionary of the common law* (Butterworths, 1984). Some other useful biographical dictionaries (and indexes to biographical material in journals) are noted in *Holborn's sources*.

C3. DIRECTORIES

Directories are a useful method of locating a lawyer ancestor. Having found an entry in one directory, a researcher can consult earlier and later editions to find other entries and establish changes of address and the approximate date on which a lawyer ceased to practise or died. Directories can be consulted at the SoG and in large reference libraries. Many have also been reprinted in book form and on microfiche, CD-ROM and web sites.

The very earliest English directories omitted lawyers. Then, in 1734 Henry Kent published the first of his London directories. This listed the 'principal traders' in London but in later years the names and addresses of lawyers were included. The edition for 1769 lists 97 attorneys and solicitors, most of them in the City of London, including Thomas Nuthall, Esq., Solicitor to the Treasury and the East India Company, 2 New Broad Street, but no barristers or notaries.

A particularly useful directory for information about lawyers is the *United British directory of trade & commerce comprehending ... London, Westminster & ... Southwark; and all the cities, towns and principal villages in England and Wales*, various editions of which were published in the period 1790-98. The law directory in this publication lists barristers, attorneys, notaries and proctors in London and elsewhere. In addition it provides other items of information about lawyers, such as the salary (£200 per annum) of Samuel Palmer, who was solicitor to the General Post Office. However, the details about lawyers in this directory are not always accurate. For example, the list of London notaries includes 40 men but the surnames of 10 of them are wrongly spelt and one notary is listed twice: by his correct name of William Deey but also as William Deep.

Holden's triennial directory for 1805, 1806 and *1807* lists attorneys, solicitors and notaries in London but not barristers. However, many barristers appear in the section of London 'Private residents', which provides the private addresses of many professional men. The second part of the directory covers the principal provincial cities and towns in England, Wales, Scotland and Ireland. It lists attorneys and solicitors such as James Bourne, attorney and Master in Chancery, of Dudley, Worcestershire. He and William Fellows are the only attorneys recorded there in that directory although the *Law list 1805* notes three attorneys in the town.

The series of directories published by James Pigot and his successor Isaac Slater, from 1818, are very useful. *Pigot's London and provincial new commercial directory*, which lists attorneys, was published in 1822 and lists the professional and business people in London and 280 towns in Cheshire, Derbyshire, Gloucestershire, Herefordshire, Lancashire, Leicestershire, Lincolnshire, Monmouthshire, Norfolk, Nottinghamshire, Rutland, Shropshire, Somerset, Staffordshire, Warwickshire, Wiltshire, Worcestershire, Yorkshire and Wales. London attorneys are listed at the end of the London section with their addresses. London notaries and proctors are included with them but barristers are not listed. The names and addresses of attorneys in the 280 cities and towns are listed under the city or town concerned. Provincial barristers are listed in this directory, for example three practising in Liverpool (as against 129 attorneys), three in Manchester, three in Norwich, four in Bath, 13 in Bristol, three in Leeds, two in Wakefield and five in York.

As noted, the lists of lawyers in directories were not always accurate. *The Post Office annual directory of Dublin and vicinity for 1840* included this warning for its readers:

Attorneys and Solicitors.
Gentlemen of the Profession are respectfully informed ... this list will not contain the name of any person who does not, by annual enrolment, appear to be a member, as numerous instances have been discovered in which persons who had no claim to the distinction of attorney have had their names inserted and published in this list.

Some lawyers who are listed in directories cannot be found in law lists. Charles Camplin, for example, who is described in the list of attorneys in Mathews' *Annual Bristol directory 1815* as practising at 3 Pembroke Court, does not appear in a law list. It is perhaps significant that the same directory for the following year contains no reference to him.

As time passed, directories became increasingly comprehensive. Illustration 14 is an extract from the Norwich section of the *History, gazetteer and directory of Norfolk and the city and county of Norwich* (2nd edn. William White, 1845). This extensive list of attorneys evidences the importance of Norwich as a cathedral city and commercial centre. This directory also included lists of barristers and proctors. Directories continued

Bunn John, jun. (city surveyor,) Tombland; house Chapelfield rd
Hinsbey Wm. Bank street
Kitton Robert, St Giles' st; house Pottergate street
Mear Wm. Horn's ln; h Lower close
Stannard Joseph, St George's plain
Stone Wm. Upper King street

(5) ARTISTS.
Marked * *are Drawing Masters, and* † *Portrait Painters.*

†Blazeby James, jun. 14 Bethel st
†Earl Wm. Elden, 4 Gun lane
*Gooch Samuel, Pottergate street
*Hodgson David, Tombland
*Hubbard Mary Ann, Surrey street
†King Reuben Webster, Palace st
†Housego Henry, Tabernacle street
*Ladbrooke John Berney, Bridge street, St Andrew
*Short Obediah, Heigham place
Stannard Alfred, (landscape,) St Faith's terrace
Thorne George, Vauxhall street

(6) ATTORNEYS.
(See also Proctors.)
Marked * *are Masters Extraordinary in Chancery.*

Asker Samuel Hurry, St Giles' st; h Lower close
Atkinson John Goldsmith, (commissioner of bankruptcy, &c.) 2 Castle street; h 6 Bank street
Bailey Elijah Crosier, Ltl. Orford st
Bardwell Everett, St Andrew's st; h Lower close
*Beckwith, Dye, & Kitton, Palace st
*Beynon John Fowler, Lower close; h St Giles' terrace
*Bignold & Field, Upper Surrey st
Blake, Keith, & Blake, The Chantry
*Blake Fras. John (supt. registrar of Norwich, and clerk of St Faith's Union,) Upper King street
Bond Edgar, 72 St Giles' street
*Brightwell Thos. & Sons (clerk to Charity Trustees) Surrey street
*Chapman & Hansell, Upper close
*Coleman Samuel, St Lawrence lane
Colman Joseph, Princes street
Cooper Jn. Norton Val., Crescent
Cooper Jonth. Whitley, Distillery st
Cuddon Jas. & Son (*conveyancers*) St Giles' plain
*Culley John Baldwin, St Martin's at Palace

Dalrymple Arthur, (under-sheriff)66 St Giles' street
*Dalton Samuel, 5 St Giles' terrace
Daveney Chas. Burton, 42 Bethel st
Day Wm. (magistrates' clerk) Guildhall; h Lakenham terrace
*Day Peter & Son, Theatre street
Deacon John,(clerk to the Norwich, Norf. Hospital,) St Stephen's sq
*Dowson John Withers, 14 Bank st; h 19 Castle meadow
*Durrant George, Surrey street
*Fickling Robert, jun. Elm hill
*Foster, Unthank, Burroughs and Robberds, Bank street
Francis Henry, Surrey street; h St Giles' terrace
*Freestone Edward, Little Orford st
Gilman Charles Suckling, Bethel street; h Newmarket road
Gilman Samuel Heyoe Le Neve, (Stamp office) St Andrews street; h Hingham
*Goodwin Jas. & Son, Willow lane
Grand John, 74 St Giles' street
Gwynn Wm. Horatio, Orford hill
Harrod Hy., King st; h Lower close
Jay & Pilgrim, Tolls ct. Briggs st
*Kerrison & Preston, Church street, St Simon's
Kitson & Rackham, Lower close
Ling Henry, Pottergate street
Long Edmd. Slingsby Drury, Broad st. St Andrews'; h 3 St Giles' ter
Mendham Wace Lockett, (dep. coroner) Post office street
Miller Henry, (registrar of Guild Hall court,) Surrey street
Mitchell and Clarke, Surrey street, (attend Saturday;) h *Wymondham*
Palmer Thos. Flitchen, Redwell st
Pulley Henry, Surrey street
Rackham Wm. 16 Castle meadow
*Rackham, Cooke, and Rackham, 77 St Giles' street
*Sharpe Daniel, Lakenham terrace
*Simpson George Edward, (clerk to magistrates for Henstead & Humbleyard Hundreds,) Tombland
Skipper John, Bank st; h Thorpe hamlet
*Sparke James Bird, Castle hill; h Scoles green
*Staff John Rising, (clk.of the peace, town clerk, &c.) St Andrew's st
*Steward Edward, Upper King st; h *Sprowston Hall*

Illustration 14: List of attorneys practising in Norwich, from a directory of Norfolk 1845.

to include errors. There is an entry in this Norwich listing for George Edward Simpson (Brian Brooks's great great grandfather) but the name 'Edward' is an error for 'Elward'.

Victorian directories often gave both the business and private addresses of lawyers. *The Post Office London directory 1859* in its 'Court directory' (a list of private residents) lists Thomas Edward Twisden of 60 Russell Square and The Mall, Chiswick. The *Law list 1859* includes William Frederick Browne Staples, a barrister, of Eldon Chambers, Devereux Court. The London directory for that year records him as living at 12 Merton Road, Kensington. Directories of large provincial towns also reveal the private addresses of some lawyers. Gore's *Liverpool directory 1875*, for instance, lists the firm of Simpson and North, attorneys and notaries, at Middleton Buildings, 1 Rumford Street, with one of the partners, Palgrave Simpson, living at Edenhurst, Princes Park.

Lawyers did not always give their private addresses as well as the addresses at which they practised to the compilers of directories. Nevertheless many Victorian lawyers practising in London lived in Middlesex, Hertfordshire, Kent, Surrey and Sussex so a search for them in directories of those counties may prove fruitful. Other lawyers lived in London and may be found in *Boyle's court guide* and, in the later years of the century, the *Royal blue book*.

C4. REGISTERS OF SCHOOLS AND UNIVERSITIES

Many lawyers, particularly since the late eighteenth century, were educated at public schools and favoured them for their children. Many schools have published their admission registers or biographical dictionaries of pupils, although the amount of information in such works varies enormously. The SoG has an extensive collection of school, college and university registers and biographical dictionaries. Some registers can also be found in reference libraries.

An excellent example, for Westminster School in London, is a two-volume biographical dictionary by G.F.R. Barker and A.H. Stenning, *The record of Old Westminsters: a biographical list of all those who are known to have been educated at Westminster School from the earliest times to 1927* (Chiswick Press, 1928). A third volume and supplements covering pupils in the period up to 1974 were published subsequently. A typical entry is that for Robert Dalzell, who was admitted to the school in 1806. The entry records that he was later admitted to Lincoln's Inn and practised as a conveyancer:

Dalzell, Robert, elder son of Robert Dalzell; b. May 7, 1794; adm. Bartholomewtide 1806; [King's Scholar] 1809; elected to Trinity college, Cambridge 1813 ... B.A. 1817; M.A. 1822; adm. to Lincoln's Inn April 19, 1822, called to the bar May 13, 1825; practised as a conveyancer; joint author with J.H. Leigh of A Treatise on the Equitable Doctrine of Conversion of Property (1852); [married], Margaret, daughter of Col. Legh, M.P., of Lyme Park, Cheshire; [died], Jan. 14, 1878.

As another example, there are a number of published registers, covering different periods, of the pupils who attended Harrow School. The third edition, *The Harrow School register 1800-1911* (Longmans, 1911) by M.G. Dauglish and P.K. Stephenson, includes entries for many lawyers, such as this admission in 1863:

White, Henry Arthur, son of H.A. White, Esq., Wellington, New Zealand. Left 1866. Solicitor, 1873; Senior Partner in Arnold and Henry White; Private Solicitor to Queen Victoria, King Edward VII and King George V; knighted 1897; C.V.O. 1907 ... 14 Great Marlborough Street, [London], W.

Advocates obtained their degrees and doctorates in civil law at Oxford or Cambridge universities. An increasing number of barristers also attended university before joining one of the Inns of Court. It was unusual before the late nineteenth century for attorneys and solicitors to have a university education but it became increasingly common after that. Until 1832, the only two universities in England were those at Oxford and Cambridge and they taught only civil law, not the common law. The number of universities gradually increased after that date and there are published lists of the students attending many of them.

There are published biographical dictionaries of the students at Oxford and Cambridge. The principal source for Oxford students is J. Foster, *Alumni Oxonienses: the members of the University of Oxford; their parentage, birthplace and year of birth with a record of their degrees, 1500-1714* (Parker & Co, 1891) and similar volumes for 1715-1886. Most entries note a student's name and age, the name and place of residence of his father, the date of his admission (and college) at the university and details of his later career, as in this example:

Brows, Nicholas, son of Nicholas, of Harberton, Devon, gent. Exeter Coll., matriculated 22 March 1676-7, aged 19; a student of Middle Temple 1669.

The principal source for Cambridge students is the 10 volume work by J. Venn and J. Venn, *Alumni Cantabrigienses: a biographical list of all known students, graduates and holders of office at the University of Cambridge, from the earliest times to 1900* (CUP, 1922-51). Most entries are very detailed and note some of the sources relied upon, as in this example:

Barlow, William Wycliffe. Adm. Pensioner at St John's, Feb. 6, 1872. S. of William, gent, of Ashford, Wilmslow, Cheshire. B. Mar. 18, 1854 at Bowdon. School, Malvern College. Matriculated, Michaelmas 1872; B.A. 1876; M.A. 1879. Adm. at Lincoln's Inn, July 24, 1875. Called to the Bar, 1883. On the Northern Circuit. Of Pitt Manor, Winchester and of Plaes Maenan, Llanrwst, N. Wales. Lord of the Manor of Maenan. J.P. for Cheshire. Permanently crippled through an accident in the hunting field, 1898 .... A keen musician and a skilled photographer. Married and had issue. Died Jan. 11, 1913, aged 58, at Pitt Manor. Buried at Hursley, Hants. (Burke, Landed Gentry; Foster, Men at the Bar; Eagle, xxxiv; The Times, Jan. 14, 1913).

C5. BUSINESS HISTORIES

There are many published histories of firms of solicitors. These commonly include lists of partners in a firm and photographs (or portraits) of senior partners and the firm's offices. Examples of these histories include J. Slinn, *Linklaters & Paines: the first one hundred and fifty years* (Longman, 1987); L. Dennett, *Slaughter and May, a short history* (Granta Editions, 1989); and H. Keenlyside, *Allen & Overy, the firm 1930-1998* (Allen & Overy, 1999). Many firms' histories are held in the Law Society library, London Metropolitan Archives, Guildhall Library and at the Business Archives Council.

Many histories of other companies and businesses that contain references to lawyers have been published. One example is P. G. M. Dickson, *The Sun Insurance Office 1710-1960* (Oxford University Press, 1960). This lists the 24 signatories of a deed of April 1710 by which the company was established. Several of the signatories were lawyers, including Sir John Bennett who was a serjeant, a judge of the Marshalsea Court and MP for Morpeth.

C6. MILITARY SERVICE AND ROLLS OF HONOUR

Many lawyers served in the British armed forces, particularly during the two world wars. Details of these men can be found in the services' surviving records (most are held at TNA) and in the vast array of published sources available at the SoG and reference libraries.

There are some published works of particular relevance to lawyers. Many rolls of honour were published after the First World War (for certain military units, towns, schools and professional groups). Some of these commemorate those who died but some list all persons who served in the conflict. One example, *The war book of Gray's Inn*, was noted above. The Solicitors' War Memorial Fund arranged the publication of *Record of service of solicitors and articled clerks with His Majesty's forces 1914-1919* (Spottiswoode, Ballantyne, 1920). This includes about 5,000 biographical entries (including entries for the 1,127 solicitors and clerks who died). Illustration 15 is a typical page. One entry is for

FRANK STANLEY WOOTTON.
Admitted July 1906. Member of Wood & Wootton, of 13 Fish Street Hill, E.C. Joined Aug. 26, 1916, as Private, 5th City of London Batt. London Regt. (London Rifle Brigade). Served in France. Killed in action May 5, 1917.

ALAN FLETCHER WORDEN.
Admitted Aug. 1912. Member of Worden & Worden, of Southport. Joined Sept. 7, 1914, as Private, 7th Batt. King's Liverpool Regt. Gazetted 2nd Lieut. 7th Batt. Lancashire Fusiliers July 20, 1916, promoted Lieut. Jan. 1918. Awarded the M.C. Served at Home and in France. Wounded at Athies, near Arras, May 4, 1917.

LEONARD WORDEN.
Admitted March 1912. Deputy Town Clerk, County Borough of Smethwick. Joined Jan. 5, 1915, as Private, 15th (Service) Batt. Royal Warwickshire Regt. and attained rank of A/Company Quartermaster-Sergeant. Subsequently gazetted Lieut. Duke of Cornwall's Light Infantry, attached Supply and Transport Corps. Served at Home, and in India and Aden.

THOMAS HOWARD WORDSWORTH.
Articled to E. B. Kite, of Taunton. Joined June 14, 1915, as 2nd Lieut., Sussex Royal Garrison Artillery (T.), subsequently promoted Lieut. Served in France March to April 1916 and Dec. 1917 to Jan. 1919 with 481st Siege Battery.

JOHN FORTESCUE WORSLEY.
Admitted Dec. 1913. Member of Morgan & Co., of Calcutta. Joined July 1915 as 2nd Lieut., Grenadier Guards, and subsequently promoted Lieut. Served in France. Killed at Fontaine Notre Dame in Battle of Cambrai Nov. 27, 1917.

FREDERICK WORTHINGTON.
Articled to J. W. Jackson, of Grimsby. Served as Capt., Lincolnshire Regt. Wounded on the Somme July 1916. Killed in action April 28, 1917.

WALTER WORTHINGTON.
Admitted June 1893, practising at Hull. Joined Sept. 14, 1914, as Capt., 12th (Service) Batt. East Yorkshire Regt., transferred to 1st Garrison Batt. East Yorkshire Regt. Oct. 1915, attached to King's Own Yorkshire Light Infantry in Sept. 1917. Served at Home and in India from Feb. 1916 to Sept. 1917.

GERALD LASCELLES WOULFE.
Admitted Nov. 1912. Member of Wakeford, May, Woulfe & Gwyther, of 37 Bloomsbury Square, W.C. Joined Sept. 1914 as 2nd Lieut., Northamptonshire Regt. Served in France 1915 to 1916. Killed at the Battle of the Somme July 14, 1916.

MARC EUGENE TOWNSEND WRATISLAW.
Admitted Dec. 1899, practising at Rugby. Joined Dec. 1916 as Lieut., Special List, attached Southern Command as Assistant Recruiting Officer,

Illustration 15: Extract from the roll of honour of solicitors and articled clerks who fought in the Great War.

75

Alan Fletcher Worden, who had been admitted as a solicitor in 1912 and was a member of the firm Worden & Worden of Southport in Lancashire. The entry provides brief service details for him, noting the award to him of the Military Cross and that he was wounded near Arras in May 1917. Another interesting entry is that for John Fortescue Worsley of the firm of Morgan & Co in Calcutta. He joined the Grenadier Guards and served in France but was sadly killed at Cambrai in 1917.

Many barristers and other lawyers also served (with many men who were not lawyers) in the Inns of Court Officer Training Corps, based at Stone Buildings in Lincoln's Inn. Lists of those who served in the corps, with brief service details, are included in F.H.L. Errington, *The Inns of Court Officer Training Corps during the Great War* (Printing Craft, 1920).

About 7,200 solicitors and 2,200 articled clerks served in the Second World War, of whom 316 solicitors and 221 clerks died and are recorded in a roll of honour that is held at the Law Society in Chancery Lane.

D. RECORDS OF THE COURTS

For many years, lawyers were formally admitted to the courts in which they practised. The legislation concerning the admission of attorneys and solicitors was noted above. The Act of 1729 required them to take an oath prior to admission and for the courts to enrol their names. The Act of 1749 required the filing at court of affidavits of due execution of articles. It was not necessary for the deeds of articles to be filed but some of them were (and many of these survive in court records). The Act of 1785 required attorneys and solicitors to obtain annual practising certificates and the courts to register those certificates. Many records of these admissions survive at TNA, principally with the other records of each court. There are also a few similar records that relate to barristers.

Until 1875, the higher courts in England and Wales were independent of each other and even competed with each other for business. However, the Judicature Act of 1873 came into force in 1875. It merged the Court of Common Pleas, the Court of Chancery, the Court of King's Bench, the Court of Exchequer, the High Court of Admiralty, the Court of Probate and the Court for Divorce and Matrimonial Causes into the High Court of Justice (the Court of Bankruptcy was added in 1883). Since 1875, the High Court has been divided into divisions (presently the Chancery, Queen's Bench and the Family divisions) that hear particular types of legal disputes, as well as some specialist courts. The High Court, the Court of Appeal and the Crown Court together constitute the Supreme Court of Judicature.

It was also in 1875 that the distinction between solicitors and attorneys came to an end and they were all named 'solicitors of the Supreme Court'. By this time, the Law Society had become responsible for the registration of articles and the issue of practising certificates. Solicitors were still admitted to practice in the High Court for some years and so many of the types of records of admissions noted below survive (in most cases at TNA) until around 1900.

The following sections do not deal with every court that has existed in England and Wales but are limited to those for which there are some substantial records of the lawyers practising in them. Researchers should however be aware of the existence of the following central courts because they may find references to them in material concerning an ancestor:

- The Court of Chivalry (since the eleventh century)
- The Court of Exchequer Chamber (fourteenth century to 1875)
- The Court for Consideration of Crown Cases Reserved (1848-1907)

- The Court of Probate (1857-75)
- The Court for Divorce and Matrimonial Causes (1857-75)
- Divisional Courts of the High Court (since 1873)
- Court of Criminal Appeal (1907-66)

Law reports of cases heard in all these courts, noting the judges and the barristers (and often the solicitors) are available as noted in section E. 5 below. Researchers should also be aware that nisi prius cases were civil disputes heard by judges on the assize circuits. These civil cases are therefore described with the criminal courts in section D. 18 below.

This section concentrates on the court records that came into being specifically to record the admission of lawyers in the courts and their right to practice. Most of the records commence after the Act of 1729 although a few are earlier. However, references to lawyers may be found in other documents in the courts' records. These provide only limited information about lawyers or are difficult to use (some are only suitable for experienced researchers or those with knowledge of Latin). There are three categories of such documents.

First, many pleadings and other documents in legal actions record the names of the lawyers acting in the case. For example, barristers (and sometimes the attorneys) signed the pleadings in many of the courts. Vast numbers of pleadings survive at TNA and in other archives. However, the task of finding any particular lawyer in these records is a daunting one.

Second, court officals kept registers of the parties to actions, their applications to the court and the lawyers that they instructed. For example, clerks in the Court of Chancery kept 'Cause books' which recorded the court's proceedings, noting the names of parties, their solicitors and the dates of their appearances. Chancery bill books (and similar documents in the Court of King's Bench and Court of Exchequer) record the applications made by the parties and name the barristers who appeared (and sometimes the attorneys or solicitors involved). Again, it is difficult to find a record of any particular lawyer.

Third, experienced researchers can make use of the rolls of 'warrants of attorney' in the plea rolls. By the end of the thirteenth century, all men could appoint an attorney to act for them in the courts and by this time, most attorneys were professionals, acting for a number of different clients. The courts took the matter of appointment of attorneys seriously (since there were cases of men falsely claiming to be attorneys for a party). From the reign of Edward I, appointments of attorneys were therefore recorded in rolls of warrants of attorney. In the courts of King's Bench and Common Pleas, these were bound with the courts' main records, the plea rolls (TNA refs: KB 27 and CP 40), at the end of the roll for each term. Warrants of attorney are also filed in the plea rolls of the Court of Exchequer (TNA ref: E 13).

Warrants of attorney are in Latin until 1733 and finding a particular lawyer in them is very difficult. They give the Christian name and surname of the attorney as well as the name and place of residence of the person or persons for whom he was acting, and the form of action on which the lawsuit was based.

Examples of professional attorneys appearing in the plea rolls of the Court of Common Pleas are noted by M. Birks, *Gentlemen of the law* (Stevens, 1960). Richard of Rockingham represented 12 litigants in 1219-20 and Stephen Bon Cristica represented 21 (from 12 different counties). Over a period of years, John Bucuinte appeared for 30 different clients. Examples from the records are also noted by C. W. Brooks, *Pettyfoggers and vipers of the Commonwealth: the 'lower branch' of the legal profession in early modern England* (CUP, 1986). For example, the warrants of attorney in KB 27/1395 for 1606 record the attorneys acting for litigants as Thomas Webb, Richard Morley, Simon Harborne, H. Turner and William Symmonds (all of whom were also clerks of the court) and William Cox, William Dandy, John Whitehead and Robert Gilbert

C.W. Brooks, *The admissions registers of Barnard's Inn 1620-1869* (Selden Society, 1995) also refers to the warrants of attorney in the plea rolls of the King's Bench and Common Pleas because the author found some members of Barnard's Inn in these records. For example, he found Ranulf Foster of Kirby Bellars, Leicestershire (admitted to the Inn on 11 May 1621) as an attorney of the Common Pleas in the plea rolls of 1630 (ref: CP 40/2251). Those rolls also listed three other members of Barnard's Inn acting as attorneys in the court. The warrants of attorney for 1630 in the plea rolls for the Court of Common Pleas (ref: CP 40/2257), included Edward Ingrey of Shepreth, Cambridgeshire (admitted to Barnard's Inn on 18 February 1623) acting as an attorney, as well as 15 other members of the Inn.

D1. THE COURT OF COMMON PLEAS

The Court of Common Pleas (initially named the Court of Common Bench) evolved in the late twelfth century as a division of the Curia Regis, that is the King's Council in which all branches of the business of government were conducted. The Court of Common Pleas sat at Westminster and was concerned principally with actions between one subject and another at common law. The Court of King's Bench competed successfully against it for business during the seventeenth century and the Court of

Common Pleas never regained its leading position. This can be seen from the fact that between 1823 and 1827 it heard 80,158 actions as against the 281,109 actions heard in the Court of King's Bench. The Judicature Act 1873 merged this court into the High Court of Justice. Its work was continued by the Common Pleas Division, which was merged into the Queen's Bench Division in 1880.

M. Hastings, *The Court of Common Pleas in fifteenth century England* (Archon, 1971) describes the administration and procedure of the court including the various clerks and officials (some of whom are listed). In particular, the court had three prothonotaries (chief clerks) who made records of the proceedings and up to 20 clerks, known as 'filazers' who issued the writs that summoned defendants to answer the complaints of plaintiffs. Records of the appointments of many of the court's officials from 1674 to 1831 are at TNA (ref: CP 4).

The earliest records of attorneys admitted in the Court of Common Pleas are some incomplete 'Supplementary admission registers'. The years covered and their reference at TNA are:

1656 – 1761   (ref: CP 69/1)

These are sheets of parchment, bound together in a book, giving the name of each attorney, the place and county of his abode and the term and year of his admission. They are arranged alphabetically by the first letter of the attorney's surname and then in chronological order. These records seem to have been carelessly kept as some dates of admission were omitted. Reference can also be made to a list, in the House of Lords Record Office, of attorneys practising in 1672/3 in the Court of Common Pleas (and in King's Bench and Chancery).

The next admission records, in order of date, are the four volumes of the 'Admission books series I'. The years covered by the these admission books and their references at TNA are:

1729-1751	(ref: CP 70/1)
1752-1775	(ref: CP 70/2)
1776-1814	(ref: CP 70/3)
1815-1848	(ref: CP 70/4)

The entries in the first two volumes give the full name of each attorney, the place and county of his abode and his date of admission. They are arranged by the first letter of the attorney's surname and then in chronological order. Illustration 16 is part of a page from

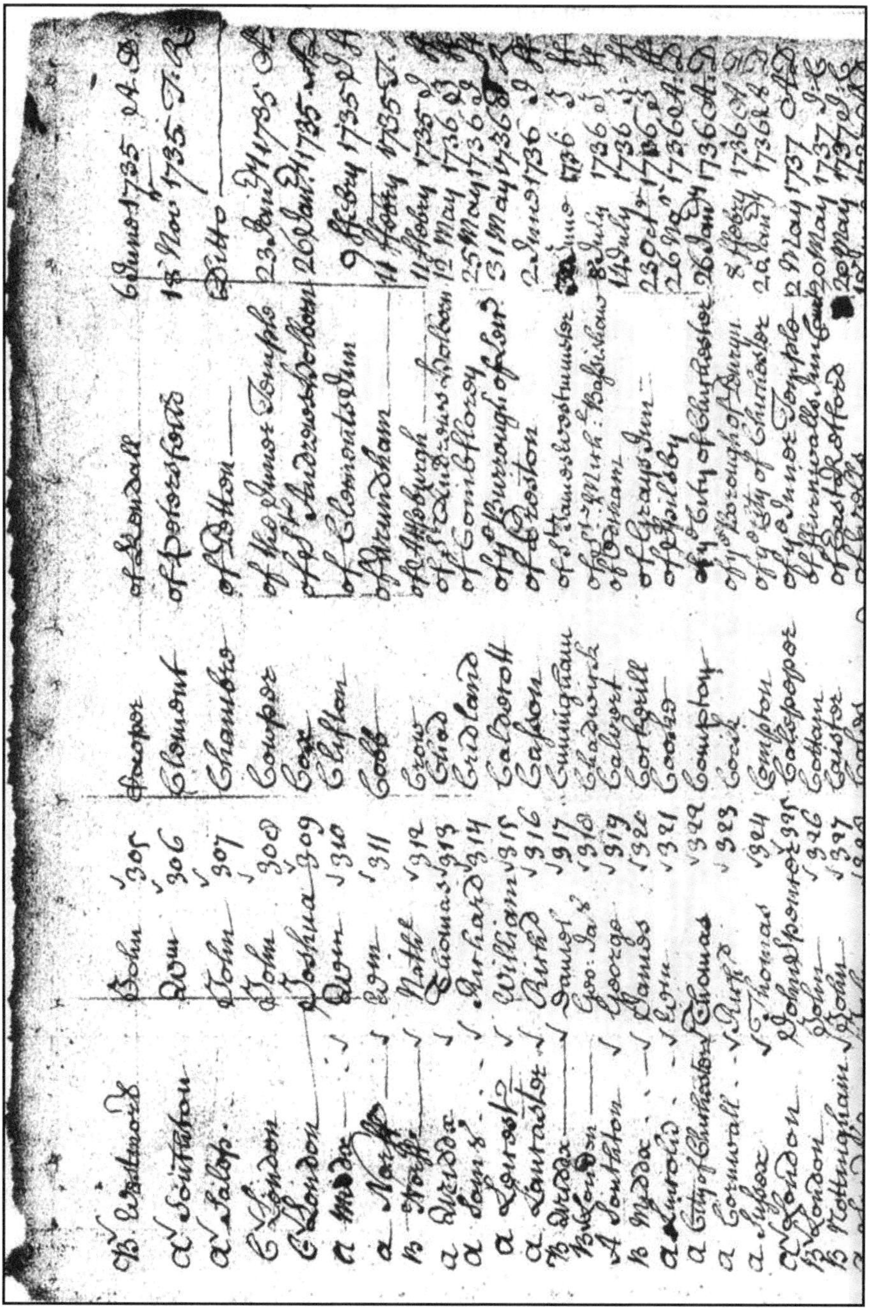

Illustration 16: An admission book of the Court of Common Pleas; extract for 1735-37 (TNA ref: CP 70/1 folio 24B).

the admission book in CP 70/1, for attorneys with surnames commencing with the letter C admitted between 6 June 1735 and 18 June 1737. A typical entry is the admission on 30 June 1736 of Daniel Cunningham of St James, Westminster. In some cases an abbreviated Latin rendering of the attorney's Christian name appears. For example, John Mellersh of Thakeham, Sussex, who was admitted on 19 November 1730, is listed as Johes. (short for 'Johannes') Mellersh. Some place names are recorded as the attorney may have pronounced them. Abraham Spooner of Uckfield, Sussex, admitted on 1 December 1730, appears as 'Abrm Spooner of Huckfield'.

The third and fourth volumes in this series give the full name of the attorney, the place and county of his abode, the date when he was sworn and the date when he was enrolled (that is admitted to practice) as an attorney of the court. Some of the attorneys admitted to this court were already practising in the Court of King's Bench.

Enrolment usually took place a few days after the attorney had taken his oath but this was not always the case. Thomas Bonnet, for example, who was 'late of Tokenhouse Yard but now of Bank Buildings, London', was sworn on 11 February 1794 and enrolled on 24 November 1803. He had been admitted as an attorney of the Court of King's Bench and also as a notary public in 1784. In that year he had also become a freeman and liveryman of the Scriveners' Company and succeeded to the practice of his father Benjamin Bonnet (who was notary to the Bank of England). He presumably had sufficient connections and work in those capacities in earlier years and had not needed to take on cases in the Court of Common Pleas.

These books include some changes of address. Thomas Edward Sherwood, for example, sworn on 11 May 1807 and enrolled on 17 November 1807, is described as 'late of Hatton Garden in the Coy of Middlesex but now of Canterbury Square, Southwark'. There are also occasional references to an attorney's change of name. Joseph Annesley, for instance, admitted as an attorney of the Common Pleas on 6 November 1787 is described as 'Joseph Annesley, formerly Joseph Abrahams, late of Fore Street, London, but now of Little Friday Street, par. St Margaret Moses'. Underneath the entry for John Hart, of Red Lion Street in the parish of St Mary, Whitechapel, admitted on 13 November 1805 is written 'altered to John Paterson by Royal Patent dated 30 March 1812 and entered 15 January 1814'.

The books also note some attorneys being struck off. Underneath the name of Charles Morris of Newport, Salop, sworn as an attorney of the court on 25 June 1814, is written 'struck out at his own request by rule of court Easter term 11th George 4th 1830'.

There are five volumes of 'Admission books series II'. The years covered and their references at TNA are:

1740-1819	(ref: CP 72/1)
1820-1853	(ref: CP 72/2)
1838-1843	(ref: CP 72/4)
1843-1862	(ref: CP 72/5)
1863-1875	(ref: CP 72/6)

These give the name of the attorney, his county of residence and year of admission only. They note some attorneys as having died or been struck off. The word 'mort' is written opposite the name of Rogers Jortin of London, admitted as an attorney of the Court of Common Pleas in 1751 and who died in 1795. Charles Aikin Holland of Middlesex, admitted in 1834, was 'struck off by rule of court of Michaelmas term 1852'.

TNA also holds an admission book of Welsh attorneys admitted to the Court of Common Pleas (ref: CP 72/3). This volume covers the period 1830-44 and gives the attorney's full name, his place of residence and the date of his admission.

There are 13 parchment rolls, covering 1730 to 1750, of attorneys practising in the Common Pleas. They may have been compiled as a result of the Attorneys and Solicitors Act of 1729. They seem to have been produced every year during the Michaelmas term but some are missing. Each roll is arranged alphabetically by the first letter of the attorney's surname, each name being preceded by the name of the county in which he lived. The word 'mort' has been added to some entries and there are references to certain attorneys being struck off. Some of the rolls are difficult to read. The dates covered by the rolls and their references at TNA are:

Michaelmas term 1730	(ref: CP 11/1)
Michaelmas term 1731	(ref: CP 11/2)
Michaelmas term 1733	(ref: CP 11/3)
Michaelmas term 1735	(ref: CP 11/4)
Michaelmas term 1736	(ref: CP 11/5)
Michaelmas term 1737	(ref: CP 11/6)
Michaelmas term 1738	(ref: CP 11/7)
Michaelmas term 1739	(ref: CP 11/8)
Michaelmas term 1740	(ref: CP 11/9)
Michaelmas term 1741	(ref: CP 11/10)
Michaelmas term 1743	(ref: CP 11/11)
Michaelmas term 1744	(ref: CP 11/12)
Michaelmas term 1750	(ref: CP 11/13)

There are also some admission rolls that were used to record the admission to the Court of Common Pleas of attorneys who had already been admitted in another court. The dates covered by these rolls and their references at TNA are:

5 November 1838 – 27 January 1844	(ref: CP 8/1)
27 January 1844 – 17 December 1844	(ref: CP 8/2)
18 December 1844 – 11 June 1850	(ref: CP 8/3)
11 June 1850 – 30 January 1860	(ref: CP 8/4)

The entries in the rolls are in chronological order. Each entry is signed by the attorney and notes his name and residence, the court or courts in which he was already practising, the date of his admission to that court or courts and the date of his admission to the Common Pleas. For example, the entry for Walter Southwood of 46 Edgware Road, Middlesex, states that he was admitted to the Court of Queen's Bench on 31 January 1838 and to the Court of Common Pleas on 5 November 1838. William Henry Cross of Surrey Street, Strand, was admitted to the Court of Great Sessions, Glamorgan, on 1 August 1826, to the Court of King's Bench on 13 November 1826 and to the Court of Common Pleas on 2 November 1844.

Some attorneys were admitted to the Court of Common Pleas after practising for many years in another court. James Edmed, for instance, who was admitted to the Court of King's Bench on 7 May 1794, became an attorney of the Court of Common Pleas over 50 years later, on 31 October 1844. His entry on these admission rolls describes him as 'then of Snowsfields, Southwark, now of Milton next Gravesend, Kent'. He must have been at least 70 years of age when he was admitted to the Common Pleas. His signature on the roll looks distinctly shaky.

As noted, an Act of 1749 required an affidavit of the due execution of articles of clerkship to be filed in court on the admission of an articled clerk as an attorney. The articles were also usually filed. The articles and affidavits for the Court of Common Pleas are in series CP/5, referred to below but the registers (containing summaries) of these documents are easier to use. The 'Registers of articles of clerkship' are two bound volumes with the entries on long sheets of parchment. The dates covered by these registers and their references at TNA are:

1756 – 1784	(ref: CP 71/1)
1785 – 1867	(ref: CP 71/2)

For each articled clerk, the register notes the attorney to whom he was articled, the date and term of the articles, the date of any assignment, the name of the person proving the articles, the date when his affidavit was sworn (and filed) and the date when the documents were read in court. Most of the articles were for terms of five years but some were for six or seven. The column headed 'when read in court' was frequently left blank. This did not mean that the articled clerk did not become an attorney. It is more likely that the court clerk simply omitted to complete that column for some reason.

There is also a 'Register of affidavits of due execution of articles'. This notes the name and address of the attorney (to whom a clerk was articled), of the clerk and of the person making the affidavit, the date of the articles and the date when the affidavit was sworn and filed. Some entries note the clerk's age and father's name. The dates covered by this register and its reference at TNA are:

1843 – 1863   (ref: CP 71/3)

TNA holds various admission papers for the Court of Common Pleas, including 251 bundles of original articles of clerkship, affidavits of the due execution of articles, affidavits of the payment of stamp duty and the court's fiats (that is orders) for admission. The dates covered by these documents and their reference at TNA are:

1729 – 1837   (ref: CP 5)

There is an index to articles of clerkship (ref: CP 5/1 to CP 5/251) with the series list in the research enquiries room at TNA. This index gives the name of the articled clerk, the attorney to whom he was articled, the year of the articles and the piece and item number.

There is a large collection of oath rolls for the Court of Common Pleas, the first 21 of which relate specifically to lawyers. These rolls came into existence because of the requirement from 1695 for all lawyers (amongst others) to take oaths of allegiance and supremacy and also an oath promising to act 'truly and honestly' in their profession. A declaration and oath suitable for Catholics was introduced in 1791 and a declaration for Quakers and Separatists in 1833. The dates covered by the rolls and their references at TNA are:

Michaelmas term 1789 – Michaelmas term 1791	(ref: CP 10/1)
Hilary term 1792 – Easter term 1793	(ref: CP 10/2)
Trinity term 1793 – Hilary term 1794	(ref: CP 10/3)
Hilary term 1794	(ref: CP 10/4)
Easter term 1794 – Michaelmas term 1794	(ref: CP 10/5)
Hilary term 1795 – Trinity term 1795	(ref: CP 10/6)

Michaelmas term 1795 – Michaelmas term 1797	(ref: CP 10/7)
Hilary term 1798 – Hilary term 1806	(ref: CP 10/8)
Easter term 1806 – Michaelmas term 1813	(ref: CP 10/9)
Easter term 1814 – Michaelmas term 1815	(ref: CP 10/10)
Hilary term 1816 – Hilary term 1820	(ref: CP 10/11)
Easter term 1820 – Michaelmas term 1825	(ref: CP 10/12)
Hilary term 1826 – Trinity term 1830	(ref: CP 10/13)
Michaelmas term 1830 – Trinity term 1833	(ref: CP 10/14)
Michaelmas term 1833 – Trinity term 1837	(ref: CP 10/15)
Michaelmas term 1837 – Easter term 1843	(ref: CP 10/16)
Undated roll	(ref: CP 10/17)
Trinity term 1791 – Michaelmas term 1814	
(Roman Catholic attorneys' Roll)	(ref: CP 10/18)
Trinity term 1816 – Easter term 1829	
(Roman Catholic attorneys' Roll)	(ref: CP 10/19)
Trinity term 1829 – Easter term 1836	
(Roman Catholic attorneys' Roll)	(ref: CP 10/20)
Easter term 1835 – Hilary term 1842	
(Quaker and Separatist attorneys' Roll)	(ref: CP 10/21)

These rolls contain the signatures of the attorneys admitted, the dates of admission and the oaths that were required. Rolls 18 to 20 were signed by Catholics. Some entries on the Catholics' rolls note the attorney's place of residence. Roll 21 contains the declaration that had to be made by Quakers and Separatists but carries only one signature – that of William Cole Fincham then (on 11 May 1835) of 1 Cloisters, Temple. He practised for many years at Blandford in Dorset.

These oath rolls include the oaths of some attorneys who had previously been admitted in other courts (and presumably swore oaths there). For example, the roll in CP 10/1 records the oath being sworn on 24 January 1791 in the Court of Common Pleas by Richard Rosser. His signature is the first appearing in Illustration 17, which is part of the roll covering the Hilary, Easter and Trinity terms in the 31st year of the reign of George III (1791). The *Law list 1790* included Rosser (of 32 King Street, Holborn) as practising in the Court of King's Bench. By the time of the *Law list 1793*, Rosser was recorded as practising in both the Court of King's Bench and in the Court of Common Pleas.

Rolls 22 to 31 in this series (ref: CP 10/22-31), are more general rolls and contain the signatures of persons holding civil or military office or places of trust under the crown. They are not individually listed here as they do not specifically relate to lawyers, but an example of an entry in these rolls is the signature dated 6 June 1801 of Lord Alvanley who had been made Lord Chief Justice of the Common Pleas the previous month.

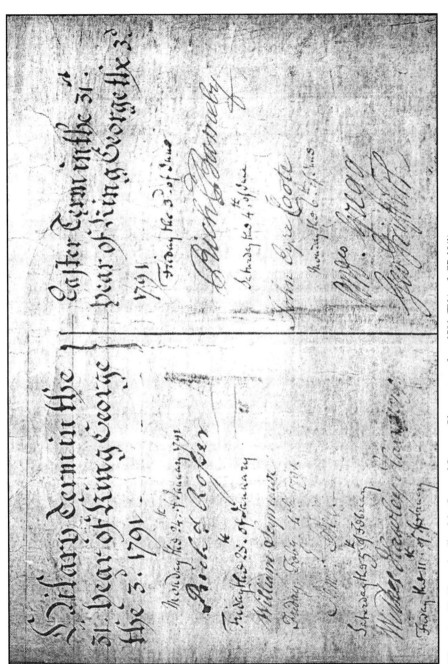

Illustration 17: The oath rolls of the Court of Common Pleas, extract from 1791 (TNA ref: CP 10/1).

As noted, from 1785, an attorney was required to obtain an annual practising certificate and produce this to the court in which he practised. The courts were required to keep registers of the certificates. TNA holds some 'Attorneys' certificate books of residence' (others have been destroyed) of the Court of Common Pleas. These give the name and abode of each attorney (arranged chronologically and then by the first letter of the attorney's surname) and the date of his certificate. TNA requires three working days' notice to produce these books for researchers. The years covered by the books and their references at TNA[6] are:

1786 – 1787	(ref: J 89/23/1)
1787 – 1788	(ref: J 89/23/2)
1788 – 1789	(ref: J 89/23/3)
1789 – 1790	(ref: J 89/23/4)
1790 – 1792	(ref: J 89/23/5)
1792 – 1793	(ref: J 89/23/6)
1793 – 1794	(ref: J 89/23/7)
1794 – 1795	(ref: J 89/23/8)
1795 – 1796	(ref: J 89/23/9)
1796 – 1797	(ref: J 89/23/10)
1797 – 1798	(ref: J 89/23/11)
1798 – 1799	(ref: J 89/23/12)
1799 – 1800	(ref: J 89/23/13)
1800 – 1801	(ref: J 89/23/14)
1801 – 1802	(ref: J 89/23/15)
1802 – 1803	(ref: J 89/23/16)
1803 – 1804	(ref: J 89/23/17)
1804 – 1805	(ref: J 89/23/18)
1805 – 1806	(ref: J 89/23/19)
1806 – 1807	(ref: J 89/23/20)
1807 – 1808	(ref: J 89/23/21)
1808 – 1809	(ref: J 89/23/22)
1809 – 1810	(ref: J 89/23/23)
1810 – 1811	(ref: J 89/23/24)
1811 – 1812	(ref: J 89/23/25)
1812 – 1813	(ref: J 89/23/26)
1813 – 1814	(ref: J 89/23/27)
1814 – 1815	(ref: J 89/23/28)
1815 – 1816	(ref: J 89/23/29)
1816 – 1817	(ref: J 89/23/30)
1817 – 1818	(ref: J 89/23/31)

1818 – 1819	(ref: J 89/23/32)
1819 – 1820	(ref: J 89/23/33)
1820 – 1821	(ref: J 89/23/34)
1821 – 1822	(ref: J 89/23/35)
1822 – 1823	(ref: J 89/23/36)
1829 – 1830	(ref: J 89/23/37)
1839 – 1840	(ref: J 89/23/38)
1842 – 1843	(ref: J 89/23/39)

D2. THE COURT OF KING'S BENCH

The Court of King's Bench evolved as a separate court in the twelfth century. It was named the Court of Queen's Bench when the monarch was a woman and the Upper Bench during the Commonwealth. At first, it was not held in a particular place. During the reign of Edward I (1272-1307), the Court of King's Bench accompanied the King, if he so required, as he travelled round the country. It was only from the late fourteenth century that the court sat permanently at Westminster. By this time, the King's Bench had both civil and criminal jurisdiction; the Plea side of the court dealt with civil matters and the Crown side dealt with criminal cases. The court was merged into the High Court of Justice in 1875, its work being continued by the Queen's (or King's) Bench Division.

M. Blatcher, *The Court of King's Bench 1450-1550, a study in self-help* (University of London/Athlone Press, 1978) is a study of the early history of the court. The court officials included a prothonotary (who made records of the proceedings), his underclerks and also clerks (known as 'filazers') who issued the writs. Many of them were lawyers.

We should first note three lists of King's Bench attorneys of the seventeenth century. First, TNA holds a list of the attorneys practising in the court during Trinity term 1653 (TNA ref: KB 140/6). Second, as noted above, the House of Lords Record Office holds a list of attorneys practising in 1672/3 in the Court of King's Bench (and in the courts of Common Pleas and Chancery). Third, the House of Lords holds a printed list of attorneys of February 1697/8 that has been published in *The manuscripts of the House of Lords, new series vol III* (HMSO, 1965). This lists 544 attorneys who were at the time permitted to practice in the Court of King's Bench, noting their place of residence. For example, only two attorneys were noted for Bedfordshire (Daniel Marsh of Dunstable and John Marsh of Leighton) but 24 for Devon and about 250 for London.

TNA holds rolls of attorneys that include the earliest records of admissions in the Court of King's Bench following the Act of 1729. These rolls are the 'Private rolls', the

'Abstract rolls'and the 'Public rolls'. The Private rolls cover the period 1729-1875. The full names of the attorneys are arranged by the first letter of their surname and then chronologically. Also given are the place and county of abode of each attorney, the date of his admission and the name of the examiner. The dates covered by these rolls and their references at TNA are:

1729 – 1788	(ref: KB 172/1)
1789 – 1803	(ref: KB 172/2)
1803 – 1821	(ref: KB 172/3)
1821 – 1832	(ref: KB 172/4)
1832 – 1842	(ref: KB 172/5)
1843 – 1851	(ref: KB 172/6)
1851 – 1861	(ref: KB 172/7)
1862 – 1869	(ref: KB 172/8)
1870 – 1875	(ref: KB 172/9)

Illustration 18 is an extract from these rolls (ref: KB 172/5 page 131) including attorneys who were admitted from April to June 1832. It includes John Hookins of Southampton (admitted on 16 April) and Edmund Hyde of Ely Place, Holborn (admitted on 8 June). The entries for attorneys who were struck off the roll were ruled out and annotated. An interesting example of such an entry is that of William Catchmayd, an attorney at Monmouth who was;

struck off the Roll at his own Request by rule of court made on Friday next after 15 days from Easter Day 20th Geo: 3. Restored and name changed to Gwinnett by his Majesty's Licence and rule of court Easter term 23 Geo. 3d.

The Abstract rolls and Public rolls are similar to the Private rolls but do not contain an attorney's full address. The Abstract rolls (ref: KB 172/16) cover the period 1729-1814. The years covered by the Public rolls and their references at TNA are:

1790 – 1810	(ref: KB 172/10)
1810 – 1838 Trinity term	(ref: KB 172/11)
1838 Michaelmas term – 1849 Hilary term	(ref: KB 172/12)
1849 Easter term – 1862 Easter term	(ref: KB 172/13)
1862 Trinity term – 1873 Michaelmas term	(ref: KB 172/14)
1874 Hilary term – 1875 Trinity term	(ref: KB 172/15)

TNA also holds rolls of attorneys previously admitted in other courts (ref: KB 172/17) covering 1843-67. They record the full name of each attorney, his place of residence (for

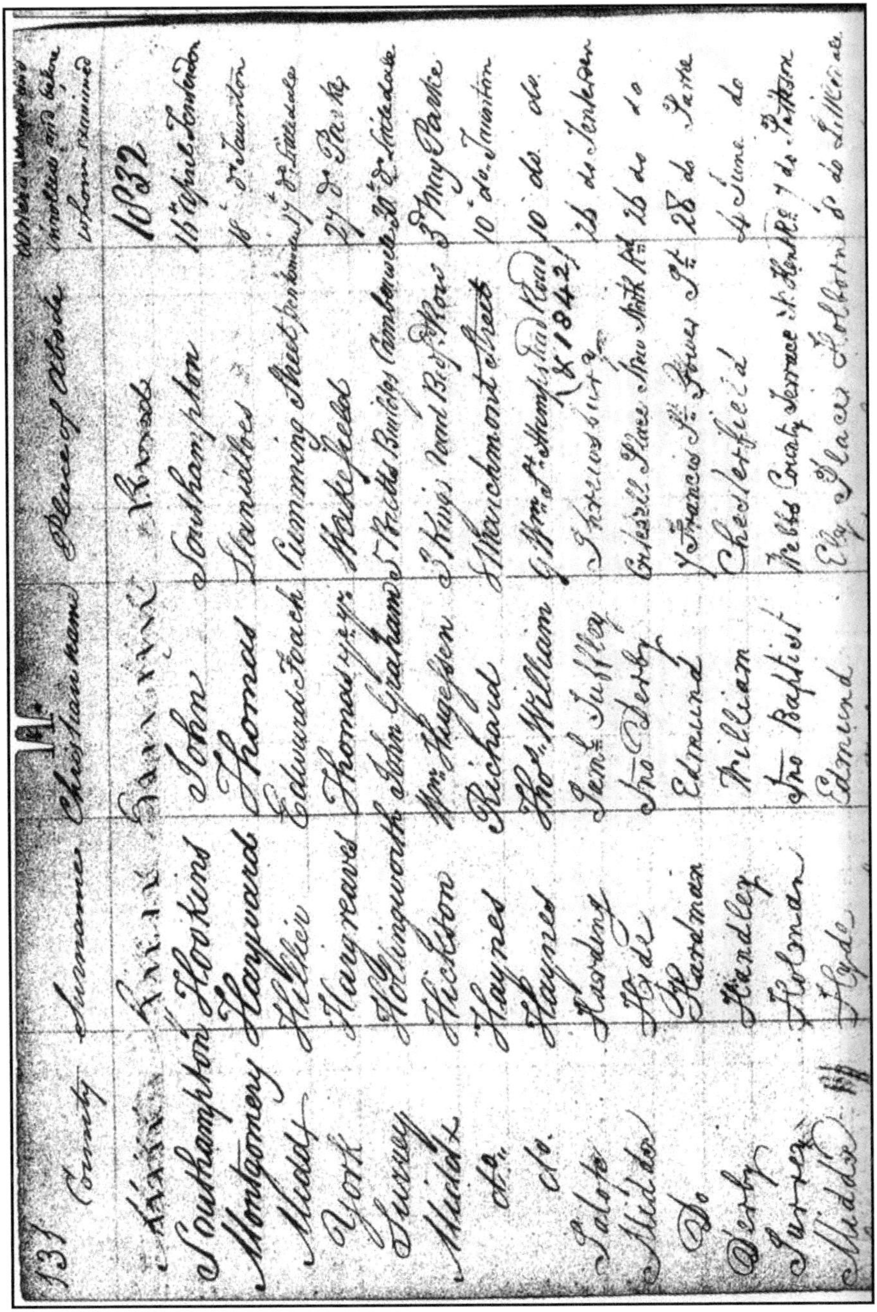

131

County	Surname	Christian name	Place of Abode	When admitted and before whom examined
[illegible]	[illegible]	[illegible]	[illegible]	1832
Southampton	Hookins	John	Southampton	15th April Jenkinson
Montgomery	Hayward	Thomas	Llanidloes	18 do Taunton
Middx	Hellier	Edward Roach	Cumming Street Pentonville	17 do Littledale
York	Hargreaves	Thomas	Wakefield	24 do Parke
Surrey	Hollingworth	John Graham	5 Prices Buildings Camberwell	30 do Littledale
Middx	Hickson	Wm Hugesson	3 Kings Road Bedf Row	3 May Parke
do	Haynes	Richard	Richmond Street	10 do Taunton
do	Haynes	Thos William	6 Wm St Hampstead Road (1842)	10 do do
Salop	Harding	Saml Jeffrey	Shrewsbury	26 do Jenkinson
Middx	Hyde	Jno Derby	Gresvill Place New North Rd	26 do do
Do	Hardman	Edmund	4 Frances St Tower St	28 do Parke
Derby	Handley	William	Chesterfield	4 June do
Surrey	Holman	Jno Baptist	Pellets Cottage Terrace St Kennington	7 do Patteson
Middx	Hyde	Edmund	Ely Place Holborn	8 do Littledale

Illustration 18: The private rolls of the Court of King's Bench; extract for the attorneys admitted April to June 1832 (TNA ref: KB 172/5 page 131).

London attorneys a street address, for country attorneys a town), the court in which he was previously admitted, the date of that admission and the date when he signed the roll in the Court of King's Bench.

It is interesting that, for some attorneys, there were a considerable number of years between their admission to the court in which they first practised and their admission to the Court of King's Bench. Boys Aldham, for example, an attorney at Lynn (King's Lynn) in Norfolk, was admitted to the Court of Common Pleas on 9 February 1797 and was admitted to the Court of King's Bench over 47 years later (on 18 September 1844). In contrast, Charles Henry Compton of 4 Alfred Place, Camberwell New Road, was admitted to practise in both the Court of Common Pleas and the Court of King's Bench on the same day, 8 May 1848.

The last of the rolls of King's Bench attorneys is the Wales Roll (ref: KB 172/18), covering 1830-34. This lists those attorneys, admitted to the Court of King's Bench, who were already practising in the Court of Great Sessions in Wales or the Court of Sessions at Chester. For each attorney, the roll gives his place and county of abode and the date of his enrolment as an attorney of the Court of King's Bench. Some entries note both a former and current place of abode. Frederick Lewis Brown, for example, who was enrolled as an attorney of the King's Bench on 4 January 1831, is described as 'of Llanelly, late of Carmarthen'.

Another useful series of records is the 'Court of King's Bench, Plea side, attorneys' oath rolls'. The dates covered by these rolls and their references at TNA are:

1750 – 1800	(ref: KB 113/1)[7]
1801 – 1820	(ref: KB 113/2)
1821 – 1840	(ref: KB 113/3)
1860 – 1874	(ref: KB 113/4)

The first three rolls are signed by each attorney and give only the term and year during which he was admitted. The fourth roll gives the attorney's name and residence, the date he signed the roll and the date of his admission. At the head of each roll are the three oaths which attorneys had to swear on their admission. The name of the monarch varies, of course, according to the date of the roll. There are also slight variations in the wording of the oaths on each of the rolls but the oaths in KB 113/1 are:

I do solemnly promise and swear that I will be faithful and bear true allegiance unto His Majesty King George the Second, So help me God

I do swear that I do from my heart abhor detest and abjure as impious and heretical that damnable doctrine and position that Princes excommunicated by the See of Rome may be deposed or murthered by their subjects or any other whatsoever And I do declare that no foreign Prince Person Prelate State or Potentate hath or ought to have any Jurisdiction Superiority Preheminence or Authority Ecclesiastical or Spiritual within these Realms, So help me God

I do swear that I will truly and honestly demean myself as an Attorney according to the best of my knowledge and ability, So help me God

The roll for 1821-40 has, filed with it, an affidavit, dated 20 June 1835, by William Reece (an attorney at Ledbury, Herefordshire). He swore that when he was admitted as an attorney the previous year, he had given his name as William Reece, which was the name recorded for him in the baptism registers of Ledbury and in his articles. He states in the affidavit that, having been informed by his mother that his name was William Henry Reece, he 'occasionally so signed his name'. The affidavit continues;

And Deponent saith he did [sign 'William H. Reece'] upon the occasion of signing the Roll of this Honourable Court by mistake, he having been admitted in the name of William Reece and this Deponent is anxious to have the said Roll corrected in that respect and that the present application is made at the earliest opportunity he had the power of making it and that there are not any proceedings taken or anticipated by this Deponent in respect thereof but that this application is made to prevent any mistake that may hereafter occur and is not made for the purpose of avoiding any proceeding whatever.

On the back of the affidavit, Sir John Williams (the judge in the Court of King's Bench at whose chambers in Serjeants' Inn the affidavit was sworn), scribbled 'I think it reasonable that the letter 'H' should be struck out, as desired. J.W.' It is interesting that Reece's name appears in the *Law list 1835* as William Henry Reece and subsequently as William Reece.

As noted, from 1785, an attorney was required to obtain an annual practising certificate and produce this to the court in which he practised. The courts were required to keep registers of the certificates. TNA holds the 'Attorneys' certificate books' of the Court of King's Bench Plea side. Each book gives the name and abode of each attorney (arranged by the first letter of the attorney's surname, then chronologically) and the date of his certificate. The years covered by these books and their references at TNA[8] are:

1785 – 1786	(ref: J 89/7/1)
1786 – 1787	(ref: J 89/7/2)
1787 – 1788	(ref: J 89/7/3)
1788 – 1789	(ref: J 89/7/4)
1789 – 1790	(ref: J 89/7/5)
1790 – 1791	(ref: J 89/7/6)
1791 – 1792	(ref: J 89/7/7)
1792 – 1793	(ref: J 89/7/8)
1793 – 1794	(ref: J 89/7/9)
1794 – 1795	(ref: J 89/7/10)
1795 – 1796	(ref: J 89/7/11)
1796 – 1797	(ref: J 89/7/12)
1797 – 1798	(ref: J 89/7/13)
1797 – 1798	(ref: J 89/7/14)
1798 – 1799	(ref: J 89/7/15)
1799 – 1800	(ref: J 89/7/16)
1799 – 1800	(ref: J 89/7/17)
1800 – 1801	(ref: J 89/7/18)
1801 – 1802	(ref: J 89/7/19)
1801 – 1802	(ref: J 89/7/20)
1802 – 1803	(ref: J 89/7/21)
1803 – 1804	(ref: J 89/7/22)
1804 – 1805	(ref: J 89/7/23)
1805 – 1806	(ref: J 89/7/24)
1806 – 1807	(ref: J 89/7/25)
1807 – 1808	(ref: J 89/7/26)
1807 – 1808	(ref: J 89/7/27)
1808 – 1809	(ref: J 89/7/28)
1808 – 1809	(ref: J 89/7/29)
1809 – 1810	(ref: J 89/7/30)
1810 – 1811	(ref: J 89/7/31)
1810 – 1811	(ref: J 89/7/32)
1811 – 1812	(ref: J 89/7/33)
1812 – 1813	(ref: J 89/7/34)
1813 – 1814	(ref: J 89/7/35)
1814 – 1815	(ref: J 89/7/36)
1815 – 1816	(ref: J 89/7/37)
1816 – 1817	(ref: J 89/7/38)
1817 – 1818	(ref: J 89/7/39)
1818 – 1819	(ref: J 89/7/40)

1820 – 1821	(ref: J 89/7/41)
1821 – 1822	(ref: J 89/7/42)
1822 – 1823	(ref: J 89/7/43)
1823 – 1824	(ref: J 89/7/44)
1830 – 1831	(ref: J 89/7/45)
1840 – 1841	(ref: J 89/7/46)
1842 – 1843	(ref: J 89/7/47)

These books include many entries of interest to family historians. For example, William Bryant obtained his first practising certificate on 2 November 1785 and gave his address as 'at the Clerk of the Paper's Office, St George's Fields.' When he took out his practising certificate the following year he said simply that he was 'of St George's Fields, Southwark' so perhaps he had left, or been dismissed from, his post.

Series KB 101 at TNA contains affidavits from the plea side of the Court of King's Bench. These include some affidavits of attorneys who had ceased to practise but then wished to be re-admitted. The dates covered by these affidavits and their references at TNA are:

1806 – 1820	(ref: KB 101/27)
1821 – 1830	(ref: KB 101/28)
1831 – 1835	(ref: KB 101/29)
1836 – 1838	(ref: KB 101/30)
1839 – 1841	(ref: KB 101/31)
1842 – 1843	(ref: KB 101/32)
1844 – 1845	(ref: KB 101/33)
1846 – 1848	(ref: KB 101/34)
1873	(ref: KB 101/35)
1873	(ref: KB 101/36)
1873	(ref: KB 101/37)
1873 – 1874	(ref: KB 101/38)
1874	(ref: KB 101/39)
1874	(ref: KB 101/40)
1874	(ref: KB 101/41)
1874	(ref: KB 101/42)

The reasons given in these affidavits by attorneys as to why they had discontinued practising (and wished to be re-admitted) are many and various. John Graham, for example, an attorney at Carlisle, swore an affidavit on 2 February 1818 at Brampton, Cumberland (before John Carrick who was also an attorney at that place and a commissioner entitled to take affidavits). Graham stated that he had been admitted as an attorney of the Court of King's Bench in 1812 and took out his certificate annually until 1816. He did not take it out in 1817, he said:

> *in consequence of being afflicted with a severe rheumatic complaint in his limbs which rendered him incapable of attending to or following his profession ... [he was] now recovered ... this Deponent further saith that it was not to avoid any censure of the Court upon this Deponent in consequence of his conduct in practice that he discontinued to act as an Attorney nor was this Deponent even under any apprehension of censure from the Court having uniformly practised with strict regard to honor and integrity and never having had any complaint made against him in respect of any part of his practice whilst he continued to act as an Attorney.*

Attached to this affidavit is another one sworn by three clerks of John Birkett, a London attorney. They stated that John Graham intended to apply for re-admission as an attorney. They had confirmed this intention by entering a notice in the court books (kept at the chambers of its various judges), affixing a copy of the notice on the outside of the Court of King's Bench in Westminster Hall and placing another in the court office.

Charles Calland, of Worthing, omitted to take out his certificate because when his father died in 1803 he felt that, as a single man, he was sufficiently independent not to need income from his legal practice. He had to think again in 1818 because by that time he had a 'very large family to maintain'. William Hamilton of London had been 'under the necessity of departing for the United States of America not for any malpractice but solely for the purpose of arranging certain affairs in that country in which he was interested'. On his return to England in 1815 he was afflicted by a 'severe indisposition' at Liverpool. John Shipman of London met with a severe accident in 1826 when a coach ran over his foot so he could not practise for four years. Jared Jackson, of Fron, in the parish of Llangefni, Anglesey, found, after being admitted as an attorney, that there was not much business so he discontinued practice as a lawyer and took up farming. He applied for readmission as an attorney in 1823.

One particularly interesting affidavit is that of John Dickson, of London, later of Shrewsbury. He was admitted in 1797 as an attorney of the courts of King's Bench, Common Pleas and Exchequer and as a solicitor of the Court of Chancery. He practised with a partner in the City of London until 1804 and then practised on his own account. By 1808, however, the profits from his work were 'inadequate to his expenditure' so he 'retired into the country' and gave up his legal practice. Unfortunately he fell into 'embarrassed circumstances' and incurred debts that he was unable to discharge. He was arrested and placed in Shropshire County Gaol where he remained until 1811 when 'he took the benefit of an Insolvent Act' and was freed. After leaving prison he worked for various attorneys in Shrewsbury 'occasionally engrossing deeds and making copies of other law proceedings'. He said in his affidavit that;

having been frequently and repeatedly urged by many very respectable farmers tradesmen and others residing in or near to Shrewsbury to resume his profession of an attorney with full assurances of support and deponent finding his present employ precarious uncertain and inadequate to his support and maintenance he is desirous of complying with the wishes and requests of his numerous friends with the full hope and confidence of being enabled by the profits of his profession to obtain a reputable and sufficient maintenance and be thereby also enabled to satisfy and pay in due course of time those creditors from whose debts the said Insolvent Act has for the present relieved him it being deponent's full intent and purpose when possessed of the means to pay every creditor's full demand.

Another interesting example is an affidavit of 1824 of Thomas Mills. He was noted as 'late of Ely Place, Middlesex (then of the firm of Mills & Trower), afterwards in the Kingdom of France, since of the parish of Rickmensworth [sic], co Hertford and now of No 12 Rue du Faubourg St Honoré in Paris in the Kingdom of France'. Mills was admitted as an attorney of the Court of King's Bench in 1797, practised in London and took out a practising certificate every year until 1814. He then retired from practice because of pecuniary embarrassment. He had been been induced to engage as a partner in a 'very extensive concern for the manufacture of lime' (at Rickmansworth). This concern then stopped payment but he was allowed by the creditors after its failure to draw from it the sum of £200 per year. During this time, he said, 'from motives of economy' he resided on the Continent but occasionally came to England when the affairs of the lime concern or other matters required him to do so. In 1819, his partner in the lime business having died, Mills took on sole management of the business. Eventually, with the trustees, he sold the business. In his affidavit, Mills stated that when his income from this source ceased he:

formed the resolution of establishing himself in France as an attorney and solicitor for the transaction of general professional business there and in England for persons resident in France and which deponent was induced to do with the patronage of His Excellency Sir Charles Stuart, the British Ambassador there, with whom this deponent has been several years acquainted and from the knowledge this deponent possesses of the language and customs of France.

The affidavit was sworn in Paris on 15 May 1824. The Ambassador's patronage was clearly useful to Mills since the *Law list 1825* describes him as Solicitor to the British Embassy.

From 1749, an affidavit of the due execution of articles of clerkship had to be filed in court on an attorney's admission. TNA holds 'Registers of affidavits of due execution of articles' of the Court of King's Bench, plea side'. The entries are in chronological order. They give the clerk's name and abode, the name and address of the attorney to whom he was articled, the date and term of the articles, the name, address and occupation of the person making the affidavit and the dates when the affidavit was sworn and filed. In the first volume the name, address and occupation of the clerk's father (or his mother or guardian if his father was dead) are sometimes given. The first entry relates to the articles of William Cadle, of Westbury, Gloucestershire to William Cooke, of Great Faringdon, Berkshire, on 9 August 1749 for five years. Most articles at this time were for five years but some were for six or seven years.

Some entries contain additional information. For example, Thomas Dennett, who was articled in 1750 to Henry Dodson, an attorney at Rye in Sussex, is described in the registers as the eldest son of John Dennett, of Woodmancote in Sussex. The years covered by these records and their references at TNA are:

1749 – 1784	(ref: KB 170/1)
1785 – 1802	(ref: KB 170/2)
1802 – 1814	(ref: KB 170/3)
1814 – 1822	(ref: KB 170/4)
1822 – 1829	(ref: KB 170/5)
1829 – 1837	(ref: KB 170/6)
1837 – 1845	(ref: KB 170/7)
1846 – 1854	(ref: KB 170/8)
1854 – 1862	(ref: KB 170/9)
1862 – 1868	(ref: KB 170/10)
1868 – 1871	(ref: KB 170/11)
1871 – 1874	(ref: KB 170/12)
1874 – 1877	(ref: KB 170/13)

TNA also holds indexes to these registers. The entries are by year of execution of the affidavit and then alphabetical by the first letter of the articled clerk's surname. Entries note the surnames of the articled clerk and attorney and the serial number of the affidavit. The dates covered by these indexes and their references at TNA are:

1749 – 1787	(ref: KB 170/14)
1787 – 1806	(ref: KB 170/15)
1806 – 1817	(ref: KB 170/16)
1817 – 1824	(ref: KB 170/17)

1824 – 1831	(ref: KB 170/18)
1831 – 1845	(ref: KB 170/19)
The index for 1845 – 1860 is missing.	
1860 – 1866	(ref: KB 170/20)
1867 – 1873	(ref: KB 170/21)
1874 – 1876 July	(ref: KB 170/22)

The surviving affidavits of due execution of articles of clerkship for the Court of King's Bench at TNA are in three series; Series I in KB 105, Series II in KB 106 and Series III in KB 107. The affidavits for 1749-75 are missing. The dates covered by Series I of these affidavits and their references at TNA are:

1775 – 1780	(ref: KB 105/1)
1781 – 1784	(ref: KB 105/2)
1784 – 1786	(ref: KB 105/3)
1786 – 1789	(ref: KB 105/4)
1789 – 1791	(rcf: KD 105/5)
1791 – 1793	(ref: KB 105/6)
1793 – 1794	(ref: KB 105/7)
1794 – 1796	(ref: KB 105/8)
1796 – 1797	(ref: KB 105/9)
1797 – 1799	(ref: KB 105/10)
1799 – 1800	(ref: KB 105/11)
1800 – 1801	(ref: KB 105/12)
1801 – 1803	(ref: KB 105/13)
1803 – 1804	(ref: KB 105/14)
1804 – 1805	(ref: KB 105/15)
1805 – 1806	(ref: KB 105/16)
1806 – 1807	(ref: KB 105/17)
1807 – 1808	(ref: KB 105/18)
1808 – 1809	(ref: KB 105/19)
1809 – 1810	(ref: KB 105/20)
1810 – 1811	(ref: KB 105/21)
1811 – 1812	(ref: KB 105/22)
1812 – 1813	(ref: KB 105/23)
1813 – 1814	(ref: KB 105/24)
1814 – 1815	(ref: KB 105/25)
1815 – 1816	(ref: KB 105/26)
1816 – 1817	(ref: KB 105/27)

The earliest surviving affidavit (ref: KB 105/1/3001) is that sworn on 6 April 1775 by Richard Ford of Lincoln's Inn, reproduced as Illustration 19. Ford's affidavit confirms the execution on 1 March 1775 of the articles of another Richard Ford, son of James Ford of Albemarle Street, a Doctor of Physic, to John Exley, an attorney in Lincoln's Inn, for five years.

Some of these records contain additional information that is helpful to family historians. For example, the affidavit relating to the articles, dated 4 May 1775, of Digory Forrest to Charles Whitefield, an attorney at Plymouth, states that the articles were signed by his stepmother (his father Austen Forrest of Plymouth, gentleman, being deceased). The affidavit also states that Digory Forrest was Austin Forrest's son by a former wife. In the case of the articles of Edward Peale of Maidstone to Thomas Dunnett, an attorney there, on 16 December 1780, the clerk is stated to be 'aged upwards of fourteen years'.

Articles were often assigned during their term to another attorney, sometimes because the attorney with whom the articles were originally made had died but sometimes for other reasons. An affidavit made under these circumstances gives the date of the assignment and the name of the deceased's executor or administrator. Some assignments of articles indicate other relationships. An example of this is found in the assignment of the articles of Edward Smith on 13 January 1781 from John Forster, an attorney in the Inner Temple, to the articled clerk's uncle Thomas Wildman, an attorney who practised in Lincoln's Inn.

The affidavits in Series II and III of these records contain similar information to those in Series I. The dates covered by Series II and their references at TNA are:

1817 30 Sept– 1818 29 June	(ref: KB 106/1)
1818 29 June– 1819 1 May	(ref: KB 106/2)
1819 12 May– 1820 28 March	(ref: KB 106/3)
1820 28 March – 1821 30 Jan	(ref: KB 106/4)
1821 30 Jan – 1821 4 Dec	(ref: KB 106/5)
1821 19 Nov – 1822 8 Aug	(ref: KB 106/6)
1822 8 Aug – 1823 29 April	(ref: KB 106/7)
1823 29 April – 1824 13 Feb	(ref: KB 106/8)
1824 13 Feb – 1824 22 Nov	(ref: KB 106/9)
1824 23 Nov – 1825 11 July	(ref: KB 106/10)
1825 11 July – 1826 16 March	(ref: KB 106/11)
1826 16 March – 1827 30 April	(ref: KB 106/12)
1827 2 May – 1828 9 June	(ref: KB 106/13)
1828 9 June – 1829 4 Aug	(ref: KB 106/14)

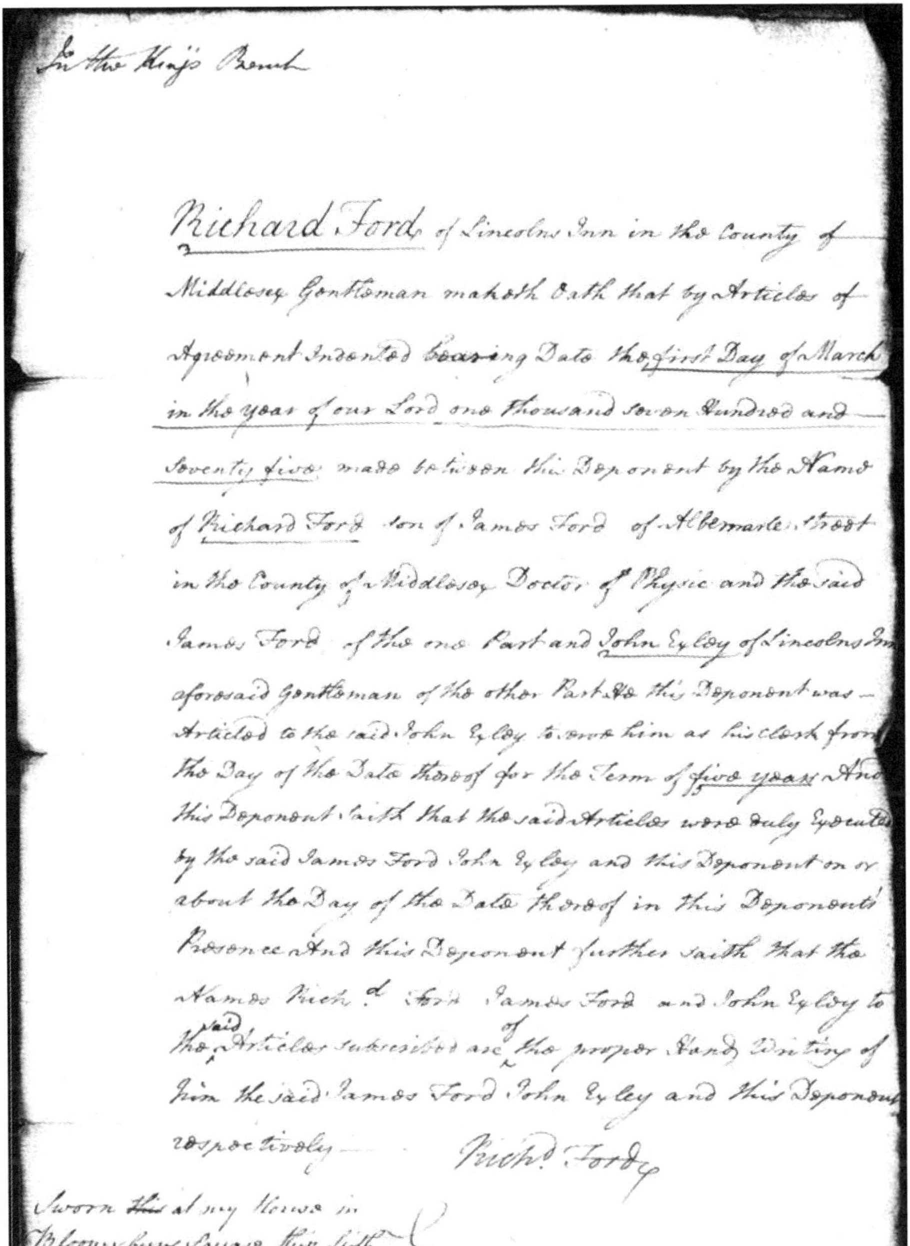

Richard Ford of Lincolns Inn in the County of
Middlesex Gentleman maketh Oath that by Articles of
Agreement Indented bearing Date the first Day of March
in the year of our Lord one thousand seven hundred and
Seventy five made between this Deponent by the Name
of Richard Ford son of James Ford of Albemarle street
in the County of Middlesex Doctor of Physic and the said
James Ford of the one Part and John Eyley of Lincolns Inn
aforesaid Gentleman of the other Part As this Deponent was
Articled to the said John Eyley to serve him as his clerk from
the Day of the Date thereof for the Term of five years And
this Deponent saith that the said Articles were duly Executed
by the said James Ford John Eyley and this Deponent on or
about the Day of the Date thereof in this Deponents
Presence And this Deponent further saith that the
Names Rich.d Ford James Ford and John Eyley to
the said Articles subscribed are the proper Hand Writing of
him the said James Ford John Eyley and this Deponent
respectively —

Rich.d Ford

Sworn this at my House in
Bloomsbury Square this Sixth

Illustration 19: Extract from the register of affidavits of due execution of articles; Court of King's Bench, plea side (TNA ref: KB 105/1/3001).

101

1829 13 Aug – 1831 1 January	(ref: KB 106/15)
1831 3 January – 1832 25 April	(ref: KB 106/16)
1832 25 April – 1833 21 June	(ref: KB 106/17)
1833 21 June – 1834 16 October	(ref: KB 106/18)

The dates covered by Series III and their references at TNA are:

| 1834 October – 1837 12 June | (ref: KB 107/1) |
| 1837 12 June – 1838 2 November | (ref: KB 107/2) |

Series KB 107 also includes further affidavits of due execution for 1837-75 (indexed in KB 171/1 to KB 171/3 noted below), some affidavits of payment of stamp duty and judges' fiats of attorneys admitted. The dates of these documents and their references at TNA are:

1840	Hilary & Easter terms	(ref: KB 107/3)
1840	Trinity & Michaelmas terms	(ref: KB 107/4)
1841	Hilary & Easter terms	(ref: KB 107/5)
1841	Trinity & Michaelmas terms	(ref: KB 107/6)
1842	Hilary & Easter terms	(ref: KB 107/7)
1842	Trinity & Michaelmas terms	(ref: KB 107/8)
1843	Hilary & Easter terms	(ref: KB 107/9)
1843	Trinity & Michaelmas terms	(ref: KB 107/10)
1844	Hilary & Easter terms	(ref: KB 107/11)
1844	Trinity & Michaelmas terms	(ref: KB 107/12)
1845	Hilary & Easter terms	(ref: KB 107/13)
1845	Trinity & Michaelmas terms	(ref: KB 107/14)
1846		(ref: KB 107/15)
1847		(ref: KB 107/16)
1848		(ref: KB 107/17)
1849 – 1853		(ref: KB 107/18)
1853 – 1859		(ref: KB 107/19)
1859 – 1867		(ref: KB 107/20)
1867 – 1871		(ref: KB 107/21)
1872 – 1873		(ref: KB 107/22)
1874 – 1875		(ref: KB 107/23)

The affidavits of due execution for 1837-75 in KB 107 are indexed in the 'Indexes to attorneys' articles of clerkship' in series KB 171. These list the names of the attorneys (arranged by the first letter of the attorney's surname, then chronologically) and give the term and year of admission. The periods covered by these indexes and their references at TNA are:

1838 – 1855	(ref: KB 171/1)
1856 – 1870	(ref: KB 171/2)
1871 – 1875	(ref: KB 171/3)

TNA also holds 'Court of King's Bench: plea side: affidavits of due execution of articles of clerkship of persons not admitted' (ref: KB 109/1), covering 1831-48. These affidavits contain similar information to the affidavits for clerks who were admitted as attorneys. Some include information about the articles being assigned to another attorney. For example, the articles of George Wickens were assigned on 7 December 1839 to a London attorney named Richard Henry Witty. The noted reason was that William John Willett, 'formerly of Essex Street, Strand but late of Margate, Kent', to whom Wickens had been articled on 1 January 1835, had died on 21 August 1839. The assignment was made by William John Willett's executors.

Series KB 111 at TNA includes miscellaneous records relating to the admission of attorneys and solicitors to practise on the plea side of the Court of King's Bench, but also for the Court of Chancery and the Chancery Division of the High Court of Justice. The second piece (ref: KB 111/2) contains some articles of clerkship for the Court of King's (or Queen's) Bench and the Queen's Bench Division of the High Court of Justice, but also affidavits of due execution and articles of clerkship for the Court of Chancery. The documents and covering dates are:

Articles of clerkship	1827 – 1888
Chancery: affidavits of due execution of articles of clerkship	1801 – 1860
Chancery: affidavits and articles of clerkship	1864 – 1875

With the articles of clerkship are some forms issued by the Law Society with questions to be answered by the clerk and the attorney. The clerk had five questions to answer:

- his age on the date of the articles,
- whether or not he had completed his articles at the office of the attorney to whom he had been articled or assigned,
- whether he had absented himself during the articles without permission,
- if so, when and for how long, and
- whether he had been employed during his articles (or since completing them) in any profession, business or employment other than as clerk to the attorney to whom he had been articled or assigned.

The attorney also had to answer five questions, by confirming:

- that the clerk had served the whole term of his articles,
- that the clerk had not been absent without permission from his work,
- that the clerk had followed no other profession, business or employment during the articles,
- that the clerk had been 'faithfully and diligently employed' during his service,
- whether the clerk, having completed his articles, had followed any other profession, trade, business or employment.

Attached to the forms are receipts from the Law Society as to payment (in 1860) of 15 shillings for 'Inspection and inquiry as to due service, previous to examination for admission in the courts at Westminster'.

The third piece in series KB 111 (ref: KB 111/3) consists of;

Applications and affidavits concerning articled clerks 1868 – 1874
Articles of clerkship 1840 – 1882.

The affidavits were sworn in support of applications for the issue of practising certificates or for leave to renew them. These affidavits give some details of an attorney or solicitor's career after admission. For example, Edward Hilder was admitted in the Michaelmas term of 1868 and then worked as managing clerk with a firm of solicitors in Chancery Lane. His affidavit, made in 1871, stated that he had never practised on his own but now wished to do so and therefore applied for a practising certificate. Many applications have the word 'Insufficient' written on them. As noted above, law lists generally listed only those attorneys and solicitors who had practising certificates. Men such as Edward Hilder would not, therefore, be included in law lists of 1868-71.

The fourth piece in series KB 111 (ref: KB 111/4) consists of articles of clerkship for 1840-84. They include receipts for the premiums paid to the attorney when the clerk was articled, details of any assignments of the articles that had taken place and the lists of questions asked by the Law Society as noted above. One example from these documents are the papers relating to George Crump, the younger, son of George Crump, the elder, of Greatfield House, in the parish of Kidderminster, Worcestershire. He was articled on 4 September 1848 for five years to George Adam Bird, a solicitor in Kidderminster. On 23 January 1851 his articles were assigned to James Thomas Woodhouse, of Leominster. On 17 November 1852, his articles were assigned to William Frederick Wratislaw Bird, of Verulam Buildings, Gray's Inn, an attorney in the courts of Queen's Bench, Common Pleas and Exchequer and a solicitor of the Court of Chancery. Mr W.F.W. Bird, in answer to the Law Society's question 'Has the said George Crump, Junr, at any time during the term of his articles been absent without your permission and, if so, state the length and occasions of such absence,' wrote, rather sensibly;

I suppose that, like other clerks, he occasionally forgot to come to the office, but I can not call to recollection anything which could be styled 'absence without permission'.

The Committee on Modern Legal Records 1966 recommended that certain documents should be preserved as specimens only. Among these were Court of King's Bench affidavits of due execution of articles of clerkship (continuing those in series KB 107 noted above). The specimens retained are from 1875, 1880, 1890, 1900 and 1903 (TNA ref: J 89/5[9]). TNA requires three working days notice in order to produce these documents for researchers. The periods covered by the documents and their references at TNA are:

1875 Jan to Dec	(ref: J 89/5/1)
1880 Jan to Apr	(ref: J 89/5/2)
1880 May to Aug	(ref: J 89/5/3)
1880 Sept to Dec	(ref: J 89/5/4)
1890 G800-G1100	(ref: J 89/5/5)
1890 G1101-G1474	(ref: J 89/5/6)
1900 H4050-H4325	(ref: J 89/5/7)
1900 H4326-H4600	(ref: J 89/5/8)
1900 H4601-H4802 and J1	(ref: J 89/5/9)
1903 J1557-J1800	(ref: J 89/5/10)
1903 J1801-J2065	(ref: J 89/5/11)
1903 J2066-J2400	(ref: J 89/5/12)

There are some indexes to to the affidavits of due execution of articles of clerkship (although many of those records have been destroyed since the indexes were compiled). The dates covered by these indexes and their references at TNA are:

November 1874 – November 1877	(ref: IND 1/29728)
November 1877 – December 1878	(ref: IND 1/29729)
January 1879 – February 1881	(ref: IND 1/29730)
March 1881 – July 1883	(ref: IND 1/29731)
August 1883 – April 1886	(ref: IND 1/29732)
May 1886 – January 1889	(ref: IND 1/29733)

Also preserved as specimens only, on the recommendation of the 1966 committee, are Court of King's Bench admission papers and articles of clerkship, including affidavits of completion of articles of clerkship. These documents have been retained for the years 1838, 1840, 1850, 1859, 1870, 1875, 1876, 1880, 1890 and 1904. The dates covered by these documents and their references at TNA[10] are:

1838	Hilary & Easter terms	A – M	(ref: J 89/4/1)
1838	Hilary & Easter terms	N – Z	(ref: J 89/4/2)
1838	Trinity & Michaelmas terms	A – E	(ref: J 89/4/3)
1838	Trinity & Michaelmas terms	F – J	(ref: J 89/4/4)
1838	Trinity & Michaelmas terms	K – N	(ref: J 89/4/5)
1838	Trinity & Michaelmas terms	P – Z	(ref: J 89/4/6)

These references continue in the same manner (but only for the years 1840, 1850, 1859, 1870, 1875, 1876, 1880, 1890 and 1904) up to:

| 1904 | October – December | M – Z | (ref: J 89/4/65) |

Indexes to the articles of clerkship were prepared (although many of the articles were subsequently destroyed). There is an index for November 1875 to November 1885 (ref: IND 1/29712) and an index for January 1886 to January 1889 (ref: IND 1/29713).

The first of the documents in piece J 89/4/1 is the deed of articles, dated 6 June 1832, of Anthony Horrex Roger Micklefield. He was articled for five years to his father Roger Micklefield, of Stoke Ferry, Norfolk, an attorney of the Court of Common Pleas and a solicitor in the Court of Chancery. The affidavit of 13 January 1838 as to the completion of those articles stated that Anthony served his father from the date of the articles until 2 November 1836. His articles were then assigned to John Wickham Flower, of 61 Bread Street, an attorney who was his father's London agent, and completed with him.

The wording of the articles of clerkship varied. Benjamin William Rawlings was articled on 23 November 1832 for five years to James Fawcett, of Lewin Street, Cripplegate and of South Sea Chambers, Threadneedle Street, London, an attorney of the courts of King's Bench and Common Pleas and a solicitor of the Court of Chancery. Fawcett undertook to provide;

all manner of necessary board and lodging and becoming wearing apparel both linen woollen and otherwise fit for the use and wear of the said Benjamin William Rawlings and also washing mending and repair thereof and also physic and surgery in case of sickness.

Richard Roberts, aged 19, son of Anne Roberts of Carnarvon, widow, was articled on 29 December 1832 for six years to George Faulkner of Bedford Row, an attorney of the Court of King's Bench. His articles provided that:

> *the said Anne Roberts her executors or administrators shall and will find and provide for the said Richard Roberts all manner of clothes and wearing apparel and also proper and sufficient board washing and lodging during the said term fit and suitable for a person in his station.*

When a premium was payable, which was not always the case, there were substantial differences between the amounts. In 1833 Henry Howlet, a London attorney and solicitor, charged five shillings to accept Charles Mason Innes Pollock as an articled clerk. In the same year John Gilbert Meymott, also a London attorney and solicitor, received £262-10s-0d for his articled clerk John Naylor Clayton.

An interesting collection of papers in this series relates to William Charles Lacey, whose period of articles was served with three solicitors in turn and then with a barrister. Lacey was articled from 13 March 1833 until 28 April 1835 to Thomas Webster, a London attorney and solicitor. He was assigned to another London solicitor, Joseph Edmond Pool, on 29 April 1835 and further assigned on 22 April 1837 to Thomas George Fynmore, also a London attorney and solicitor. On 27 November 1837 he became a pupil of John Wright, of Hare Court, Inner Temple, a barrister with whom he remained until 13 March 1838. Lacey duly qualified as a solicitor and practised in the City of London and at Wareham in Dorset.

The records of the Court of King's Bench include some records of barristers. Series KB 24 at TNA includes rolls of various oaths of allegiance and supremacy taken since 1672.[11] It also includes oaths by barristers and eight volumes of oaths taken by judges, magistrates and recorders during the twentieth century, with indexes. Series KB 4 includes rolls of oaths taken by barristers on their being admitted to practise in the Court of Queen's Bench and in the Queen's (or King's) Bench Division of the High Court from 1868 (when they were no longer required to take an oath of allegiance) until 1986. There is one roll for each legal term and they include the barristers' names, Inns of Court and signatures.

D3. THE COURT OF CHANCERY

The establishment of the Chancery (the 'Cancellaria' or writing department of government) as a separate entity from the Curia Regis, and headed by the Lord Chancellor, dates from the reign of Henry III. During the fourteenth century the

Chancery developed its own court, which became known as the Court of Chancery (or the High Court of Chancery). From the fifteenth century this court became the most important of the English 'courts of equity', that is those courts that attempted to apply rules of justice and fairness to ameliorate the harshness of some aspects of English common law. Accordingly, the court dealt with cases in respect of which the common law provided no remedy (such as those concerned with trusts) and cases concerning land, companies or some aspects of maritime and ecclesiastical law. The Court of Chancery was merged with other courts in 1875 to form the High Court of Justice, its work being continued by the Chancery Division.

W.J. Jones, *The Elizabethan Court of Chancery* (Clarendon Press, 1967) describes the administration and procedure of the court in the second half of the sixteenth century. It also describes the responsibilities of the court's officials, including the masters in chancery (also known as masters in ordinary), the 'six clerks' (who filed pleadings and issued writs) and the registrars (who took minutes and noted the court's decrees). The six clerks had deputies to assist them, named the 'sworn clerks' from 1668. Each of the six clerks had up to 10 sworn clerks.

The office of master in chancery (master in ordinary) lasted from the late twelfth century until 1852. They undertook a large amount of quasi-judicial work, for example preparing reports for the court on executors', trustees' or business accounts and on title to property, and also taking recognizances and affidavits. By 1540, there were 11 masters at any time. Most of them were barristers but some were advocates from Doctors' Commons. E. Heward, *Masters in ordinary* (Barry Rose, 1990) describes their work and lists all known masters, with some biographical information about them. For example, Thomas Lane was a master from March 1749 until his death in January 1773. Lane was the son of John Lane of London and admitted to Inner Temple (of which he later became a Bencher and Treasurer) on 23 May 1715. Lane was also a Commissioner of Bankruptcy and chairman of the Middlesex justices.

The 'clerks of records and writs' replaced the masters in chancery (and were later given the title of masters of the Supreme Court). They kept cause books which recorded the court proceedings, noting the names of parties, their solicitors and the dates of their appearances.

In the sixteenth century, the 'six clerks' were often called the only 'attorneys' of the Court of Chancery (although many of them were in fact barristers). They not only filed pleadings but also acted as a medium between the solicitors of the Court of Chancery and the court itself. The office of the six clerks was abolished in 1842 and the duties passed to other officials. The names of the six clerks (and of the Sworn Clerks who worked for them) were included in the law lists. All of the six clerks from 1522 to 1842 are listed in E.A. Fry, *Index of Chancery proceedings (Reynardson's division), vol I A to K, 1649-1714* (British Record Society, 1903). The six clerks who were barristers included Edward Vernon Utterson of Elm Court, Temple (a clerk from 1814 to 1842) and Randle Ford (a clerk from 1795-1807), who was also a Commissioner of Bankrupts. Some of the six clerks were special pleaders, including Walden Henry Hanmer of 2 Old Square, Lincoln's Inn (a clerk from 1787 to 1825) and John Anthony Noguier of 3 Stone Buildings (a clerk from 1807 to 1814).

In contrast to the common law courts (in which attorneys practised), most practitioners in the courts of equity until 1875 were solicitors, although attorneys were also admitted after the Act of 1729. The earliest surviving records of admissions of solicitors in the Court of Chancery are the solicitors rolls of the 'Petty Bag Office' at TNA. There are five rolls covering the period 1729 to 1875.[12] The years covered by these rolls and their references at TNA are:

1729 – 1791	(ref: C 216/22)
1791 – 1823	(ref: C 216/23)
1824 – 1836	(ref: C 216/24)
1836 – 1858	(ref: C 216/25)
1859 – 1875	(ref: C 216/21)

The earliest roll is in a bound volume. On the first page is the following heading:

The Names of such Solicitors who are sworn and admitted to Act as such in the High Court of Chancery (pursuant to an Act of Parliament [the 1729 Act] ... Intitled an Act for the better Regulating of Attorneys and Solicitors) with the days of Admittance, their Names and places of abode, before whom admitted, and time when Inroll'd or Entred in the Office of the Petty Bagg.

This is followed by a list of the names (but without addresses) of 36 solicitors and then some entries for solicitors who had ceased to practise and applied to the Master of the Rolls for their names to be struck off the roll. Walter Pryer, for example, who practised at Castle Yard, Holborn, petitioned on 14 March 1744 to be struck off as he had 'retired to the country and does not intend any more to practise as a solicitor'. Edmund Hooke of Norwich stated in his petition of 9 May 1746 that he wished to be struck off the roll of solicitors of the Court of Chancery in order to be called to the bar. Landon Jones was discharged from being a solicitor of the Court of Chancery and struck off the court roll after conspiring with two other men to obtain money from Thomas Severne by charging him with 'the Crime of Sodomy'. He had previously been struck off the roll of attorneys of the Court of Common Pleas. Mr Jones and his fellow conspirators were convicted of the conspiracy at the session of oyer and terminer held at Hertford on 26 July 1743, fined one shilling and:

> committed to the Gaol of Hertford ... to be set in and upon the Pillory at the said Town of Hertford to be imprisoned for six months and until they should severally Give Security for their good behaviour for two years from the time of their severally finding sureties as aforesaid.

The entries in the second and third rolls are in a similar form to those in the first roll. Sometimes they give additional information. Abraham Cortissos, for instance, admitted as a solicitor of the Court of Chancery on 26 June 1795, described himself as 'late clerk to Ephraim Franco of Salvadore House, Bishopsgate Street, London, Gent.' Francis Cohen, a solicitor of Basinghall Street in the City of London was struck off the roll at his own request in 1823. Of Jewish origin, he became a Christian, changed his name to Palgrave (his mother-in-law's maiden surname) and qualified as a barrister in 1826. He was appointed Deputy Keeper of Her Majesty's Records in 1838 when the Public Record Office was established.

TNA holds some indexes to the solicitors' rolls in C 216/21-25, noting a solicitor's name and year of admission. The years covered by these indexes and their references at TNA are:

1800 – 1842	(ref: IND 1/4613)
1842 – 1851	(ref: IND 1/4614)
1874 – July 1876	(ref: IND 1/29736)

Attorneys were also permitted by the Act of 1729 to practise in the Court of Chancery. TNA holds certificates of the admission of attorneys to practice as solicitors in the Court of Chancery 1730-87 (ref: C 203/7). These give names, addresses and dates of admission. There is also a name and address book of attorneys 1849-61 (ref: C 220/11/6).

Alphabets of solicitors taking out practising certificates, arranged by the first letter of the solicitor's surname, are in C 220/11. The years covered and references at TNA are:

1785	C 220/11/1
1786	C 220/11/2
1787	C 220/11/3
1788-93	C 220/11/4
1794-1843	C 220/11/5

The court's records at TNA include two oath rolls of Roman Catholic solicitors. The first (ref: C 217/180/5) covers Trinity term 1791 to Hilary term 1813. In this period of 22 years, only three Catholic solicitors were admitted to practise in the court: Jasper Gibson (1791), John Rosson (1812) and William Wilson (1813). The roll includes the following statement that had to be signed by any Catholic wishing to be admitted as a solicitor:

I AB [name of solicitor] do hereby Declare that I do profess the Roman Catholick Religion.

I AB do sincerely promise and Swear that I will be faithful and bear true Allegiance to His Majesty King George the Third and him will defend to the utmost of my power against all Conspiracies and Attempts whatever that shall be made against his Person Crown or Dignity and I will do my utmost Endeavour to disclose and make known to his Majesty his heirs and successors all Treasons and traitorous Conspiracies which may be formed against him or them

And I do faithfully promise to maintain support and defend to the utmost of my power the Succession of the Crown which succession by an Act intituled 'An Act for the further Limitation of the Crown and better securing the Rights and Liberties of the Subject' is and stands limited to the Princess Sophia Electress and Duchess Dowager of Hanover and the heirs of her Body being Protestants hereby utterly renouncing and abjuring any obedience or allegiance unto any other Person claiming or pretending a Right to the Crown of these Realms, And I do swear that I do reject and detest as an unchristian and impious Position that it is lawful to murder or destroy any Person or Persons whatsoever for or under Pretence of their being Hereticks or Infidels and also that unchristian and impious Principle that Faith is not to be kept with Hereticks or Infidels. And I further declare that it is not an article of my Faith and that I do renounce reject and abjure the Opinion that Princes excommunicated by the Pope and Council or any Authority of the See of Rome or by any Authority whatsoever may be deposed or murdered by their subjects or any Person whatsoever. And I do promise that I will not hold maintain or abet any such Opinion or any other Opinions contrary to what is expressed in this Declaration. And I do declare that I do not believe that the Pope of Rome or any other Foreign Prince Prelate State or Potentate hath or ought to have any Temporal or Civil Jurisdiction Power Superiority or Pre-eminence directly or indirectly within this Realm. And I do solemnly in the presence of God profess testify and declare that I do make this Declaration and every part thereof in the plain and ordinary sense of the Words of this Oath without any Evasion Equivocation or mental Reservation whatever and without any Dispensation already granted by the Pope or any Authority of the See of Rome or any Person whatever and without thinking that I am or can be acquitted before God or Man or absolved of this Declaration or any part thereof although the Pope or any other Person or Authority whatsoever shall dispense with or annul the same or declare that it was null or void.
So help me God

I AB do swear that I will truly and honestly demean myself in the Practice of a Solicitor according to the best of my knowledge and ability.

So help me God

The second oath roll of Catholic solicitors admitted to practise in the Court of Chancery (ref: C 214/23/1) covers the period June 1838 to June 1867 and contains 129 entries. Each entry gives the solicitor's full name and date of admission. The oath sworn by each applicant during that period was in similar terms to that set out above. It reads as follows:

Of the first year of the reign of our Sovereign Lady Victoria by the Grace of God of the United Kingdom of Great Britain and Ireland Queen Defender of the Faith

I AB do sincerely promise and swear that I will be faithful and bear true allegiance to her Majesty Queen Victoria And will defend her to the utmost of my power against all Conspiracies and Attempts whatever which shall be made against her person Crown or Dignity, And I will do my utmost endeavour to disclose and make known to her Majesty her Heirs and Successors all Treasons and Traitorous Conspiracies which may be formed against her or them And I do faithfully Promise to maintain, support and defend, to the utmost of my power, the succession of the Crown which succession by an Act intituled an Act for the further limitation of the Crown, and better securing the rights and liberties of the subject, is and stands limited to the Princess Sophia, Electress of Hanover and the Heirs of her body, being Protestants: hereby utterly renouncing and abjuring any obedience or allegiance unto any other person claiming or pretending a right to the Crown of the Realm. And I do further declare that it is not an article of my faith And that I do renounce, reject and abjure the Opinion that Princes Excommunicated or deprived by the Pope or any other authority of the See of Rome may be deposed or murdered by their subjects or by any person whatsoever : And I do declare that I do not believe that the Pope of Rome or any other Foreign Prince, Prelate, Person, State or Potentate hath or ought to have any Temporal or Civil Jurisdiction, Power, Superiority or Preheminence, directly or indirectly within this Realm. I do swear that I will defend to the utmost of my power the Settlement of Property within this Realm, as established by the Laws : And I do hereby disclaim, disavow and solemnly abjure any intention to subvert the present Church Establishment as settled by Law within this Realm : And I do solemnly swear that I never will exercise any privilege to which I am or may become entitled to disturb or weaken the Protestant Religion or Protestant Government in the United Kingdom : And I do solemnly in the presence of God profess, testify and declare that I do make this Declaration and every part thereof, in the plain and ordinary sense of the words of this Oath, without any evasion, Equivocation or mental reservation whatsoever.

So help me God.

As noted, some articles of clerkship and affidavits of due execution of articles, for solicitors admitted to practise in the Court of Chancery, are in KB 111/2. Many others are in 'Chancery miscellanea' (ref: C 217) at TNA. This series contains many other relevant documents (that the authors have not had the opportunity to review). These include 'solicitors admission papers', admission certificates and some certificates of enrolment of attorneys and solicitors in the King's Bench (presumably lodged by those men when applying for admission to practise in the Court of Chancery). The entries in the catalogue of TNA are:

C 217/21: Certificates of enrolment of attorneys and solicitors in the King's Bench 1778-1840
C 217/22: Certificates of enrolment of attorneys and solicitors in the King's Bench 1792-1843
C 217/23-40: Solicitors' affidavits of due execution 1730-1839:
 C 217/23 for 1730
 C 217/24 for 1730-69
 C 217/25 for 1770-78
 C 217/26 for 1779-84
 C 217/27 for 1783-92
 C 217/28 for 1793-1802
 C 217/29 for 1803-1804
 C 217/30 for 1805-12
 C 217/31 for 1810-15
 C 217/32 for 1817
 C 217/33 for 1818-31
 C 217/34 for 1821-23
 C 217/35 for 1824-26
 C 217/36 for 1827-29
 C 217/37 for 1830-32
 C 217/38 for 1833-35
 C 217/39 for 1836
 C 217/40 pre 1800; and for 1839
C 217/41-54: Solicitors' admission papers:
 C 217/41 for 1876
 C 217/42 for 1877
 C 217/43 for 1878
 C 217/44 for 1879
 C 217/45 for 1880
 C 217/46 for 1881
 C 217/47 for 1882

C 217/48 for 1883
C 217/49 for 1884
C 217/50 for 1885
C 217/51 for 1886
C 217/52 for 1887
C 217/53 for 1888
C 217/54 for 1889

C 217/181-183: Solicitors' admission papers:
C 217/181 for 1828-37
C 217/182 for 1812-35
C 217/183 for 1738-1818 (also affidavits as to the qualifications of attorneys and solicitors, 1803-37)

C 217/184: Certificates and articles of clerkship 1801-31

C 217/185:Certificates and articles of clerkship 1809-25

C 217/186: affidavits as to qualifications of attorneys and solicitors 1800-39; articles and affidavits of due execution of articles, 1818-31; admission papers (surnames commencing B, C, D, F, H, I, J, N, R, U, V, W) 1815-42; miscellaneous affidavits and certificates, 1839; and receipts for certificates of admission, 1839-40.

C 217/187: affidavits as to qualifications of attorneys and solicitors, 1807 and 1813-17; admission papers (surnames commencing M, S, W); articles and affidavits of due execution of articles, 1823-36; miscellaneous affidavits, 1842-43.

D4. THE COURT OF EXCHEQUER

The Exchequer became a separate organisation from the Curia Regis in the twelfth century. It was headed by the Barons of the Exchequer and had two sides, the financial and the judicial. By the end of the thirteenth century the Exchequer's judicial side had acquired characteristics of a court of law and by the beginning of the fourteenth century the Court of Exchequer had become a separate entity. Some of the Barons of the Exchequer were lawyers and they acted as judges of the court. In its early years, the Court of Exchequer dealt mainly with revenue cases but its jurisdiction was gradually extended, so that it eventually dealt with both common law and equity cases as well as those involved merely with the state's revenue.

W.H. Bryson, *The equity side of the Exchequer* (CUP, 1975) describes the procedures and records of the equity side of the Court of Exchequer and includes lists and biographies of the Barons (judges) and senior court officers. For example, the Deputy King's Remembrancers serving between 1698 and 1729 included Robert Barker of Gray's Inn, John Morgan of Middle Temple, Thomas Jones of Lincoln's Inn and John Harding of Inner Temple.

The printed list of attorneys in 1697/8 (noted above for the Court of King's Bench)[13] notes that there were then only four attorneys admitted to practice in the Court of Exchequer: Thomas Arden, Samuel Anderson, David Fielder and Thomas Owen, all of London.

The earliest list at TNA of lawyers practising in the Court of Exchequer is a certificate book of 1729-30 (ref: E 109/1), for solicitors admitted to practice on the equity side of the court after the passing of the 1729 Act. The names are arranged by the first letter of the solicitor's surname, and then chronologically, for example (from the list of names beginning with A):

Ashfield, Thomas *20 Feby 1729*
Appleton, Robert *24 Feby 1729*

The certificate book gives the solicitor's full name, his abode and the date of his admission to the court. In certain entries additional information is provided. The entry for Benjamin Palmer of Solihull, Warwickshire, for instance, who was admitted to practise in the Court of Exchequer on 21 April 1730, includes this note that reveals that Benjamin Palmer was already practising as an attorney of the Court of Common Pleas:

admitted by Mr Baron Carter haveing been admitted by the Honble Mr Justice Price, one of the Justices of his Maty's Cort of Common Pleas the 20th June 1729.

TNA also holds a certificate book of 1794-1841 (ref: E 109/2), which gives the solicitor's full name, his place of residence and the dates of his admission and enrolment as a solicitor of the court. Some changes of a solicitor's address appear in the book. For example, the entry for Andrew Edge, admitted to the Court of Exchequer on 11 February 1794, describes him as 'late of Ipswich but now of Palsgrave Place'. There are some references to solicitors being struck off. William Dalton, of Lincoln's Inn, for instance, who had been admitted and enrolled on 11 February 1794, was struck off the roll 'pursuant to order dated 9th May 1839'. Edward Donne, of Furnival's Inn, admitted and enrolled on 17 November 1806, was struck off 'at his own request the 12th of June 1830 pursuant to order of 11th June 1830'.

TNA also holds some 'certificates of admission to the Court of Exchequer (ref: E 109/3). Most are unfit for production because of their condition but five certificates, issued in 1730 and 1731, may be examined at TNA (under supervision). The certificate of John Sawyer of New Windsor, Berkshire is dated 10 February 1730/1. His application for admission is supported by testimonials from four barristers.

TNA also holds the solicitors' oath rolls for the equity side of the Court of Exchequer. They bear the signatures of the solicitors, dates of admission and, sometimes in the earliest roll but always in the later ones, the solicitor's place of residence. In some entries only the solicitor's initials are given. The dates covered by these rolls and their references at TNA are:

1730 – 1739	(ref: E 200/2)
1772 – 1841	(ref: E 200/1)

The Act of 1785 required certificates to be obtained by solicitors (and by clerks) in the Court of Exchequer. TNA holds a certificate book (ref: E 108/1) that records certificates from the period 1785-1843. The entries are arranged by year and then in alphabetical order by the first letter of the clerk's or solicitor's surname. They give a man's full name, address and the dates when the 'licences' (certificates) were issued. Sometimes additional information is provided. For example, William Cooper, whose licence was issued on 31 October 1785, is described as of King's Bench Walk in the Temple but also 'Solicitor of his Majesty's Customs for the northern parts of England and Wales'. Bolt Henry Cay, barrister at law of Cursitor Street in the parish of St Andrew Holborn, Middlesex, Solicitor of Excise, was granted a licence to act as a solicitor of the Court of Exchequer on 2 November 1785. Alexander Bennett, one of the sworn clerks in the office of his Majesty's Remembrancer, received his licence to act as a clerk in the Court of Exchequer on the same day. The application by Thomas Bonnet of Bank Buildings in the City of London, for a licence to practise (stating that he 'hath this day entd his annual certificate as an attorney and notary public') is crossed out. A note opposite the entry reads 'Retd Mr B. not being enrolled a Solr of this Court. 12th November 1800'.

The Exchequer of Pleas was the common law side of the Court of Exchequer. The rolls of attorneys who were admitted to practise in this court are in bound volumes, the entries being arranged alphabetically by the first letter of the attorney's surname, then chronologically. The years covered by these records and their references at TNA are:

1830 – 1836	(ref: E 4/1)
1830 – 1837; 1844	(ref: E 4/2)
1836 – 1846	(ref: E 4/4)
1846 – 1861	(ref: E 4/5)
1861 – 1875	(ref: E 4/6)

The first of these volumes notes the attorney's full name, his address and the date of his admission to practise in the court. There are also references to some attorneys being struck off. For example, Edward Duke of Brighton, late of Bedford Row, Middlesex, was struck off on 3 June 1870 pursuant to an order of the Master of the Rolls and at his own request. The entry of 25 April 1835 for Titus Hibbert of 24 Grafton Street East, Middlesex, is annotated 'vide letter W, the surname of 'Ware' added pr rule of court dated 31st Janry 1838'. He is shown in the *Law list 1839* practising in Manchester under the name Titus Hibbert Ware.

The second of these volumes lists attorneys of the Court of Sessions in the County Palatine of Chester or the Court of Great Sessions in Wales (reviewed below) who were also permitted to practise in the Court of Exchequer by an Act passed in 1830. The names are listed in the same way and give the same information as those in the previous volume.

The third, fourth and fifth volumes in this series give the attorney's name and residence, the court in which he had previously been admitted and the date of his admission to that court.

TNA holds 10 large parchment oath rolls of attorneys admitted to the Court of Exchequer. The rolls give the name of the attorney, his place of abode (an address for London attorneys, otherwise town only) and the date of his admission. The first three rolls list attorneys who were Protestants. The fourth roll lists Catholic attorneys and the fifth roll lists Quakers. The Quakers did not swear an oath on their admission but instead made an affirmation. The remaining five rolls list attorneys who were already practising in other courts but wished to practise also in the Court of Exchequer. These five rolls identify the courts in which those attorneys were already practising and the dates of admission to those courts. The dates covered by these rolls and their references at TNA are:

Michaelmas term 1830 – Michaelmas term 1833	(ref: E 3/1)
Hilary team 1834 – Michaelmas term 1836	(ref: E 3/2)
Hilary term 1837 – Trinity term 1842	(ref: E 3/3)
January 1831 – May 1837	(ref: E 3/4)
April 1831 – May 1835	(ref: E 3/5)
Michaelmas term 1838 – Michaelmas term 1839	(ref: E 3/6)
Hilary term 1840 – Trinity term 1843	(ref: E 3/7)
October 1843 – January 1850	(ref: E 3/8)
November 1853 – June 1858	(ref: E 3/9)
June 1858 – September 1872	(ref: E 3/10)

TNA also holds a register of affidavits of due execution of articles of clerkship for the

Court of Exchequer (ref: E 4/3). This register covers the period 1833-55 but contains only 27 entries. These note a clerk's full name and address, the name of the attorney to whom he was articled (or to whom his articles were assigned), the term and date of the articles (and date of any assignment), the name of the person swearing the affidavit, the dates when the affidavit was sworn (and filed) and the date when the articles were enrolled.

D5. THE HIGH COURT OF ADMIRALTY

In the early medieval period most maritime disputes were heard by local courts, such as the Shipway Court of the Cinque Ports, or by the Admiralty Court, established by Edward III, of which the Lord High Admiral of England was a judge. By the fifteenth century, a High Court of Admiralty sat in London and Vice-Admiralty Courts sat in some ports (for example Sunderland and Exeter) replacing many of the local courts. Appeals from the Vice-Admiralty Courts were heard in the High Court of Admiralty. Many boroughs (such as Bristol and Southampton) were permitted to continue holding their own admiralty courts. The High Court of Admiralty became part of the Probate, Divorce and Admiralty Division of the High Court of Justice in 1875 and later part of the Queen's Bench Division.

Judges and senior officials of the Court of Admiralty are listed in J.C.Sainty, *Office-holders in modern Britain: vol IV, Admiralty officials 1660-1870* (University of London Institute of Historical Research, 1975).

Advocates and proctors practised in the admiralty courts until the nineteenth century. Some material about proctors is included in the records of the High Court of Admiralty at TNA. The series 'High Court of Admiralty miscellanea 1727-1841' (ref: HCA 30) includes a volume of admissions of advocates and proctors to this court. The first admission noted is that of Thomas Collins on 4 November 1761 and the last noted admission is that of Charles Sladen on 25 June 1841. With this volume are various forms of certificates relating to proctors.

This series also includes 'Original appointments of proctors in prize causes 1801-1803' (ref: HCA 30/538). This is a register of proctors appointed by the owners of private ships of war pursuant to an Act of 1801 entitled 'An Act for the better regulation of his Majesty's prize courts in the West Indies and America and for giving more speedy and effectual execution to the decrees of the Lords Commissioners of Appeals'. The register is arranged alphabetically by the first letter of the ships' names and identifies the proctor appointed in a case (and the date of his appointment), the commander of the ship and the ship's owner or owners.

There are also minutes of a committee for a dinner given by proctors admitted in 1727 (ref: HCA 30/539). The minutes list the surnames of those who attended the dinner, including not only proctors but also doctors of law and some articled clerks.

The 'Admiralty muniment books' at TNA (ref: HCA 50) cover the period 1585 to 1973. These are entry books containing commissions, letters patent and warrants for the appointment of Lords High Admiral, Vice-Admirals, judges, registrars and other officers of the High Court of Admiralty. They include warrants for the appointments of proctors.

D6. THE COURT OF BANKRUPTCY AND THE COURT FOR INSOLVENT DEBTORS

A law of bankruptcy was introduced in the reign of Elizabeth I in respect of persons in trade or business. The Lord Chancellor was given various powers over a bankrupt's person and property and empowered to appoint commissioners to exercise those powers. Certificates of discharge for bankrupts were introduced in 1705. This system lasted until January 1832, when jurisdiction in bankruptcy matters was transferred from the Lord Chancellor to a new Court of Bankruptcy with a Chief Judge in Bankruptcy, assisted by three other judges and six commissioners. The bankruptcy law was extended to all persons (not just those in trade or business) in 1861 and the Court of Bankruptcy became part of the Supreme Court of Judicature in 1883, as the High Court of Justice in Bankruptcy.

Insolvent persons who were not in trade or business could not be made bankrupt prior to 1861, although they could be imprisoned (sometimes for years) until their debts were paid. Debtors had to petition the justices of the peace for their release until 1813, when a Court for Insolvent Debtors was established in London. Cases were also heard outside London by the court's commissioners, by quarter sessions or (from 1847) by county courts. Everyone became subject to the law of bankruptcy in 1861 and the jurisdiction of the Court for Insolvent Debtors was passed to the Court of Bankruptcy.

The solicitors and attorneys who were admitted to practise in the Court of Bankruptcy are listed chronologically in the court's admission rolls. They cover the period 1832-83 and are at TNA (ref: B 2/8). When a solicitor was struck off, his entry on the rolls was crossed out. The entry for John Page Sowerby, for instance, shows that he was admitted as a solicitor in the court on 7 February 1832. He practised for many years at Stokesley, Yorkshire, and became coroner, clerk to the magistrates and a county court registrar. A note under his entry on the admission roll of the Court of Bankruptcy reads:

John Page Sowerby having been struck off the Roll of the Court of Chancery by order dated 3 May 1865 is not now entitled or qualified to act as a solicitor of this Court – see 6 & 7 Victoria c. 73 ss. 2-27. 26 May 1865.

More details of attorneys and solicitors who were admitted to practise in the Court of Bankruptcy are contained in three registers at TNA, which are arranged alphabetically by the first letter of the lawyers' surnames and then chronologically. The first register is the 'Town attorneys book 1832-83' (ref: B 2/9). This names the solicitors and attorneys practising in London and gives their addresses and the dates of their admissions to practise in the court. Attorneys and solicitors who practised outside London are listed in two 'Country attorneys books' for January 1832 to January 1859 (ref: B 2/10) and January 1859 to August 1883 (ref: B 2/11). The entries contain the same information as the town attorneys' book but also name the London agents of the country attorneys. One interesting entry is the admission on 22 June 1854 of George William Frederick Grylls of Melbourne, Australia.

Only a few records of the Court for Insolvent Debtors survive at TNA and so one must turn to other sources for records of the attorneys and solicitors who practised in that court. Fortunately, they were recorded in some law lists. Thus in the *Law list 1833*, James Chilton of 1 Freeman's Court, Cornhill in London was noted as 'an attor. of insolv. Debt. Court', as were Thomas Kirk of 10 Symond's Inn, London, James Crump of Birmingham and Thomas Ambrose Clarke of Reading.

A report to the House of Commons in 1822, entitled: *Returns of the names of the commissioners and officers employed in the Court for the Relief of Insolvent Debtors in England ... and other matters relating to the said court*, included the names and places of residence of 103 London and 218 country attorneys who were entitled to practise in the court. Seven of the attorneys, for example Robert Westfield Benjamin (of Belvedere Place in the King's Bench), Edward Cole (of 16 Southampton Street, Bloomsbury) and Thomas Harle of York, were noted as having been discharged from their debts under the Insolvent Debtors Act. The report also listed thousands of debtors, including a solicitor Gabriel Tahourdin of Walcot Place, Lambeth, whose debts amounted to £66,531 2s 7d, an enormous amount at that time.

D7. THE COURT OF STAR CHAMBER

The King's Council had both administrative and judicial functions. The Court of Star Chamber was the King's Council sitting judicially (without a jury); the judges being the King's councillors and two judges of the common law courts. The court originated during the reign of Henry VII and was abolished in 1641. It dealt with civil disputes but also criminal or quasi-criminal cases, in particular local disorder and official maladministration. The court and its records are described in J.A. Guy, *The Court of Star Chamber and its records to the reign of Elizabeth I* (HMSO, 1985) and in J.A. Guy, *The Cardinal's court, the impact of Thomas Wolsey in Star Chamber* (Harvester, 1977).

The surviving records of the court (at TNA, the British Library and the Huntington Library in California) are principally the pleadings in the cases heard by the court and do not include lists of the lawyers who practised there. However, the names of some barristers and attorneys (initially limited to two but later numbering four) are known from the surviving case records. Examples are the barristers Robert Chydley (of Inner Temple), John Densell (Lincoln's Inn), John Hynde (Gray's Inn) and John Orenge (Middle Temple) and (between 1520 and 1550) the attorneys William Mill, John Valentine and John Taverner.

D8. THE COURT OF REQUESTS

This court sat from about 1493 until 1642 and was intended for poor litigants or for cases of little value. The records of the court are at TNA (ref: REQ) but do not include any admission registers of lawyers or similar material. L.M. Hill (ed), *The ancient state, authoritie and proceedings of the Court of Requests by Sir Julius Caesar* (CUP, 1975) describes the court's procedure in the sixteenth century and refers to many cases heard by the court. Detailed information about the court and some case reports are also contained in I.S. Leadam, *Select cases before the King's Council in Star Chamber, commonly called the Court of Star Chamber, vol I: 1477-1509, vol II: 1509-44* (Selden Society, 1903-11).

The lawyers who practised in the court were barristers and attorneys (limited to three at any time). Some of them are identified in Hill's edition of Sir Julius Caesar's work, for example Simon Sampson, attorney and barristers named Gaudy, Carell and Suliard of the Inner Temple who acted for John Atmore in a case in October 1539. In November 1575, an attorney named William French was committed to the Fleet Prison for contempt of court, because he had issued proceedings for his client at common law (in a *nisi prius* case at the Norfolk Assizes), in breach of an injunction.

D9. THE COURT OF WARDS AND LIVERIES

This court sat from 1540 until 1660, dealing with the Crown's rights of livery and wardship (over minors who were the heirs of deceased tenants in chief of the Crown). The court's records are at TNA (ref: WARD), including property records, surveys, accounts and court proceedings, but they do not include any admission rolls of lawyers. The organisation and procedure of the court is described in H.E. Bell, *An introduction to the history and records of the Court of Wards and Liveries* (CUP, 1953). It includes references to some cases before the court and also to many of the court's officials and the lawyers who practised in the court.

The second most senior officer of the court was the surveyor-general of the liveries. Many lawyers held this post, such as John Hynde (a serjeant at law and recorder of Cambridge), Thomas Seckford of Gray's Inn (treasurer of the Inn in 1565) and Richard Kingsmill (a bencher of Lincoln's Inn). The attorney of the wards was the court's chief legal officer. The 15 men who held this post from 1540 are listed in Bell's work and most (and possibly all) of them were benchers of the Inns of Court. Richard Goodrich (appointed in 1546) was also attorney of the Court of Augmentations[14] and Richard Onslow, Thomas Wilbraham and Henry Calthorpe were also recorders of London. The clerk of the wards (and the underclerks) dealt with most of the records of proceedings in the court. The clerk Ralph Bosseville had been a barrister, practising extensively in the Court of Wards, prior to his appointment. John Hare was an attorney with chambers in Inner Temple

The lawyers who practised in the court were barristers (such as Ralph Bosseville noted above) and attorneys. The number of attorneys practising was initially limited to two but increased to four by 1635. Some are identified in Bell's work, for example John Hare (later a clerk of the wards) and John Winthrop (later governor of Massachusetts).

D10. THE PALATINATE COURTS OF DURHAM

A Palatinate was an area in which a noble or senior ecclesiastic exercised administrative and legal rights that, elsewhere in the country, were exercised by the monarch. The County Palatine of Durham (the county of Durham and parts of Northumberland and Yorkshire), was for centuries a separate legal jurisdiction from the rest of England and subject to the authority of the Bishop of Durham. The bishop exercised his spiritual authority through church courts (in which advocates and proctors practised) and his temporal authority through a system of courts, the Durham Palatinate courts, modelled on the King's courts. They are described in detail in K. Emsley and C.M. Fraser, *The courts of the County Palatine of Durham* (Durham County Local History Society, 1984).

The most important courts for civil actions were the Durham Court of Pleas (administering the common law) and a Court of Chancery (exercising equitable jurisdiction). There was also a county court that dealt mainly with small debts or criminal cases. Serious criminal cases were heard at the Durham assizes and by a Durham court of gaol delivery until Durham was included in one of the national assize circuits (the Northern circuit) in 1654. Justices of the peace also dealt with many civil and criminal cases from the mid-sixteenth century.

The temporal jurisdiction of the Bishop of Durham was abolished in 1836. The Durham courts were then gradually brought within the national court system. The Palatinate's county court was abolished in 1836 and the Durham Court of Pleas was merged into the High Court of Justice in 1875. The Durham Court of Chancery was also merged into the High Court but remained a separate entity, within the Chancery Division, until its abolition in 1971.

Most of the judges who presided over the Durham courts were already judges of the King's courts at Westminster and so records of them (and of the barristers appearing in the Durham courts) can therefore be found in the records noted above for judges, barristers and serjeants. Solicitors acted in the Durham Court of Chancery in the same manner as solicitors of the Court of Chancery in London (but no admission records appear to survive).

There are however records of attorneys being formally admitted to practise in the Durham Palatinate courts. The oldest records of practitioners are the admission rolls of the Court of Pleas held at TNA. These give the name of the attorney being admitted and the date of his admission. The years covered by the rolls and their reference at TNA are:

1660 – 1723   (ref: DURH 3/218)

The earliest admission recorded is that of Theophilus Brathwaite on 3 November 1660. The rolls usually name the attorney to whom a petitioner had been apprenticed (or articled), note the term of the articles and state whether the attorney (master) practised in more than one court. For example, the petition of Ralph Adamson dated 7 September 1662, stated that:

> he hath beene educated a Clerke with Mr Richard Hutchinson, one of the Attorneys of the Court of Common Pleas at Westmr and of all ye temporall Courts at Durham for five years and one halfe ... during which time yor petitioner hath beene imployed in all ye business of ye said Mr Richard Hutchinson and fronted and defended in the Courts at Westmr and Durham.

The period of articles varied. The most common term in the late seventeenth century was four years but Abraham Hilton, admitted on 28 May 1661, was articled for seven years. His petition states that he was 'son of Lancelot Hilton, gent., now Countie Clerke and one of the Attorneys of Durham'. George Warcup, admitted on 7 April 1694, served nine years of articles with George Bowes, Esquire, 'Councellor at Law and Solicitor General to the Right Reverend Father in God Nathanael, Lord Bishop of Durham'.

Some petitions are vague as to the length of the articles served. Francis Peacock, for instance, was admitted as an attorney on 10 August 1686. He stated that he had served Michael Alnwicke, one of the attorneys of the courts of Durham, as his clerk by 'the space of these many years last past'. Fleetwood Davenport of Staple Inn, London, was admitted as an attorney of the Durham courts on 1 April 1685. His petition stated that he was a clerk of the Court of King's Bench at Westminster but;

> *haveing married into this County of Durham and having urgent concerns here, is earnestly importuned by yor petitioners' relations to continue here, and to make his addresses to Yor Worpp to be admitted an Attorney of the Courts of this County.*

TNA holds oath rolls of the Durham courts, containing the signature of the attorneys being admitted to the court and the dates of their admission. The years covered by these rolls and their reference at TNA are:

1730 – 1843 (ref: DURH 3/217)

The earliest entries are on 1 September 1730 when a number of attorneys were re-admitted following the Attorneys and Solicitors Act of 1729. The rolls are arranged by year and then in alphabetical order by the first letter of the lawyer's surname. They give only the name of the attorney and the date. Several entries have the word 'dead' written in the margin.

TNA also holds 'affidavits of due execution of articles and service of clerkship' for the Durham courts. The years covered by these affidavits and their references at TNA are:

1750 – 1769	(ref: DURH 9/1)
1768 – 1794	(ref: DURH 9/2)
1794 – 1834	(ref: DURH 9/3)

The affidavits give the name and address of the clerk, his father's name, address and occupation, the name and address of the attorney to whom the clerk was articled, the court or courts in which that attorney practised, the term of the articles and the date when they were signed. Some affidavits note the name and address of the mother (if the father of the clerk was no longer alive when the articles were executed). Nearly all the articles were for a five year term but occasionally they were for six or seven years. Sometimes a clerk's articles were assigned from one attorney to another, both usually Durham attorneys. However there is one instance of a clerk (John Williamson) being articled for five years in 1756 to John Dixon of Durham, his articles then being assigned in 1759 for the remainder of their term to William Masterman, an attorney in London.

Another source of information at TNA about attorneys who practised in the Durham courts is the 'Register of certificates to practise' for 1785-1842 (ref: IND 1/10152). The certificates were required under the Act of 1785 noted above. The register gives the full name of the attorney, his place of residence and the date of the certificate. As the importance of the Durham Palatinate courts declined, so did the number of certificates. In 1785 and 1786, for example, certificates were issued to 35 attorneys. From 1 November 1799 to 1 November 1800, 16 attorneys received certificates. In 1815, only two attorneys obtained certificates. In the last section of the register, for certificates from 1841 to 1842, there is only one entry; for the certificate issued on 19 December 1842 to William Francis Hartley of Durham.

D11. THE PALATINATE COURTS OF CHESTER

The County Palatine of Chester was created by William I and entrusted to his nephew Hugh. Like Durham (and Lancaster, *see* below) it had its own system of Palatinate courts, of which the most important were the Court of Sessions of Chester and the Court of Exchequer of Chester. These were abolished in 1830 and attorneys who had practised there were allowed to enrol in the Westminster courts. The records of the Chester Palatinate courts are held at TNA.

The oldest of the Palatinate's records that evidence the lawyers who practised there are attorneys' admission rolls (ref: CHES 36/3/1) for the Chester Court of Sessions. These are sheets of paper bound into one volume. They cover the period 1697-1729 and are in Latin.

TNA also holds five oath rolls for attorneys admitted in this court following the Attorneys and Solicitors Act of 1729. The dates covered by these rolls and their references at TNA are:

1729 – 1754	(ref: CHES 36/3/2)
1787 – 1793	(ref: CHES 36/3/3)
1794 – 1800	(ref: CHES 36/3/4)
1783 – 1821	(ref: CHES 36/3/5)
1821 – 1830	(ref: CHES 36/3/6)

The rolls include the text of the attorney's oath and the signatures of the attorneys admitted. Some signatures are clear and others can be deciphered but some are illegible. Some entries give the date of admission opposite an attorney's signature. A few entries on the first three rolls also give the place where the attorney practised. The fourth and fifth rolls give the date of each attorney's admission and the place where he practised.

Most of the attorneys practised in Cheshire but others practised in Lancashire, North Wales or elsewhere. The word 'dead' is written against the entries for several of the attorneys.

TNA also holds three bundles of 'Affidavits of due execution of articles of clerkship' (ref: CHES 36/1) for the periods 1728-35 and 1749-1830. These affidavits give the name of the articled clerk, the attorney to whom he was articled, the term of articles, the date of their completion and the date of the affidavit. Many of the affidavits attach a copy of the articles and a certificate that the clerk had served his apprenticeship.

The periods of articles vary considerably. For example, the first bundle includes the articles of Daniel Ashley (son of Jonathan Ashley of Frodsham, yeoman) for four years to Edward Daniell, who practised as an attorney at Frodsham. Daniel's father paid a premium of 60 guineas to Edward Daniell. The amount of information contained in the affidavits also varies. For example, there is an affidavit of 11 September 1733 as to the execution of the articles of William Smith to serve five years with Thomas Weston, an attorney at Middlewich. This reveals that the articles stipulated that the clerk was to be paid £20 per annum by Mr Weston. The deponents to the affidavit state that 'they have heard and believe that Mr Weston was an attorney of the Court of Session at Chester and a solicitor in the High Court of Chancery and in other Courts of Equity'.

These bundles also contain some other miscellaneous documents. The first bundle includes a certificate dated 11 September 1733, by R. Wilbraham and Andrew Kenrick, stating that they know John Wicksted, of Nantwich and

> have known him to be a Practiser of the Law as an Attorney for twenty years and upwards last past and do humbly conceive him to be a person of integrity and duly Qualified for such Practice and to be admitted an Attorney pursuant to the direction of the late Act of Parliament.

Two days later, on 13 September 1733, John Wicksted himself swore an affidavit stating that:

> upwards of forty years ago he served his Father who was an Attorney as well in the County of Chester as in the Court of King's Bench at Westminster as his Clerk for three years and upwards and until his death and after his said Father's death he this Deponent served under Mr Jonathan Bradley who was likewise an Attorney of the said Court of Session for two years and upwards ... sometime before the Qualification of Attorneys pursuant to the Act of Parliament [of 1729, he was] seized with a stroack of the Palsie which in a Great Measure deprived him of the use of his left side under which he lay a considerable time in a very weak Condition and thereby prevented this Depon from his Qualification sooner pursuant to the said Act.

The affidavits of due execution in the second bundle are similar to those in the first bundle but clipped together in reverse date order. Some affidavits relate to articles of clerks to attorneys who also practised in courts other than those of the Palatinate of Chester. For example, William Bancroft was articled on 3 August 1787 to Thomas Royle of Chester, an attorney of the Chester Court of Session, the Court of King's Bench at Westminster and the Court of Great Sessions for Flint, Denbigh and Montgomery. One affidavit relates to Evan Foulkes, the son of a miner, who was articled on 28 July 1770 for five years to Thomas Jones of St Asaph, an attorney at law and proctor. Jones undertook 'to do his best to have Evan Foulkes admitted as a proctor of the Consistory Court of St Asaph at the end of the five years'.

The third bundle contains similar material, including an affidavit relating to the articles dated 12 March 1795 for a term of 8½ years of John Jubal Sutton to Alexander Eaton of Chester. Eaton practised as an attorney or solicitor in the Chester Court of Session, the Chester Court of Exchequer, the courts of Chancery and Exchequer at Westminster and in the Court of Great Sessions of Flint, Denbigh and Montgomery.

These records refer to some attorneys who practised in the Chester courts but did not live in Cheshire. Some, as already indicated, lived in North Wales. Others lived in Lancashire. William Maire, for instance, who took an articled clerk in 1789, lived at Warrington. Some of the records mention the partner of the attorney who took an articled clerk. For example, Thomas Cotton, son of the Dean of Chester, was articled to Philip Humberston of Chester, attorney, on 9 April 1799. The affidavit of due execution of Cotton's articles states that Humberston was 'co-partner with William Massey of Moston Hall, in the said County of Chester, Esquire, in the profession of an Attorney and Solicitor'.

TNA also holds a register (ref: CHES 36/2) of 'Affidavits of due execution of articles' of 1749-92. This volume is easier to use than the bundles of affidavits in CHES 36/1 because it is clearly written but it only contains what are described as 'memorandums' of the affidavits. For example, the first entry (dated 28 December 1749) relates to the articles, dated 3 October 1749, by which John Barlow (son of Thomas Barlow, a tanner) undertook to serve Robert Baxter of Chester. Baxter was an attorney of the Chester Court of Exchequer and the Chester Court of Session and a solicitor of the courts of Chancery and Exchequer at Westminster.

TNA holds three rolls of solicitors and attorneys admitted to practise in the Chester Court of Exchequer. The years covered by these records and their references at TNA are:

Admissions of attorneys 1777 – 1806   (ref: CHES 36/3/7)
Admissions of solicitors 1750 – 1787   (ref: CHES 36/3/8)
Admissions of solicitors 1787 – 1806   (ref: CHES 36/3/9)

These rolls include the text of the oath that had to be sworn on admission, the date of the attorney's or solicitor's admission and, for most solicitors, the place where he practised.

The second roll of solicitors (for 1787-1806) lists the men admitted, their place of residence and the dates of admissions. For example, the entry for Griffith Williams' admission on 15 February 1798 simply reads 'Griff: Williams, of Holywell, co Flint'. Some entries give more information or are marked 'admitted as an attorney'. The entry for John Eaton, admitted on 11 September 1806, reads 'Jno Eaton, of the City of Chester, admitted an Attorney after having taken the usual Oaths before David Fras Jones, Dep. Baron'.

The roll for attorneys includes notes, at the entries for Samuel Humphreys (admitted on 14 June 1798) and John Eaton (admitted on 11 September 1806), stating that they had been admitted to practise on the deaths of other practitioners (William Dicas and Alexander Eaton). The oaths to be taken by attorneys before being admitted in the Court of Exchequer were:

I AB, do sincerely Promise and swear that I will be faithfull and bear true Allegiance to his Majesty King George. So help me God.

I AB do swear that I do from my Heart Abhor Detest and Abjure as Impious and Heretical that Damnable Doctrine and Position that Princes Excommunicated or deprived by the Pope or any Authority of the See of Rome may be deposed or murthered by their Subjects or any other whatsoever. And I do Declare that no Foreign Prince, Person, Prelate, State or Potentate hath or ought to have any Jurisdiction, Power, Superiority, Preheminence or Authority Ecclesiasticall or Spiritual within this Realm. So help me God.

You shall swear that well and truly according to your best Skill Knowledge and Understanding you shall use and carry yourself as an Attorney of this Court whereunto you are now admitted as well in your Behaviour towards the Court, as in your Care and Diligence in and about your Client's Causes to perform what thereunto belongeth. The Authority Jurisdiction Libertys and Privileges of this Court and County Palatine you shall to all your Knowledge and Power maintain and defend and not do or cause to be done any thing that you know may be to the Infringement thereof. Also shall satisfy and pay the Fees and Dutys of this Court such as shall be due for your Clients to pay without any Diminution or Concealment thereof so far forth as shall rest in your knowledge as you well may or can; And otherwise to be at the Appointment thereof in all dutifull Regard. So help you God.

D12. THE COURT OF THE DUCHY OF LANCASTER

In the fourteenth century, Edward III conferred the title of 'duke' on his cousin Henry, Earl of Lancaster. Since then, the Duchy of Lancaster has held extensive properties in Lancashire and other parts of England. The title and lands of the Duchy have been held by the monarch since Henry IV (whose father John of Gaunt married the heiress of Henry, Duke of Lancaster). The Chancellor of the Duchy of Lancaster presided over a court, on behalf of the Duke of Lancaster, known as the Court of the Duchy of Lancaster. The court sat at Westminster and heard cases relating to the Duchy's lands, wherever they lay, but it has not sat since 1835.

Records of the Duchy of Lancaster are held at TNA (ref: DL). They do not appear to include any lists of lawyers practising in the Duchy Court. However, the list of attorneys and solicitors registered under the Attorneys and Solicitors Act of 1729 and presented to the House of Commons in 1731 does include those practising in the court.

Officers of the Duchy are listed, with biographical information, in R. Somerville, *History of the Duchy of Lancaster, vol I 1265-1603* (The Chancellor and Council of the Duchy of Lancaster, 1953) and in R. Somerville, *Office-holders in the Duchy and County Palatine of Lancaster from 1603* (Phillimore, 1972). The lists include the Attorney Generals of the Duchy and the serjeants at law, barristers and attorneys retained by the Duchy. However, many other office-holders, such as some of the Chancellors and most of the clerks of the council and deputy chief stewards were also barristers or attorneys. For example, William Tusser was a barrister of Middle Temple and clerk of the council of the Duchy of Lancaster from 1572 until his death in 1587.

D13. THE PALATINATE COURTS OF LANCASTER

At the same time as creating his cousin Henry the Duke of Lancaster, Edward III also raised the county of Lancaster into a Palatinate and granted palatine powers in that county to Henry for his life. This included the right of the duke to have his own Chancery and Exchequer and to appoint justices (to hear common law disputes), sheriffs, coroners and other officers to administer the law within the Palatinate. This grant of the Palatinate terminated on Henry's death in 1361 but it was revived in 1377 in favour of John of Gaunt (Edward III's son and Henry's son-in-law) who had been created Duke of Lancaster in 1362. In 1396, the Duchy and Palatinate of Lancaster were granted to John of Gaunt and his heirs male in perpetuity.

The Palatinate's judicial system included a Court of Common Pleas, a Court of Chancery, justices (of assize, oyer and terminer and of gaol delivery) and also justices of the peace. The Court of Common Pleas of Lancaster was merged into the High Court of Justice in 1875 but the Court of Chancery of Lancaster operated until 1971. Most of the records of the superior courts of the Palatinate of Lancaster are held at TNA under the reference PL (the records of justices of the peace are held at Lancashire Record Office in Preston).

Officers of the Palatinate are listed, with biographical information, in R. Somerville, *History of the Duchy of Lancaster, vol I 1265-1603* (The Chancellor and Council of the Duchy of Lancaster, 1953) and in R. Somerville, *Office-holders in the Duchy and County Palatine of Lancaster from 1603* (Phillimore, 1972). The offices staffed primarily by lawyers included those of the vice-chancellor, the clerk of the crown, the clerks of the Common Pleas, the clerk of the peace and the chief clerk of the Chancery Court. For example, Peter Catterall was an attorney at Preston and held the last of those offices from 1846. He died in 1873.

The list of attorneys and solicitors registered under the Attorneys and Solicitors Act of 1729 and presented to the House of Commons in 1731 included those practising in the Lancaster Court of Common Pleas.

TNA holds two rolls of attorneys admitted in the Lancaster Court of Common Pleas. These are in one volume with the attorneys listed by year and then in alphabetical order by the first letter of their surnames. The years covered by these rolls and their reference at TNA are:

1730 – 1875   (ref: PL 23/6)

These rolls also indicate which attorneys were struck off. Henry Blackhurst, for example, who was admitted on 31 August 1812 and practised at Preston, was struck off on 25 August 1823 'by order of Mr Justice Bayley and Mr Justice Holroyd dated 22nd inst'. The *Law list 1823* describes Blackhhurst, rather inappropriately one may think, as 'solicitor to the Association for the Prosecution of Felons'. Perhaps he became too friendly with the criminals whose activities he was employed to curtail. Nicholas Starkie, admitted to the court on 27 August 1757, had his name withdrawn from the rolls at his own request on 23 March 1760. The reason for this is not recorded.

At TNA there is also a 'Register of certificates to practise in the Palatine Court of Lancaster' for 1785-1871 (ref: PL 23/5). The certificates were entered in the register alphabetically by the first letter of the attorney's surname and in batches of years. They show that many attorneys took out their practising certificates every year but some did not. Simon Dearden of Rochdale, for instance, obtained his certificate in 1787 and 1789 but not in 1788. The records can sometimes assist to establish the date of death of a practitioner. For example, Richard Beckett of Manchester took out a practising certificate only on 4 November 1785. The word 'dead' is written opposite his name in the register.

An oath roll of attorneys admitted in the Lancaster Court of Common Pleas is at TNA (ref: PL 23/7/1). It covers the period 1730-93, is signed by the various attorneys at the time of their admission and dated. Frequently several attorneys were admitted and sworn on the same day. On 23 August 1748, for example, there were six.

TNA also holds two registers of 'Affidavits of due execution of articles' for clerks being admitted to practise as attorneys in the Lancaster Court of Common Pleas. The dates covered by these registers and their references at TNA are:

1749 – 1781	(ref: PL 23/3)
1781 – 1823	(ref: PL 23/4)

They show that most clerks contracted to serve their masters for five years but a number of entries note the period of service as six or seven years. John Rose, for example, who later became an attorney in Liverpool, was articled to Thomas Aspinwall of Liverpool for six years on 18 December 1748. In the margin opposite the entry for the affidavit as to the execution of his articles (which was made by a widow named Mary Bennet) is a note reading 'John Rose admitted'. Some affidavits reveal family relationships. William Crowther of Manchester swore an affidavit on 23 June 1781. He had witnessed the execution of an indenture of clerkship between Robert Crowther of Heaton Norris, co. Lancaster, silk throwster, Richard Tunnadine (his nephew) and Richard Tunnadine of Manchester, attorney at law, whereby Richard Tunnadine the younger, was articled to his father Richard Tunnadine for five years.

Some affidavits show that the attorney to whom a clerk was articled had died and that the articles were assigned to another attorney. For example, John Wilson was articled on 3 October 1777 for seven years to John Webster, an attorney at Lancaster. Webster died and John Wilson's articles were assigned on 21 March 1781 by Webster's executors (whose names and occupations are given in the affidavit), for the remainder of the term to George Fletcher, another Lancaster attorney.

The information in the second registere is presented in columns headed 'date of articles', 'clerk', 'master', 'term', 'witnesses', 'affidavits sworn' and 'affidavits filed'. The attorneys are described in some entries as 'gentleman' and in others as 'attorney' or 'attorney at law'. In 1822 a revised format was introduced, with the headings 'name', 'place of abode', 'name of the attorney to whom articled', 'place of abode of such attorney' and 'when entered'.

In addition to the registers of affidavits, some original articles and affidavits of due execution also survive. The dates covered by these documents and their references at TNA are:

1749 – 1785	(ref: PL 23/1)
1785 – 1814	(ref: PL 23/2)

The descriptions of the masters (the attorneys) in these affidavits vary. For example, in an affidavit referring to a clerk articled on 6 October 1777, John Gardner of Preston, the master, is noted as an attorney of both the Court of King's Bench at Westminster and the Lancaster Court of Common Pleas. In the case of the articles dated 30 June 1784 of a clerk to Robert Richmond of Liverpool, he is described as an attorney of the Court of Common Pleas of the County Palatine of Lancaster and a solicitor of the High Court of Chancery. The wording of the affidavits also varies. Some omit the period that the articled clerk had to serve.

The details contained in these records can be very helpful to genealogists. An affidavit of 7 April 1784 refers to the articles of James Spencer to Richard Smith of Chorley, dated 12 January 1780, being assigned (on 20 January 1784) to William Hough of Chorley, then assigned for the remainder of the five-year term to Robert Lawe of Preston, an attorney of the Lancaster Court of Common Pleas. The articled clerk is stated to be the only son of James Spencer, the elder, of Newburgh within Lathom, co. Lancaster.

An interesting group of records at TNA are the 'Minutes of meetings of attorneys of the County Palatine to dine together' (ref: PL 23/7/2). These begin on 10 August 1790, when a meeting at the White Hart in Lancaster resolved that the attorneys practising in the county of Lancaster, 'in order to support the dignity of the profession and to promote harmony and conviviality' should form a society to meet and dine together on the fourth day of every assizes. The resolution bore 27 signatures. Other attorneys subsequently attended meetings and joined the society. In the early nineteenth century, the society took in some honorary members, such as Alexander McGregor, W.S. (Writer to the Signet) of Glasgow (in 1804) and Willoughby Rackham, a London attorney (in 1805). The last meeting for which records survive at TNA was held at the Commercial Inn, Lancaster, on 10 August 1807.

D14. THE COURT OF THE KING'S PALACE

The Court of the King's Palace was established in 1630 and had jurisdiction over all personal actions that arose within 12 miles of Whitehall that were not in the jurisdiction of the City of London or other liberties. It incorporated the ancient Court of the

Marshalsea (that had jurisdiction over many disputes involving members of the King's household). The court sat at Westminster until its abolition in 1849. At any one time, only four barristers and six attorneys were admitted to practise in the court, the records of which are at TNA. Those that contain useful information about lawyers, with their TNA references, are:

Oaths of office: attorneys   1782-1843   (ref: PALA 9/4/2)

These are the original oaths, each a separate document, bearing the attorney's signature.

Notices of appointment; attorneys 1821-44   (ref: PALA 9/5/8)
Warrants for admission to office, counsel
(1737-1811), attorneys (1722-1811)   (ref: PALA 9/5/2)

The warrants name the attorney vacating office by surrender or death as well as the attorney admitted to office.

Surrenders of office: attorneys 1743-1844   (ref: PALA 9/5/3)

The earliest of the surrenders reads as follows:

I Thomas Cotton Gentleman one of the six sworn Attorneys as well of the Antient Court of the Marshalsea as of the Court of our Sovereign Lord King George the Second of his Majestie's Palace at Westminster Do hereby surrender into the hands of the Most Noble Lionel Duke of Dorset and of the Honble. Sir Phillip Medows Knight Marshal Judges of the said Courts my Place or Office above specifyed to the use of Richard Jackson of Clifford's Inn London Gentleman. Witness my hand and seal the twenty-fourth day of June in the year 1743
Thos Cotton (L.S.)
Sealed and Delivered (being first duely stampt.)
In the presence of Michl Barrow,
Clerk to Mr Stainbank, Deputy Prothonotary of the abovesaid Court.
Wm Smyth, Attorney, Somersett House, Stable Yard.

I do desire the above named Richard Jackson Gentleman may be admitted and sworn into the said Place or Office of one of the six Attorneys of the said Courts vacant by my Surrender. Witness my hand the day and year first above written.
Thos Cotton
Witness : Michl Barrow, Wm Smyth.

An item of particular interest in this series of documents is the surrender of his office on 20 July 1821 of an attorney named John Ferdinand Lumsden. He had fallen on hard times and was confined in the Marshalsea Prison on the date when he signed his deed of surrender (in the presence of Robert Long, also an attorney).

Profit books 1644-1846 (some gaps in earlier years)   (ref: PALA 7)

These books (150 volumes) record the fees charged by each of the six attorneys of the court at each session. They note the type of service provided, the title of the case and the charges.

Habeas corpus books (37 volumes) 1700-1849   (ref: PALA 4)

These books record the issue of writs. Each entry is signed by the defendant's attorney or his clerk. By the later eighteenth century, and sometimes earlier, the attorney's address is given. Attorneys' names can also be found in 66 volumes of bail books covering 1692-1836 and 23 volumes of custody books covering 1754-1842, of which the following are examples:

Bail book 1819-22 (indexed)   (ref: PALA 1/61)
Custody book Dec 24 1818 to April 12 1822 (indexed)   (ref: PALA 2/16)

Some of this court's attorneys are noted in the law lists. For example, the *Law list 1833* notes Joseph Arden of 2 Clifford's Inn Passage, Fleet Street as an attorney of the Palace Court.

D15. THE MAYOR'S AND CITY OF LONDON COURT

The Lord Mayor's Court was originally ancillary to the City of London's principal civil court, the Court of Husting (which dealt primarily with transfers of, and actions to recover, land in the City) and developed because of the large amount of work which overflowed from the Court of Husting. The *Law list 1790* explains that:

> *the Lord Mayor's Court of Record in Law and Equity is held every Day (except Saint Days, Sessions at the Old Bailey, Sessions in Southwark and Common Council's Courts of Conservancy) where the Recorder sits as Judge and the Lord Mayor and Alderman [sic] may sit with him. Actions of Debt, Trespass, Attachments, Apprenticiality ... and others arising within the City and Liberties may be entered and tried in this Court. An Action may be removed by Habeas Corpus or Certiorari into a superior Court if the Debt be above £5 ... This Court has ... a Register, Deputy Register, 4 Attorneys and 6 Serjeants at Mace'.*

In addition to the officers of the court mentioned above, the *Law list 1790* lists the four barristers who practised in the court.

The Lord Mayor's Court was opened to all attorneys from 1853 and was amalgamated in 1921 with the City of London Court to form the Mayor's and City of London Court. It was abolished in 1971 (a new county court, also known as Mayor's and City of London Court, was established). The records of the court (until recently held at the Corporation of London Record Office but being transferred to the London Metropolitan Archives) include:

Roll of attorneys admitted to practice 6 May 1860 to 22 February 1939
Attorneys' bill books 1694-1723 (5 volumes)
Private account books of Robert Champante, an attorney 1741-52

D16. THE COUNTY COURTS

There were county courts in medieval times that dealt with a variety of local (primarily civil) disputes. The modern county courts were established by the County Court Act of 1846 to deal with small debts and other civil claims (some also hear bankruptcy and matrimonial cases). They replaced many different local courts, such as courts of request that had previously dealt with small claims. There are presently about 320 county courts. They are presided over by district judges and solicitors have rights of audience.

County and city archive offices hold some records of county courts, including references to the lawyers acting there. For example, a search in archive catalogues, through Access to Archives' website, reveals that Devon Record Office holds a roll of attorneys working in Tiverton County Court, with their addresses, signatures and dates of admission between 1812 and 1933.

D17. THE HIGH COURT OF JUSTICE AND THE COURT OF APPEAL

As noted, the Judicature Act of 1873 amalgamated most of the higher courts into the High Court of Justice. The High Court is divided into divisions (presently the Chancery Division, the Queen's Bench Division and the Family Division) and, with the Court of Appeal and the Crown Court, constitutes the Supreme Court of Judicature.

Solicitors were admitted as 'solicitors of the Supreme Court' by the Law Society but the court also kept its own records of admissions of solicitors. Some records of admissions in the Supreme Court from 1875 to 1904, that is articles of clerkship, affidavits of due execution and affidavits of due completion of articles (TNA refs: KB 111, C 217, J 89/4 and J 89/5), were noted in the section above that dealt with the Court of King's Bench.

In addition, some 'Applications for certificates', that is solicitors' applications to take out or renew practising certificates, have been preserved as specimens only. The dates and references at TNA of these specimen documents[15] are:

1875 November	(ref: J 89/6/1)
1880 Jan to April	(ref: J 89/6/2)
1880 May to Dec	(ref: J 89/6/3)
1889 Jan to Feb	(ref: J 89/6/4)

Some records of the High Court of Justice are included in series KB 111. The first piece (ref: KB 111/1) includes the following documents relating to solicitors and articled clerks:

High Court of Justice: applications and affidavits concerning articled clerks	1879 – 1889
Testimonials concerning the service of articled clerks	1868 – 1881
Orders to strike off, restore or alter names on the Roll of Solicitors	1875 – 1888

The fifth piece in series KB 111 (ref: KB 111/5) includes some documents from the Chancery Division of the High Court relating to articles of clerkship and practising certificates. The dates covered by these documents are:

1876 May – 1876 Oct	Petty Bag Office: register of Articles, 1st entries and receipts and applications to dispense with preliminary examinations
1878 Apr – 1889	Petty Bag Office: register of applications to take out and renew certificates

Many cases heard in the Supreme Court are included in published law reports (*see* section E.5). These note the judges hearing cases, the barristers appearing before them and some of the firms of solicitors instructed by clients.

D18. THE CRIMINAL COURTS

The courts considered above dealt primarily with civil actions, although the Court of King's Bench had jurisdiction over some criminal matters (hearing writs of 'habeas corpus' and some appeals from other criminal courts). The Court of Star Chamber also heard cases that involved allegations of criminal conduct. A separate structure of courts dealt with most criminal cases.

Assizes

Serious offences were tried from the twelfth century by the King's justices, who travelled from Westminster round the country, and sat with local juries. These itinerant justices (the 'justices in eyre') dealt with both criminal and civil matters. By 1300, the system developed into a more formal system of 'assize' circuits. Most English counties were included in one of the circuits and the justices of assize visited each county (usually twice a year) to dispense justice at the assizes held at certain towns on each circuit. The justices had three functions:

- to try people in custody (commissions of gaol delivery),
- to try cases passed to them by the local justices of the peace (commissions of oyer and terminer; that is to hear and determine), and
- to hear the trials of common law civil actions started in the courts of King's Bench, Common Pleas and Exchequer (plea side) so as to save the parties and witnesses travelling to the courts at Westminster (cases heard at *nisi prius*).

Administration on each assize circuit, including the making and storage of records, was the responsibility of clerks of assize and their associate clerks, most of whom were barristers. The surviving records of the justices in eyre and assizes are held at TNA (references JUST and ASSI). The assizes were abolished in 1971 and replaced by Crown Courts located permanently in cities such as Birmingham, Leeds and Manchester. Appeals are heard by the Court of Appeal (Criminal Division) which sits at the Royal Courts of Justice in London.

The cities of London and Westminster and (for many years) Middlesex were excluded from the assize circuits. Serious crimes committed there were heard by justices at sessions under commissions of oyer and terminer and of gaol delivery from Newgate Gaol. These sessions took place at the Old Bailey Sessions House or, from 1834, at the Central Criminal Court (also in Old Bailey). Records of the Old Bailey Sessions are held at the Corporation of London Record Office. Records of cases heard at the Central Criminal Court are at TNA. Published reports (known as the 'Old Bailey Proceedings') of cases at the Old Bailey Sessions and the Central Criminal Court are held at Guildhall Library and TNA (and can be accessed online). However, although they refer to the judges who heard cases, very few other lawyers are mentioned.

Bristol was also excluded from the assize circuits and had its own sessions until 1832. The records are at Bristol Record Office. The Palatinates of Durham, Chester and Lancaster were also excluded from the assize circuits until the nineteenth century. Records of the sessions held in the Palatinates are at TNA under references DURH, CHES and PL respectively.

Very few of the eyre, assize and session records are indexed and they include little information about the lawyers who appeared. Most of the records before 1733 are in Latin. Nisi prius cases were conducted by barristers and attorneys, as in the London courts, and reports of some nisi prius cases are included in published law reports (*see* section E.5 below). However, in criminal matters, although a prisoner was often allowed to use lawyers this was rare before the 1730s and there was no legal right to representation by a barrister at a criminal trial until 1836. Research in original eyre and assize records for a lawyer is therefore likely to be a long (and fruitless) task. Those who wish to make the attempt should first review D. Crook, *Records of the General Eyre* (PRO, 1982), J.S. Cockburn, *A history of the English assizes* (CUP, 1972) and TNA legal records information leaflet 13 'Assizes: criminal trials'.

Searches are best undertaken in published material. Cockburn's work lists the judges on each assize commission from 1559 to 1714 and provides biographical details of the clerks of assize for the same period. For example, Nicholas Hearne of Arminghall, Norfolk, was a clerk of the Norfolk circuit between 1605 and 1612. He matriculated at St John's College, Cambridge in 1577/8 and was admitted to Lincoln's Inn from Clement's Inn in 1582. He was appointed as a justice of the peace for Norfolk in 1608 and died in 1612. Some attorneys also acted as clerks. Cockburn refers to Simon Spatchurst, a junior clerk on the Western circuit who also appeared as an attorney at the Somerset assizes in 1611. Jonas Pinsent was an associate clerk who also practised as an attorney at the Devon and Somerset assizes between 1610 and 1630. Barristers (and some attorneys) practising on the circuits are named in assize records. Cockburn's work identifies 10 of the barristers practising on the Western circuit between 1630 and 1650; William Lenthall, William Noy, Peter Ball, Thomas Bedingfield, Francis Crawley, Robert Foster, Thomas Gates, Robert Nicholas, Edmund Reeve and Hugh Wyndham.

D. Lynch, *Northern circuit directory 1876-2004* (Bluecoat Press, 2005) is a very detailed biographical dictionary of 3,417 judges and barristers who served on the Northern circuit between 1874 and 2004, with many photographs. A. May, *The bar and the Old Bailey 1750-1850* (University of North Carolina Press, 2003) includes a list (with some biographical details) of many of the barristers who appeared at the Old Bailey sessions or at the Central Criminal Court between 1783 and 1850. Other studies of particular circuits, such as J.S. Cockburn, *Somerset assize orders 1640-1649* (Somerset Record Society, 1971) and J.S. Cockburn, *Western circuit assize orders 1629-1648, a calendar* (Royal Historical Society, 1976) identify many barristers and some attorneys. For example, the barristers John Glanville, Henry Rolle, Nathaniel Finch and Mr Morgan and the attorney William Champion were appointed to represent Elizabeth Stile. She had been tried and acquitted of witchcraft in 1636 and was given permission of the court to sue her accusers, with the help of the lawyers, for malicious prosecution.

Many of the cases heard at the assizes were reported in newspapers and those reports (considered below) often referred to the lawyers involved.

Quarter sessions, petty sessions and magistrates' courts
Less serious offences were tried without juries by justices of the peace, now known as magistrates, most of whom are laymen rather than lawyers. Justices of the peace sat at quarter sessions (held four times a year) in each county. They were assisted by clerks of the peace (*see* section B.18), who were lawyers and are now known as magistrates' clerks. Except in a few places (such as Bodmin), only barristers had a right of audience before the quarter sessions. Many boroughs (about 100 by 1660) had the right to hold their own quarter sessions, often with a paid judge (a recorder) rather than lay justices. Crown Courts replaced the quarter sessions in 1971.

From the 19th century, magistrates also sat, between the quarter sessions, at petty sessions, now known as magistrates' courts. Solicitors had rights of audience. Magistrates examined defendants and witnesses prior to a trial and conducted committal hearings to decide whether there was sufficient evidence for a defendant to be tried. The City of London and City of Westminster had their own sessions. City magistrates sat at Guildhall and Mansion House. Middlesex magistrates sat at Guildhall in Westminster and Clerkenwell Sessions House.

London also had police courts. Justices of the peace were unpaid (and originally made money from court fees and offenders' fines). Before the institution of a police force, the justices of the peace and parish constables were quite insufficient to deal with crime in a major city. However, the first Bow Street magistrate, Sir Thomas de Veil, and his successors Henry and Sir John Fielding effected important changes. De Veil was justice of the peace for Westminster and Middlesex in the early 18th century and, like most justices, worked from his own home or office. He moved to a house in Bow Street in 1739, establishing the first court known as a police office there. De Veil and the Fieldings commanded paid constables and kept registers of known criminals.

This concept of a court with a justice of the peace, commanding professional constables to detect crime and arrest offenders, was very successful. Bow Street became the model for eight new police offices in London and Middlesex between 1792 and 1821. Each office was staffed by stipendiary (that is paid) full-time magistrates with paid constables to assist them. A statute of 1839 removed the constables from the magistrates' control and renamed the offices as police courts. They are now known as magistrates courts. The use of stipendiary magistrates spread to other busy magistrates' courts around the country. The stipendiary magistrates are now known as district judges and there are presently 126 of them.

Appointments of justices of the peace from the sixteenth to the twentieth centuries are recorded in series C 202 at TNA and, from 1665, were also announced in *The London Gazette* (*see* section E.1 below). Although most magistrates today are not lawyers, this has not always been the case. From the fourteenth century, commissions of the peace (appointing men to serve as justices of the peace) were required to include two 'men of the law'. In the late sixteenth century perhaps 20% of the justices in some counties were lawyers. J.H. Gleeson, *The Justices of the Peace in England 1558-1640* (Clarendon Press, 1969) is a detailed study of the education and background of justices. It includes lists of the justices in Kent, Norfolk, Northamptonshire, Somerset, Worcestershire and the North Riding of Yorkshire from 1558 to 1640 (and for most English counties in 1609), with biographical information on many of them. Some justices were also judges in the Westminster courts, serjeants at law or barristers. For example, the 1636 commission for Kent included the barristers John Honiwood, Henry Dixon, Richard Parker, Reginald Edwards and Robert Filmer.

Most records of the justices of the peace have been deposited in county and city archives. The records, indexes, transcripts and abstracts are listed in J. Gibson, *Quarter Sessions records for family historians, a select list* (4th edn. FFHS, 1995). Very few of the documents refer to the lawyers who appeared in cases. However, there are some exceptions. The records of the clerk of the peace held at Cheshire Record Office include lists and registers of magistrates, solicitors and barristers for the period 1846-1969. Lawyers may also be found in the series of rolls of oaths of allegiance, dating from the late seventeenth to nineteenth centuries. It is also worthwhile reviewing any published selections from the records, or indexes held at archives, for references to a lawyer ancestor.

Many cases before the justices of the peace were reported in newspapers and those reports (considered below) often referred to the lawyers involved.

D19. COURTS OF THE SHERIFFS OF LONDON AND MIDDLESEX

The sheriffs of London and Middlesex were responsible for gaols (known as compters) but they also held courts at the Poultry Compter and Wood Street Compter. A description of these courts in the *Law list 1790* reads as follows:

> *The Sheriffs have two courts, which are Courts of Records for Trial of Debt, Case, Trespass, Account, Covenant, Attachment and Sequestration, held on Thursdays and Saturdays for the Poultry [Compter], and on Wednesdays and Fridays for Wood Street. To these Courts belong 8 Attorneys, 2 Secondaries, 2 Clerks of the Papers who return all Writs, and copy Declarations; 8 Clerk-sitters, who enter Actions and take Bail ... 36 Serjeants at Mace for both Compters and 36 Yeomen.*

Law lists give the names and addresses of the sheriffs, under sheriffs and sheriffs' officers for both compters, as well as the judges, counsel and attorneys who appeared in the courts. For example the *Law list 1856* lists three barristers and 28 attorneys practising in the courts.

The sheriffs' courts were later transferred from the compters to Guildhall, merged into the City of London Court in 1867 and amalgamated with the Mayor's Court in 1921.

Most of the early records of these courts do not survive because the sheriffs, elected each year, considered them as their personal property which they needed to retain in case they were required to account for their actions after their terms of office. The surviving records of these courts (until recently held at the Corporation of London Record Office but being transferred to the London Metropolitan Archives) include rolls of attorneys admitted to practise from 1860 to 1867.

D20. ECCLESIASTICAL COURTS

The ecclesiastical or church courts were of great importance in medieval England, having jurisdiction over, inter alia, probate, matrimonial disputes and defamation as well as discipline of the clergy. However, the powers of these courts were gradually transferred to the secular courts (for example probate and matrimonial matters in 1857). By 1900, the church courts dealt almost exclusively with matters concerning church buildings and clergy discipline.

The main church courts of first instance were the archdeacon's court, the bishop's (that is diocesan) consistory court and the prerogative courts of the archbishops of Canterbury and York. There were also courts that had jurisdiction over one or more parishes (the peculiar courts and the courts of deans and chapters) and courts with specialist jurisdiction, such as the Court of Faculties (the court of the Archbishop of Canterbury for granting dispensations). Appeals from the lower courts could be made to the Court of Arches of the Archbishop of Canterbury and the Chancery Court of the Archbishop of York. Final appeals were made to the Court of Delegates until it was abolished in 1832 (appeals were then heard by the Judicial Committee of the Privy Council).

The procedure and records of the church courts are described in A. Tarver, *Church court records, an introduction for family and local historians* (Phillimore, 1995) and C. Chapman, *Sin, sex and probate: ecclesiastical courts, officials & records* (2nd edn. Lochin Publishing, 1997). The lawyers who practised in the church courts were the advocates and proctors noted above. Most surviving church court records are held in diocesan record offices (usually county or city record offices) and can be found in archives' catalogues, some of which can be accessed through Access to Archives' website. Advocates' and proctors' admissions to practise in a church court were recorded in act books; Tarver's work includes an illustration of an act of court, for the admission of Thomas Buckeridge as proctor in the Consistory Court of Lichfield in 1784.

Archbishops, bishops and archdeacons did not preside over courts themselves but appointed someone (usually an advocate or later a barrister) to do so on their behalf. A consistory court was presided over by the chancellor of a diocese and an archdeacon's court was presided over by the archdeacon's official or by the bishop's commissary. C. Ritchie, *The ecclesiastical courts of York* (Herald Press, 1956) describes the church courts in York in the sixteenth century, identifying some of the judges, advocates and proctors in those courts.

The records of the Prerogative Court of Canterbury are at TNA. These refer to many proctors acting in that court. The acts of court books (ref: PROB 29), covering 1536-1819, are minutes of the court, mostly in Latin until 1732. Most of the business relates to the granting of probate or related matters but the earlier volumes include appointments of proctors. More accessible to the researcher is a biographical index of proctors that is filed with the series list for PROB 39 in the research enquiries room at TNA.

G. Duncan, *The High Court of Delegates* (CUP, 1971) describes the history, procedure, officials and records of that court. Many judges of the court were advocates but some were judges of the common law courts. The principal official of the court was the registrar, who was usually a notary public (the registrars are listed in Duncan's work). Advocates and proctors who had been admitted to practice in the Court of Arches (*see* sections B.11 and B.12) were also entitled to practice in the High Court of Delegates. Barristers could also appear with leave of the court and they made increasingly regular appearances. The records of the court are at TNA (ref: DEL). They include written proxies by which parties appointed proctors to conduct their appeals. Act books (ref: DEL/4) record the court's business, with entries for each case noting the names of the parties and their proctors. The names of the parties' advocates are not generally recorded in the act books but they can be ascertained from certain case documents, that the advocates signed, such as sentences (draft court orders).

D21. OTHER LOCAL COURTS

The introduction of the feudal system resulted in the establishment of manorial courts; the court leet and court baron. These dealt with the transfer of copyhold land (abolished in 1922) and with disputes between a lord of the manor and his tenants or between those tenants. These courts were generally presided over by a steward (often a lawyer) on behalf of the lord. As the manorial system fell into decline in late medieval times, so did the manorial courts. Surviving manorial court rolls and other documents may refer to lawyers appearing in those courts.

From medieval times up to the establishment of the new county courts in the nineteenth century, there were many other courts in England and Wales that had jurisdiction in personal actions, particularly those for small debts. There were ancient hundred courts (a hundred was part of a county) but most of them had been obsolete for many years prior to their abolition in 1867. Most cities and boroughs were granted extensive rights and freedoms by charter that included the right to hold a variety of courts. For example, Bristol was granted the right to hold its own courts of assize, oyer and terminer and gaol delivery (until 1835). It also had quarter and general sessions, a court of piepowder (to regulate fairs), a court of orphans, a staple court and courts (the Tolzey Court, the Mayor's Court and the Court of Requests) to deal with claims for small debts, trespass and other civil actions.

In 1840 there were 328 of these local courts in England and 22 in Wales. Some counties had a larger number of courts of this nature than others. In Sussex in 1840, for example, there were four: the Dumpford Hundred Court, Arundel Borough Court, Chichester Court of Record and Hastings Court of Record. In Kent there were 19 such courts. Over 140 borough courts, such as the Oxford Court of Husting, were abolished in 1972.

Unfortunately, many of the records of these courts have not survived and those records that have survived often include little material about the lawyers who practised in those courts. The surviving records of these courts are held in county, city or borough record offices. West Sussex Record Office, for example, has a minute book for Arundel Borough Court 1753-1835. Searches can also be made in archives' catalogues through the web site of Access to Archives. For example, a search for records of attorneys held at Devon Record Office revealed a roll of the names of attorneys in the Tiverton County Court (ref: 1532-O/H/1), with their addresses, signatures and dates of admission.

D22. THE PRIVY COUNCIL AND THE HOUSE OF LORDS

The House of Lords is not only one of the Houses of Parliament but also a final court of appeal. Until the nineteenth century any member of the House (even those with no legal knowledge) could hear such an appeal. However, appeals are now heard by members of the Appellate Committee of the House of Lords consisting of the Lord Chancellor, the Lord Chief Justice and the Lords of Appeal in Ordinary (senior judges who have been made life peers). Records of appeals are in series KB 34 at TNA and at the House of Lords Record Office, and most cases are included in published law reports (*see* section E.5) noting the judges, the barristers appearing before them and some of the firms of solicitors involved.

The Privy Council was a legislative, judicial and administrative body, consisting of the king's most important ministers, which evolved from the King's Council in the fourteenth century. It received many petitions for justice to be done, many of which were referred to the Court of Chancery. The Judicial Committee of the Privy Council (now consisting of the Lords of Appeal in Ordinary and other senior judges) was established in 1833 as the final court of appeal from the ecclesiastical courts. It also heard appeals from the Court of Admiralty (until 1876) and from the Isle of Man, Channel Islands, Crown colonies and dominions. Records of appeals are at TNA (ref: PCAP) and most cases are included in published law reports.

E. MISCELLANEOUS SOURCES

E1. NEWSPAPERS AND JOURNALS

Newspapers and journals included death and obituary notices for many lawyers and are also useful for their reports of court cases and announcements of births, marriages and bankruptcies. National and local newspapers are held at the British Library Newspaper Library in Colindale, London and its catalogue can be accessed online. Local newspapers are also held in county and city archives. *The Times tercentary handlist of English and Welsh newspapers 1620-1920* (Times Publishing, 1920) lists all newspapers known to have been published during those years. The best guide to the location of copies of local newspapers (and to indexes of their contents) is J. Gibson, B. Langston and B.W. Smith, *Local newspapers 1750-1920 England and Wales, Channel Islands, Isle of Man* (2nd edn. FFHS, 2002).

There are some indexes to newspaper birth, marriage and death announcements. *Palmer's index to The Times*, which dates from 1790 to 1905, is in most reference libraries and includes the births, marriages and deaths announced in *The Times* from 1790 to 1837. *Gentleman's magazine* was published from 1731 and the *Annual register* from 1758. These also included obituaries and birth, marriage and death notices, many relating to lawyers. In *Gentleman's magazine* in 1751, for example, there is an entry reading 'Died 21 April Mr Thos. Blagden, attorney and deputy chamberlain of Bristol'. In June 1750, there was a report of the marriage of 'Mr Merefield, Attorney and Steward to Lord Ilchester to Miss Shirley of Bagber, Dorsetshire'. There are various indexes to *Gentleman's magazine*, described in *Herber's Ancestral trails*, including two published volumes that cover 1731-86 and 1786-1810. There is also a published index to the *Annual register* covering 1758-1819.

Information about lawyers is also available in local newspapers. They contain obituaries and announcements of marriages and deaths of prominent citizens in their area. *The Bristol Mirror*, for example, on 7 April 1860 included an entry reading 'Deaths. April 2 at 36 Prince Street, in his 67th year, Henry Day, Esq., solicitor, surviving his wife only five months'.

The London Gazette, first published under that name on 5 February 1665/1666, contains notices of bankruptcies and insolvent debtors. Copies of *The London Gazette* can be consulted at Guildhall Library, TNA, at other large reference libraries and are being made available online. There are annual indexes.

Newspapers included information (usually copied from *The London Gazette*) about bankrupts and the dissolution of partnerships. For example, *The Times* of 18 June 1892 reported that Christopher Anderson of Leeds, a barrister and George Henry Booth, a solicitor of Moorgate Street in the City of London and of Sydenham, had been adjudicated bankrupt. *The Newcastle Journal* of 13 April 1833 reported the dissolution of the partnership of F.K. Drawbridge & Co, attorneys of Maidstone.

Newspapers' reports of court cases sometimes included reference to the lawyers involved in a case. *The Times* of 18 June 1892 reported on the case of Taylor v. Garnett (concerning an alleged breach of contract) being heard in the Queen's Bench Division of the High Court. The barristers Mr Candy Q.C. and Mr Lewis Thomas appeared for one party and Mr L.E. Glyn for the other. The same paper reported that William Maunsell Collins was charged at Marlborough Street Police Court with forgery with intent to defraud. Arthur Newton was noted as the defendant's solicitor, with the prosecution conducted by George Lewis.

The Newcastle Journal of 13 April 1833 reported the names of solicitors acting in some bankruptcies. In the case of the bankrupt William Garbutt, a brick manufacturer of Kirby Moorside, Yorkshire, the solicitors dealing with the matter were noted as Mr Soulby in Leeds and Messrs Wiglesworth & Co of Gray's Inn Square in London. The same paper had a lengthy report on the civil trial at Lancaster Assizes, heard by Mr Baron Gurney, of a disputed probate case, Tatham v. Wright. The number of barristers involved probably indicates the amount of money at stake. The barristers for the plaintiff (Admiral Tatham) were Sir James Scarlett, Mr Williams (the Attorney General), Mr Starkie, Mr Armstrong and Mr Cresswell. His attorney was Mr Higgin. The defendant's counsel were Mr Pollock, Mr Sergeant Jones, Mr Wightman, Mr Tomlinson and Mr Martin. His attorney was Mr Sharp.

Lawyers sometimes engaged in activities that brought them to the attention of the local press. *The Derby Mercury* published, on 3 June 1813, this account of an incident in Derbyshire:

> *DUEL. On Saturday last a meeting took place in a field near Swanwick between Colonel Hall of the Belper Regiment of Local Militia and Joseph Wilson, Esq., of Alfreton (in consequence of a misunderstanding at a meeting of the Commissioners of the Alfreton Enclosure), the former attended by Major Hunter of the Same Regiment, and Mr Smith as Surgeon; the latter by Captain Wilkinson of the Derbyshire Militia. After an exchange of shots the seconds interfered, when the affair was amicably and honourably adjusted to the satisfaction of all parties.*

Colonel Hall was John Cressy Hall, a solicitor who practised at Alfreton. Joseph Wilson was a solicitor in the same town. There were only three solicitors practising at Alfreton in 1813 so the duellists may well have opposed one another in court as well as in a field.

A number of journals were published for lawyers (the magazine of Gray's Inn, *Graya*, was noted above) from the early nineteenth century. These included included law reports, notes of new statutes as well as information on lawyers, for example judicial appointments and lawyers' obituaries. These journals included the *Law Journal* (from 1822 until 1965), *The Law Times* (from 1843 until 1965) and the *Solicitor's Journal* (1857 to date). The obituaries of judges, barristers and solicitors in the *Solicitor's Journal* are indexed from 1859 to 1941.

Useful information about lawyers in the late nineteenth and early twentieth centuries can also be found in the journal *The weekly notes* (it was actually published every two weeks), from 1866 until 1952. Copies are held at Guildhall Library and in law libraries. Editions of *The weekly notes* were in two parts. The first part consisted of reports of cases in the House of Lords, the Court of Appeal and the High Court of Justice, to assist lawyers keep up to date with legal developments. These reports noted the names of the judges who heard cases, the barristers who appeared for the parties and the firms of solicitors acting.

The second part of this journal included useful information about the legal profession. In the 1908 volume for example, there were announcements of honours for lawyers, such as the grant of a knighthood to Francis Beaufort Palmer of 5 New Square, Lincon's Inn and legal appointments, for example;

26 March; Joseph John Heaton (Indian Civil Service) to be a judge of the High Court of Judicature, Bombay.
26 March; Arthur Stewart Duffield of 3 Lawrence Pountney Hill, Cannon Street, London and of Chelmsford, appointed Clerk to the County Justices of the Chelmsford Petty Sessional Division, Clerk to the Guardians and Superintendant Registrar, in succession to his father, William Ward Duffield, who has retired from those appointments.
29 June; the barrister John Castleman Swinburne-Hanham to be Recorder of the borough of Faversham.
10 November; Simon John Fraser Macleod, KC, to be a Commissioner in Lunacy.

The weekly notes also included lists of dissolved partnerships (or partnerships from which certain partners had retired) and some notices of partners joining firms:

Graham Keith and Charles Humphries (Keith & Humphries), solicitors, 43 Chancery Lane, WC, by mutual consent as from December 25, 1907.
Messrs Longbourne, Stevens & Powell of 7 Lincoln's Inn, WC, solicitors, have taken into partnership Mr Arthur Collin Moore.
John Cameron, Thomas Heath Thornely and Thomas Basil Duguid (Thornely & Cameron)

solicitors and notaries public, Liverpool, by effluxion of time on December 31, 1907, from which date the said T.H. Thornely will retire. J. Cameron and T.B. Duguid will carry on the business at the same address, under the style Cameron, Duguid & Co.

An index to the appointments and partnership changes appeared in the list of contents of *The weekly notes*. The journal also listed many cases that were due to be heard in the superior courts (noting the firms of solicitors acting in those cases). More usefully to genealogists, it listed the results of the Law Society's preliminary, intermediate, final and honours examinations, the bar examinations as well as lists of barristers called to the bar. These extensive lists of names are unfortunately not indexed. The results of the Law Society's honours examinations noted the solicitor with whom a candidate had served his articles. For example, George Finch Hotblack obtained second class honours in January 1908, having previously obtained a B.A. and LL.B at Cambridge University. He had served his articles with Sydney Cozens-Hardy of Norwich and Messrs Waterhouse & Co in London. The bar exam results noted the Inn of Court to which a student belonged. The lists of calls to the bar noted a barrister's Inn of Court and, in most cases, the university at which he had obtained a degree. For example, E.G. Eardley-Wilmot was called to the bar in Hilary term 1908 by Lincoln's Inn. He had obtained a certificate of honour from the Council of Legal Education (for the bar exams) and an M.A. at Oriel College, Oxford.

The Law Society's own journal, the *Gazette*, was first published in 1903 as the *Gazette and register*. At first, it concentrated on providing information about the society's activities but the very first issue included an obituary of William Dawes Freshfield, the senior partner of the firm Freshfields (then and now one of the best-known London law firms). Later issues included information on legal and professional developments, such as lists of those persons applying for admission as solicitors, persons joining or leaving partnerships and details of solicitors struck off the roll or otherwise disciplined. During both world wars, the *Gazette* included lists of solicitors who had been killed.

It is worth mentioning here the *Handbook of the Law Society* (The Law Society, 1938). This includes a list of the solicitors who achieved first, second or third class honours (and various prizes) in the Law Society's examinations from 1919 to 1937. For example, in October 1919, L. Marks, G.R.J. Duckworth, J.W.T. Holland, J.H. Whittingham, S.L. Peter and C.A. Fell each obtained first class honours and received the Law Society's Prize. F.E. Nash achieved first class honours and was awarded the Clifford's Inn Prize.

D2. BANKRUPT LAWYERS

A large number of lawyers have been made bankrupt, for example 55 solicitors in 1901. The Law Society was given the power to refuse a practising certificate to bankrupts in

1906 and was then able to remove bankrupts from the roll of solicitors (24 names were removed in 1928). Information may be obtained about bankrupt lawyers. Bankruptcy proceedings before 1710 are in the records of the Court of King's Bench. After that date they are in the records of the Court of Bankruptcy and the Court for Insolvent Debtors. Many of these records are at TNA although some records of insolvent debtors are also included in the records of quarter sessions in local archives.

Bankrupts and insolvent debtors are also listed in *The London Gazette*, noted above, to which there are annual indexes. Another useful index to bankrupts is G. Elwick, *The bankrupt directory, being a complete register of all the bankrupts with their residences, trades and dates when they appeared in The London Gazette from December 1820 to April 1843, alphabetically arranged affording easy reference for bankers, merchants, solicitors, commercial travellers etc* (Simpkin, Marshall & Co, 1843). Although the index covers nearly 23 years, there are only three references to solicitors; Cornelius Benson, of Edgbaston, Birmingham, solicitor and metal manufacturer, in 1840, and George Thompson and Edward Creswell, who were in partnership with one another and became bankrupt in 1843. There are 14 references to bankrupt attorneys. One of these, William Oliver Bright of Chancery Lane, who became bankrupt on 2 August 1839, is listed as an attorney and jeweller. He is noted in the *Law list 1839* as an attorney and as a commissioner for affidavits in Essex, Kent, Hertfordshire, Middlesex and Surrey. Five of the other attorneys are also described as scriveners. Daniel Sharp of Southampton, who became bankrupt in 1841, is noted as a merchant and attorney-at-law. Robert Webber and Thomas Bland of Bedford Row, also declared bankrupt in 1841, are noted as attorneys and bankers.

Elwick's list includes other bankrupt attorneys and solicitors. It does not describe them as such but there is no doubt that they were attorneys or solicitors because they appear in law lists. Charles More Ullithorne, an attorney in Red Lion Square, Holborn, who became bankrupt in 1835, is listed by Elwick simply as a broker. Algernon Wallington became bankrupt in 1829 and is listed as a coach proprietor, of Aldersgate Street, London. He was, in fact, an attorney who practised at the Castle & Falcon, a hotel and coffee-house in Aldersgate Street, from which a coaching business was also run. The occupation of most of these bankrupt lawyers is given as 'scrivener' or 'money scrivener' and some of them also had other occupations. Edward Charlton of Newcastle-upon-Tyne, for instance, who was declared bankrupt in 1840, is listed as a scrivener and brewer. George Cooke, an attorney in Northampton, bankrupted in 1841, is referred to as a miner and money scrivener. The occupations of Luke Evill, of Bath, an attorney who was made bankrupt in 1822, are noted as money scrivener and builder. Jonathan Foster, of Easingwold, Yorkshire is noted as a scrivener and a cattle jobber.

Devon Record Office holds a register of insolvent debtors for the period 1824-47 (reference QS 36/2). Devon Family History Society has published two volumes, *Register of insolvent debtors 1824-1834* and *Register of insolvent debtors 1835-1847* (Devon Family History Society, 2004) listing the debtors brought before the court to answer questions about their affairs. The first of these volumes includes 15 attorneys, two scriveners and an attorney's clerk. The latter volume also includes many lawyers. For example, John Attersol Gifford, an attorney of Plymouth, appeared before the court on three occasions in 1843.

E3. FAMILY HISTORIES, BIOGRAPHIES AND DIARIES

The best place to search for published family histories is the library catalogue of the SoG, which can be accessed online. There are also lists of published pedigrees in:

- G. W. Marshall, *The genealogist's guide* (Genealogical Publishing Co, reprint 1973),
- J. B. Whitmore, *A genealogical guide: an index to British pedigrees in continuation of Marshall's genealogist's guide* (Harleian Society, 1947-52, reprinted 1953),
- G.B. Barrow, *The genealogist's guide, an index to printed British pedigrees and family histories 1950-75* (Research Publishing Co, 1977), and
- T.R. Thomson, *A catalogue of British family histories* (Research Publishing Co, 1980).

As examples of the histories of families to which lawyers belonged, there is C.J. Palmer and S. Tucker: *Palgrave family memorials* (Miller & Leavins, 1878). W. Rye, *Norfolk families* (Goose & Son, 1913) contains information about many lawyers in Norfolk. R. Maugham, *Somerset and all the Maughams* (Longmans, 1966) is an account of a family that produced a number of lawyers, including an attorney, Robert Maugham (the first secretary of the Law Society) and Frederick Herbert Maugham (who was appointed Lord Chancellor in 1938).

Biographies have been written of a number of successful lawyers, such as Sir Edward Marshall Hall Q.C., who appeared in the sensational Russell divorce case of 1923. References to lawyers and legal families may also be found in biographies of individuals who were not legal practitioners. N. Vine Hall, *My name is Blacket* (Sydney: 1983), is the biography of an Australian architect but it contains a considerable amount of information about his relatives, the Freshfield family, members of which were solicitors to the Bank of England. Guidance on finding published biographies and autobiographies of lawyers is provided in *Holborn's sources*.

Diaries are a useful and fascinating source for family historians. Your lawyer ancestor may have written a diary (which may have been published) or another person's diary may refer to your ancestor. Information about an ancestor's lifestyle can also be gleaned from diaries of people who undertook the same work as him or who lived at about the same time. Many lawyers have written diaries and these can be located using the finding aids noted in *Herber's Ancestral trails*.

An example of a lawyer's diary that has been published is J. Bruce (ed), *The diary of John Manningham, of the Middle Temple, and of Bradbourne, Kent, barrister-at-law, 1602-1603* (Camden Society, 1868). Manningham was a student of Middle Temple from March 1597/8 until 1605 and noted a wide range of matters in his diary (the original is in the British Library). Another example is R. Hardstaff and P. Lyth, *Georgian Southwell as seen in the journals of the George Hodgkinsons, attorneys at law, 1770-81* (Newark & Sherwood District Council, undated). This volume includes extracts from daybooks of 1770 and 1771 of George Hodgkinson, an attorney in Southwell, Nottinghamshire and from the journal (dating from 1781) of his son, also named George, who was then training in his father's practice. They provide much information on the Hodgkinsons' practice as country attorneys (and many references to their clients) and useful background information as to their social life.

E4. DICTIONARIES OF THE PEERAGE AND LANDED GENTRY

The entries in *The complete peerage*, by G.E. Cokayne, originally published in eight volumes but subsequently revised and enlarged to 14 volumes by various editors (St Catherine Press and Sutton Publishing, 1910-98) include many references to lawyers. Volume V, for example, contains information about John Scott, a barrister and MP, who was created Baron Eldon when he was appointed Lord Chief Justice of the Common Pleas in 1799. Volume VIII has an entry for Thomas Parker, Lord Chief Justice of the Queen's Bench in the reign of Queen Anne, who was created Baron Parker by her successor, George I, in 1716. He became Lord Chancellor in 1718 and Earl of Macclesfield in 1721. He was the son of a Staffordshire attorney also named Thomas Parker.

The various editions of *Burke's peerage, baronetage and knightage* and *Burke's landed gentry* also refer to many lawyers. One example in *Burke's peerage* is in the entry for the family of Baynes. Walter Francis Baynes (1823-1914) practised for many years as a solicitor in Carey Street, Lincoln's Inn (his father was a baronet). One of his clients shown in law lists was the Brewers' Company, a City livery company.

The 1886 edition of *Burke's landed gentry* includes an entry for the Dayrell family of Lillingstone Dayrell in Buckinghamshire. In 1807, Richard Dayrell, then head of this family, married Frances Elizabeth Dax, daughter of John Dax, a London attorney who, at the time of the marriage, was deputy clerk of the Exchequer Office of Pleas.

Walford's county families, a number of editions of which was published between 1860 and 1920, is also useful as a source of information about lawyers. The entries relate to individuals, in similar format to the volumes of *Who's who*.

E5. PUBLISHED LAW REPORTS

From medieval times, lawyers have prepared reports of many cases heard by the courts, principally for the information of other lawyers and so that a ruling in one case can be used as a precedent for future cases. Only a minority of cases were reported and family historians should be aware that law reports concentrate on the relevant legal issues and so many reports contain little information of genealogical value.

Most law reports note the judge hearing the case and the barristers (and more recently the attorneys or solicitors) who acted in a particular case. For example, N. Simons and J. Stuart, *Reports of cases decided in the High Court of Chancery by Sir John Leach, Vice-Chancellor of England, vol 1, 1822-24* (J. & W.T. Clarke, 1824) includes the case of Packwood v. Mason in 1823. This was a dispute as to whom was entitled to certain money bequeathed by the will of Ann Brimyard. The barristers were noted as Mr Rose for the plaintiff, Mr Parker for the relatives of the legatee noted in the will and Mr Latham for the executors.

It is difficult to locate published reports of cases in which a particular lawyer acted because few volumes of law reports include indexes to the lawyers (an exception is the series of early law reports published by the Selden Society). Searches are however becoming easier due to the publication of law reports on CD-ROM or online (which allow name and word searches). You may become aware, from biographical dictionaries or similar sources, of a particular case in which your ancestor was involved as the lawyer for one of the parties or for the accused. You then need to ascertain whether there is a published report of that case.

From about 1272 until 1536, notes of cases were made by lawyers and these were collected together in what are known as the 'Year Books', many of which have been published, for example by the Selden Society and the Ames Foundation. From 1536 until 1865, cases were reported by private law reporters (usually barristers) and these reports were published in a large number of different series, listed in *Guide to law reports and statutes* (4th edn. Sweet & Maxwell, 1962). These reports gradually included more references to the barristers arguing each case, but rarely the names of the attorneys or solicitors involved. They have been reprinted, in book form and on CD-ROM, as the *English reports*. From 1865, cases were reported in one series of volumes: *The law reports* (also available on CD-ROM). These generally identified the barristers and the firms of solicitors instructed by the parties. Some other series of reports were published, such as the *Times law reports* and the *All England law reports*, and the number of series of reports (especially covering specialist aspects of the law) has increased in recent years. In addition, the online database LEXIS includes almost every case reported since 1945.

There are many other published accounts of court cases, particularly famous criminal trials. Some include reference to the lawyers who acted. The series of volumes entitled *Notable British trials* (William Hodge: various dates) consists of about 50 volumes, each providing a detailed account of a notorious or important criminal trial, for example the trials of Crippen, the Seddons and Neill Cream. These volumes record the lawyers who were involved in each trial and some of the volumes include portraits of the judges and the barristers.

E6. FREEDOM AND BURGESS RECORDS

It was not unusual for lawyers to become freemen of the cities in which they practised. The records of admissions to the freedom of the City of London (until recently held at the Corporation of London Record Office but being transferred to the London Metropolitan Archives) date mainly from 1681 although there are some earlier records. Before 1835 anyone who wished to become a freeman of the City was obliged to join one of the City livery companies. Detailed coverage of City freedom records is to be found in V.E. Aldous, *My ancestors were freemen of the City of London* (SoG, 1999).

The records of most of the livery companies of the City of London are deposited in Guildhall Library which has produced a guide to those records and published material: *City livery companies and related organisations* (Guildhall Library, 1989). Some companies (including the City of London Solicitors' Company, founded in 1908) have retained their records but information may be obtained in response to written enquiries.

The records of freemen of other cities and boroughs are generally held at city and county record offices. For example, the freemen in Bristol were known as burgesses. The burgess books of Bristol begin in 1559 and are deposited in the Bristol Record Office, which also holds an index to the books. Attorneys in these records are usually described as 'gentleman' rather than by their actual profession. This is an example of an entry in the burgess books for Henry George Windey, a Bristol attorney whose father was also an attorney in that city:

25 May 1796. Henry George Windey, Gentleman, is admd into the Liberties of this City for that he is the son of Nathan Windey Gentleman decd and hath taken the Oath of Obedce and pd 4s 6d.

Enquiries about lawyer ancestors who may have been freemen of the city in which they lived should be made to the relevant record office which may also hold records of individuals who were apprenticed to freemen. Many of these records have been published. One example of a published register of freemen is Peter Ripley and John Jurica, *A calendar of the registers of freemen of the City of Gloucester 1641-1838* (Bristol and Gloucestershire Archaeological Society, 1991). This includes references to 43 attorneys, three barristers, four doctors of law, one notary and one proctor (and some judges and court officers).

E7. POLL BOOKS

Poll books were lists of electors that were published between 1696 and 1868 and intended to prevent irregularities in parliamentary elections. Poll books indicate for whom an elector voted and frequently give the elector's occupation. The best guide to the location of copies of poll books is J. Gibson and C. Rogers, *Poll books c1696-1872: a directory to holdings in Great Britain* (3rd edn. FFHS, 1994). Many are held at the SoG.

The poll books for Westminster are particularly useful. For example, that for 1818 includes very large numbers of lawyers, particularly in the parishes of St Clement Danes and St Mary le Strand (the lists include barristers, attorneys and solicitors in Clement's Inn, Lyon's Inn, New Inn and parts of Lincoln's Inn).

Although a solicitor or attorney would often be described as such in a poll book, sometimes he would be listed as 'esquire' or 'gentleman'. The Bristol poll book for 1781 lists as a voter John Thornhill, of the parish of St James, gentleman. He also appears in the *Law list 1780*, the previous year, as an attorney in that city. The *Law list 1826* notes four attorneys or solicitors as practising in Maldon, Essex. However, the poll book for Maldon of 1826 lists only two of them – William Lawrence Hance and William Wright – as solicitors, one of them – William Lawrence – as 'esquire' and the fourth – Henry Stevens – not at all.

References to lawyers can also be found in the addenda to poll books, which consist of lists of out-voters, that is to say, individuals who did not live in the place where the election occurred but had a property qualification entitling them to vote there. The 1826 poll book for Maldon noted above lists the out-voters who lived in 'London and its environs'. They include four barristers, eight solicitors and one notary public. All the barristers appear in the *Law list 1826* but only five of the eight solicitors are listed there. The notary (Isaac Routledge) is not included in any law list although he appears in several London directories of the period.

E8. LOCAL HISTORIES

Information about lawyers may be found in local histories. For example, W.J. Pinks, *The history of Clerkenwell* (2nd edn. Charles Herbert, 1881, Francis Boutle reprint, 2001) refers to a London solicitor named Abraham Rhodes as one of the trustees appointed in 1788 for the building of St James's Church, Clerkenwell and also as one of the grantees of a lease in 1789 for the building of Pentonville Chapel. C. Brent, *Georgian Lewes 1714-1830: The heyday of a county town* (Colin Brent, 1993) contains a chapter on the learned professions in the town which includes information about several attorneys there.

Information about lawyers is included in some local studies, many of them published by county record or archaeological societies. For example, an article 'Norfolk lawyers' by B. Cozens-Hardy in volume 23 of *Norfolk archaeology* (Norfolk and Norwich Archaeological Society, 1965), lists about 180 lawyers from medieval times up to about 1800 who were born, educated or died in Norfolk and provides some biographical details about them. Many other local studies are listed in *Holborn's sources*.

The 'Victoria county histories', that contain histories of towns and parishes, also include information about lawyers. The series is still in production and a number of counties (but not all) have been covered. The *Victoria history of the county of Stafford* refers, in the section dealing with East Cuttlestone hundred, to John Birch, an attorney of Cannock, who was imprisoned by the Parliamentarians in 1643, his estates being sequestered. The volume contains some information about his family and property.

The volumes of the *Survey of London* also refer to lawyers. *The parish of St Mary, Lambeth: part two, southern area* (Athlone Press/University of London, 1956), for example, includes the following information about Beulah House, 274 South Lambeth Road:

This house was first leased in 1798 to Horatio Clagett. From 1825 until his death in 1849 it was occupied by John Poynder, clerk and solicitor to Bridewell Hospital. He was the author of several theological tracts and 'Literary Extracts from English and other Works, collected during Half a Century'. He was also a stock-holder in the East India Company, and as a result of his passionate campaigning the practice of suttee was in 1829 declared to be punishable as culpable homicide.

References to lawyers may also be found in esoteric works that deal with particular aspects of a city's life. For instance, W. Ison, *The Georgian buildings of Bath* (London: 1948) contains a reference to Richard Bowsher, an attorney in Bath, who in 1792 leased the land on which Norfolk Crescent was eventually built. F. Johnson, *A catalogue of the collection of engraved Norfolk & Norwich portraits in the possession of Russell J. Colman, Esq.* (H.W. Hicks, 1911) lists portraits of three Norwich solicitors who succeeded one another as town clerk in the late eighteenth and early nineteenth centuries; Elisha De Hague, senior, Elisha De Hague, junior, and William Simpson.

E9. FREEMASONS

Many members of the freemasons have been lawyers. Freemasons' records are described in P. Lewis, *My Ancestor was a freemason* (SoG, 1999). Many records are held in the library of the United Grand Lodge of England at Freemasons' Hall, Great Queen Street, London WC2 5AZ.

The registers of freemasons begin in 1750. There are gaps in these records until 1799 when the Unlawful Societies Act required registration of freemasons. Since that date the registers are more complete. They are arranged by lodge but there are alphabetical indexes to the members' names. The registers sometimes give an individual's age and address. They also give the member's trade or profession at the time of entry to the lodge. If the individual became a member of another lodge this fact is stated.

Biographical details of lodge members may also be available. Two weekly Masonic newspapers, containing obituaries, were published from 1870 until the early 1950s. Minute books of some lodges also survive. The library at Freemasons' Hall holds an index to the names found in the minute books of some lodges. Searches are made for enquirers by the library personnel for a fee.

There are many published lodge histories. One of these is J. Johnstone, *History of Lodge of Harmony No. 255 1785-1937 and Chapter of Iris No. 255 1807–1937* (London: 1938). This lists the lodge's members since 1785 with, in most cases, the member's occupation and in some cases the date of the member's initiation into the lodge. The list includes several lawyers. For instance, a barrister, Thomas Dunckerley joined on 11 July 1785. Anthony Steventon, who was initiated into the lodge on 29 August 1787, was an attorney. Alexander Ridgway, a London notary, was initiated on 2 October 1849.

Some county record offices have material relating to freemasons. East Sussex Record Office at Lewes, for instance, has lists of members of lodges in Lewes, Shoreham, Brighton, Arundel and Chichester in the early nineteenth century. Most of the members of these lodges, a number of whom were lawyers, lived in the towns where the meetings took place but this was not always the case. One of the members in 1844 of Royal Clarence Lodge, which met in Brighton, was Thomas Hart, a solicitor who practised at Reigate.

E10. JEWISH LAWYERS

The first Jewish solicitor in England was admitted in 1770 and many Jews have had successful legal careers. Jewish notaries had existed in this country from an earlier date.

Those researching Jewish ancestry should refer to A. Joseph, *My ancestors were Jewish, how can I find out more about them?* (SoG, 2002). The collections in the library of the SoG include the Hyamson papers and the papers of Sir Thomas Colyer-Fergusson, Bt., who assembled a considerable amount of information about Jewish families. References to Jewish barristers and solicitors are also to be found in the collections of the Jewish Historical Society of England, which are kept at the Jewish Museum, 129-131, Albert Street, London NW1 7NB.

Edgar Roy Samuel read a paper on the subject 'Anglo-Jewish notaries and scriveners' to the Jewish Historical Society on 20 December 1949. This was later published privately.

E11. RECORD OFFICES

County and city record offices hold material deposited by lawyers. The majority of these papers are property records and other client files but they may include business or personal papers of a lawyer or a law firm, including accounts, precedent books, deeds of partnership and other documents. A family historian interested in a particular ancestor who was a lawyer should make enquiries at the record office of the city or county in which he practised in case he or the firm for which he worked has deposited such material.

For example, Bristol Record Office holds a collection of documents relating to Sir Samuel Astry, a coroner and attorney of the Court of Queen's Bench (who was living in 1704), personal and professional papers of Jarrit Smith (an eighteenth-century Bristol attorney), account books of 1728-36 and other professional papers of the Bristol attorney Henry Woolnough and an account book of 1795-1846 of the solicitors Broad and Lewis.

Dorset Record Office has the diaries for 1757-77 of William Filliter, an attorney who practised at Wareham. Essex Record Office holds professional papers from 1795-1810 of a barrister, John Round of Colchester, accounts and papers from 1725-76 of Charles Gray, a Colchester attorney and bill books (containing full copies of clients' bills) from 1785-1840 of William Mason and his son, Colchester attorneys.

Papers of the firm of Fryer & James of Coleford have been deposited at Gloucestershire Record Office. These include office papers of H.H. Fryer, solicitor of Tewkesbury 1786-1821 (including accounts of 1814-24) and papers of Thomas James, solicitor of Coleford (including correspondence and bills of 1740-1850 and his papers as steward of the Manor of Longhope and recorder of St Briavels Court of Requests). There are also office papers of Thomas James of Coleford from 1815-22 and of H.H. & R.H. Fryer from 1811-98.

Due to the merger of legal practices over the years, papers of one lawyer or firm may have been deposited with another firm's papers. For example, papers of Wilmot & Co of Fairford (deposited at Gloucestershire Record Office) include papers of T. Stevens, solicitor of Cirencester (1743-1837), of T. Lediard, solicitor of Cirencester and Fairford (1839-44), of G.S. White, solicitor of Fairford (1845-76) and of Hitchman, Iles & Son, solicitors of Fairford (1869-1927).

Documents can also be found at ephemera fairs. For example, Illustration 20 is the first page of a bill of an attorney Mr Wyche to the mayor, aldermen and burgesses of the borough of Stamford in its case against Edward Holcott in 1733. The bill was endorsed on the rear by Mr Wyche to confirm that he had been paid. The bill's entries reveal that Holcott was alleged to owe a debt to the borough. Mr Wyche drew up an affidavit about the debt and then arranged for Holcott to be arrested and imprisoned in the Fleet Prison. He then attended on Mr Hardcastle of counsel in respect of drawing up a 'return' to Holcott's writ of 'habeas corpus', attended at the courts at Westminster with the defendant Holcott and also served the 'return' on Holcott in the Fleet (paying the turnkey – the gaolor) his fee. Mr Wyche also travelled to Lincoln on the same case.

The Mayor Aldermen and Capitall Burgesses of the Town or Borough of Stamford against Edward Holcott

Vacation after Easter Term 1733

	£	s	d
Drawing Affid:t of Debt Copy Oath and Stamp	-	5	-
Writt Letter Stamp and fee	-	12	-
Sherriffs Warr:t thereon	-	2	-
Paid Bailiff for Arrest	-	10	-

Trinity Term 1733

Habeas Corpus for removal of Def:t to the Fleet	1	2	8
Term fee of Attorney and Agent 5:s Let:s 1:6	-	6	6

Michmas Term 1733

Drawing long Return to Habeas Corpus	-	5	-
P. Mr Hardcastle to Settle it 5:s Attending him 3:4	-	8	4
Ingr:d Return 3:s Attend at Westm:r to Surrender Def:t 6:8	-	9	8
Paid Secondary 15:s Tipstaff 9:6	1	4	6
Drawing Decl:n & Copy fo:(9) 9:s Copy sent to Agent 3:s	-	12	-
Entring Declaration and paid	-	6	10
Ingrossing Copy & Duty to leave at the Fleet	-	3	2
Paid Turnkey 1:s Attending there 3:4	-	4	4
Drawing Affid:t of Service Copy Oath and Duty	-	5	6
Rule to appear & plead 3:s Searching & Calling for plea 3:8	-	9	4
Drawing Judgement Ingr: & Duty 7:4	-	7	4
Paid signing & Entring	-	10	8
Term fee 5:s Warr:t & Dogget 3:8 Let:s 4:9	-	13	5

Hillary Term 1733.

Retein:r Mr Roak 1:1: Gave his Clerk 2:6: Attend:g him 6:8	1	10	2
Retein:r Mr Abney 1:1: John Clerk 2:6: Attend him 6:8	1	10	2
Term fee of Attorney and Agent	-	5	-
Writt of Enquiry 12:7: Do Notice, & 2 Copys & serving 9:4	1	1	11
Searching rules 3:4 Letters 1:6	-	4	10

Vacation after Hillary Term 1733

Illustration 20: Bill of Mr Wyche to the borough of Stamford in its case against Edward Holcott.

F. LAWYERS IN WALES, IRELAND AND SCOTLAND

F1. LAWYERS IN WALES

Following the conquest of Wales by the English in 1282, justice in the principality (north and west Wales) was administered by royal governors through courts known as 'Great Sessions' in each county. South Wales was controlled by the marcher lords who had their own courts and the king was represented there by the Council in the Marches, which also had its own court. Only a few records of these sessions and march courts survive (at TNA).

Following the union of England and Wales in 1536, the march was abolished and a new system of courts was established. Justices of the peace were appointed to deal with minor criminal cases at quarter sessions. Records of the justices are in the National Library of Wales or local record offices. A Court of Great Sessions was also established in 1543 for the whole of Wales except Monmouthshire (which was part of an English assize circuit). This court had jurisdiction until its abolition in 1830 over all criminal cases and those civil cases that, in England, could be heard by the courts of Common Pleas and King's Bench.[16] The Court of Great Sessions operated by way of four circuits; the Chester circuit (which covered Denbighshire, Flintshire and Montgomeryshire), the North Wales circuit (Anglesey, Carnarvon and Merioneth), the Carmarthen circuit (Carmarthenshire, Cardiganshire and Pembrokeshire) and the Brecon circuit (Breconshire, Glamorgan and Radnorshire).

Records of the judges who sat in the Welsh courts can be found in the sources noted above for English judges and barristers. Detailed biographies of Welsh judges are also included in W.R. Williams, *The history of the Great Sessions in Wales 1542-1830 together with the lives of the Welsh judges and annotated lists of the chamberlains and chancellors, attorney generals and prothonotaries of the four circuits of Chester and Wales; the Lord Presidents of Wales and the attorney generals and solicitor generals of the Marches* (Edwin Davies, 1899).

Each circuit of the Court of Great Sessions had a prothonotary (or chief clerk), a secondary, a marshal, a clerk of the indictments and a king's attorney (who acted for the Crown in prosecutions). Williams' work includes lists of these officials (with some biographical details). Many of them were lawyers. For example, the prothonotary of the Carmarthen circuit from 1772 to 1783 was George Rous. He had entered Inner Temple in 1764 and was called to the bar in June 1768. He was also MP for Shaftesbury 1776-80, standing counsel to the East India Company from 1781 until his death and a bencher of Inner Temple. He died in 1802.

Barristers practising in the Welsh courts had to be members of one of the English Inns of Court, so information about them may be found in the records of the Inns to which they belonged. For example, this is an entry from the Middle Temple admission registers:

1810: May 5: Henry Allen, eldest son of Henry Allen of Cava Way, Brecon, esq.

Attorneys and solicitors practising in the Court of Great Sessions had to be formally admitted. The court's records are held in the National Library of Wales and described in great detail by G. Parry, *A guide to the records of Great Sessions in Wales* (National Library of Wales, 1995). Many of the records of admission of attorneys and solicitors are very similar to those of the Court of Common Pleas and the other Westminster courts. This is because the legislation noted above, the 1729 Act (requiring a lawyer's oath prior to admission), the 1749 Act (requiring affidavits of due execution of articles) and the 1785 Act (requiring a court to register practising certificates) applied in Wales. The most useful records for researching lawyer ancestors (and their 'Great Sessions' library references) as described by Parry are:

1) *Chester circuit (Denbighshire, Flintshire and Montgomeryshire)*
   i. Admission rolls, Flintshire, 1732 (ref: 1/4/1A).
   ii. Articles of clerkship and affidavits of due execution for Denbighshire and Montgomeryshire 1749-71 (with prothonotary's papers, ref: P 828-72, 1158-1202), 1774-1815 (ref: 1/1/2) and for 1817-30 (ref: 1/1/4).
   iii. Articles of clerkship and affidavits of due execution, mainly for Denbighshire 1772-92 (ref: 1/1/1).
   iv. Articles of clerkship and affidavits of due execution for Montgomeryshire 1784-91 (ref: 1/1/3).
   v. Register of affidavits, Denbighshire and Montgomeryshire: 1776-1801 (ref: 1/6/1).
   vi. Register of articles 1820-27 (ref: 1/6/2).
   vii. Attorneys' oath rolls, Denbighshire and Montgomeryshire: 1729-43 (ref 1/4/1), 1767-72 (ref: 1/4/2), 1773-76 (ref: 1/4/3), 1776-1801 (ref: 1/4/4) and 1802-30 (ref: 1/4/5).
   viii. Abjuration oath roll 1714 & 1725 (ref: 1/4/6).
   ix. Register of solicitors admitted to practise on the equity side 1804-30 (ref: 1/5/1). For admissions before 1804, *see* Great Sessions ref: 10/3-5 and 27/5.
   x. Register of attorneys' certificates 1792-1830 (ref: 1/6/3).
   xi. Attorneys' certificates 1800-19 (ref: 1/6/4).

2) *North Wales circuit (Anglesey, Carnarvonshire and Merioneth)*
    i.   Register of admissions of solicitors in the court of equity 1731-43 (ref: 1/7/1).
    ii. Articles of clerkship and affidavits of due execution 1816-1822 (ref: 1/2/1). There are only five of these on file.
    iii. Attorneys' oath roll 1729-59 and records of admission 1729-1827 (ref: 1/5/2).
    iv. Attorneys' oath roll 1750-1830 (ref: 1/5/3).
    v.   Register of attorneys' certificates 1785-97 (ref: 1/7/2). This includes a list of attorneys and solicitors who were in practice on 1 November 1785 and gives the dates of admission back to 1748.
    vi. Register of attorneys' certificates 1797-1822 (ref: 1/7/3). This includes a list of attorneys and solicitors practising on 11 December 1797, with their addresses and dates of admission. The word 'dead' is written opposite several names. One of the attorneys, Thomas Wyche, admitted on 1 August 1795, is described as 'of Carnarvon' but noted as residing in London. He is included in the *Law list 1800* as practising at 2 Orange Street, Red Lion Square, London and at Baker Street, Enfield, Middlesex. He was then London agent for two Carnarvon solicitors. Another attorney, John Chidlaw, admitted on 5 August 1796, is noted as 'of Bala, Merionethshire' but also as 'in America'.

3) *Carmarthen circuit (Carmarthenshire, Cardiganshire and Pembrokeshire)*
    i.   Articles of clerkship 1807-30 and affidavits of due execution 1749-1829 (ref: 1/1/3).
    ii. Register of affidavits 1772-98 (ref: 1/9/1).
    iii. Registers of articles 1794-1825 (ref: 1/9/2) and 1825-30 (ref: 1/9/3).
    iv. Attorneys' oath roll 1773-1830 (ref: 1/5/5).
    v.   Records of admissions of attorneys 1781-1828 (ref: 1/5/6).
    vi. Register of attorneys' certificates 1788-1829 (ref: 1/9/4).
    vii. Attorneys' certificates 1810-25 (ref: 1/9/5).

4) *Brecon circuit (Breconshire, Glamorgan and Radnorshire)*
    i.   Register of admissions of solicitors in the court of equity 1730-1801 (ref: 1/8/1).
    ii. Register of articles 1796-1830 (ref: 1/8/2).
    iii. Affidavits of execution of articles 1806-20 (ref: 1/2/2) and 1820-30 (ref: 1/2/3).
    iv. Certificates of articles 1818-30 (ref: 1/8/3).
    v.   Register of attorneys' certificates 1788-1830 (ref: 1/8/4).
    vi. Attorneys' oath roll 1791-1830 (ref: 1/5/4). Many oaths from 1779 to 1790 for Breconshire, Glamorgan and Radnorshire are on the court's plea rolls.

There are no convenient lists of attorneys practising in the Court of Great Sessions prior to 1729. However, their names do appear in documents in various classes of the Great

Sessions records. Parry suggests, in his work noted above, that the most informative of these records are the plea rolls (Great Sessions refs: 16-26 and 30), the precipe books (refs: 28/63-84, 134-62 and 192-205) and the rule and minute books (ref: 14).

From 1830, most civil actions involving Welsh litigants were heard by the English courts noted above and Welsh barristers, attorneys and solicitors will be found in the records of those courts. Welsh counties were also incorporated into the English assize system as the North and South Wales circuit (split into two circuits in 1876).

F2. LAWYERS IN IRELAND

In 1921, most of Ireland became the Irish Free State but six northern counties remained part of the United Kingdom, as Northern Ireland, with its own parliament and legal system. The best guides to genealogical research in Ireland are J. Grenham, *Tracing your Irish ancestors* (2nd edn. Gill & Macmillan, 1999) and I. Maxwell: *Tracing your ancestors in Northern Ireland* (Public Record Office of Northern Ireland & HMSO, 1997), although they contain few references to records of lawyers.

Family historians wishing to research ancestors who were lawyers in Ireland should read two detailed books on the subject: C. Kenny, *King's Inns and the Kingdom of Ireland: the Irish Inn of Court 1541-1800* (Irish Academic Press, 1992) and D. Hogan and W. N. Osborough, *Brehons, serjeants and attorneys: studies in the history of the Irish legal profession* (Irish Academic Press, 1990). These also list many other sources that can be consulted.

The courts and legal profession in Ireland have been very similar to those of England since medieval times when Ireland was brought under English sovereignty. Indeed, many judges and lawyers practising in Ireland before 1922 were trained in England. The Irish law courts were modelled on those of England, with courts of Common Pleas, Chancery, King's (or Queen's) Bench, Exchequer, Admiralty, Probate and Matrimonial Causes by the mid-nineteenth century. As in England, these courts were merged, by the Supreme Court of Judicature (Ireland) Act 1877 to form the High Court of Justice in Ireland that, with the new Court of Appeal in Ireland, formed the Supreme Court of Judicature. The Act also provided that all courts could apply rules of common law and equity. As in England, the High Court was divided into five divisions, Common Pleas, Chancery, King's (or Queen's) Bench, Exchequer and the Probate, Matrimonial and Admiralty (Common Pleas and Exchequer were subsequently merged into the Queen's Bench Division). There were also a number of county courts.

The principal courts in Northern Ireland since 1922 have been the magistrates' courts, the county courts and the Supreme Court. The magistrates' courts were presided over by lay magistrates until 1935 when they were replaced by resident magistrates (who are barristers or solicitors). The county courts have had both civil and criminal jurisdiction since 1935. The Supreme Court was created in 1920, consisting of the High Court (with Chancery and Queen's Bench divisions) and a Court of Appeal. A Court of Criminal Appeal was established in 1930. Final appeals can be made to the House of Lords.

The Irish legal profession consisted of barristers and solicitors. The Irish Bar was regulated by the benchers of King's Inns, Dublin. Attorneys and solicitors (all known as solicitors from 1877) also had to be members of King's Inns until the nineteenth century. The Incorporated Law Society of Ireland (formed in 1830 as the Law Society of Ireland) was granted a charter in 1852. The Incorporated Law Society of Ireland was required to maintain a roll of attorneys and solicitors and they no longer had to be members of King's Inns from 1 January 1867.

In 1921, qualified barristers and solicitors were permitted to practise in the new courts of both north and south. New entrants to the profession had to qualify in one of the jurisdictions.

The Incorporated Society of Northern Ireland was created in 1922 (from the Northern Ireland Law Society and other societies). It controls the education, admission and discipline of solicitors in the north. The Inn of Court of Northern Ireland was established in 1926.

The judges of each of the superior courts in Ireland and the men who have been appointed as the law officers in Ireland, the Attorney General for Ireland, the Solicitor General for Ireland and the King's Serjeant, are listed in Haydn, *The book of dignities* (noted above). Biographies of Irish judges are contained in F.E. Ball, *The judges in Ireland 1221-1921* (John Murray, 1926). Many were of English ancestry and trained at the Inns of Court in London.

Until 1885, those wishing to practice at the bar in Ireland had to join one of the four Inns of Court in London (for many barristers, this meant little more than an annoying expense and having to eat a few dinners at the Inn). The records of those Inns therefore contain many Irishmen, as in these examples from the Middle Temple admission registers:

1809: Oct 31: Charles Putland, second son of George Putland of the City of Dublin.

1871: Jan 23: Alexander Bruce Hawkins, B.A.: Queen's University, Ireland, student of King's Inns, Dublin, and of Kin-Edar, Strandtown, Belfast ([age] 22), fourth son of Henry Hawkins, of Belfast, Antrim, merchant.

The archives of King's Inns are described in an essay by C. Kenny in the work by Hogan and Osborough noted above. Many admission papers of King's Inns, covering barristers, attorneys and solicitors, have been published in E. Keane, P.B. Phair and T.U. Sadleir, *King's Inns admission papers 1607-1867* (Irish Manuscripts Commission, 1982). The later admission papers of King's Inns and various other sources have been used to prepare the brief biographies of King's Inn barristers for the period 1868-1968 (and lists of the barristers up to 2004) that are contained in K. Ferguson, *King's Inns barristers 1868-2004* (The Honourable Society of King's Inns, 2005). For example, James Head Staples is noted as born on 13 October 1849, the second son of Sir Nathaniel Alexander Staples, Baronet, of Lissan, County Tyrone and Elizabeth Lindsay Head. He was admitted as a student to Lincoln's Inn in 1873, to King's Inns in 1876, and was called to the Irish bar in 1880. Ferguson's work also contains a detailed history of the Irish bar since 1867, information on some other research sources and lists of the barristers who served or died in the First World War.

Law lists were published in similar form to those for England and Wales. These may be found in reference libraries in Ireland and a few copies can be seen in libraries in England. The SoG has a copy of *The Incorporated Law Society's calendar and directory for 1915* (The Incorporated Law Society of Ireland, 1915). This lists judges, the benchers of King's Inns, law officers, King's Counsel, barristers and solicitors. The entries for barristers note their address and the term and year of their admission to the bar. There are two lists for solicitors; one is alphabetical and one is arranged by place and then alphabetical. The entries in the alphabetical list note each solicitor's address and the term and year of his admission.

Directories of Dublin include references to many lawyers. Wilson's *Dublin directory* for 1814 for example lists the benchers of King's Inns: barristers, with the terms and years when they were called to the Irish bar (and noting those who had also been called to the English bar); and attorneys, with their addresses and a note of the courts in which they practised.

F3. LAWYERS IN SCOTLAND

The following is only a brief guide to the most important records of lawyers in Scotland. For more information, researchers should refer to works on Scottish genealogy and records, such as *Tracing your Scottish ancestors: the official guide* (3rd edn. The National Archives of Scotland, 2004), which is a useful guide to the records available at the National Archives of Scotland ('NAS') that are helpful to family historians.

Scotland's legal system is separate from that of England and Wales except that final appeals in civil cases are heard by the House of Lords. The three principal courts in

Scotland are the Court of Session, the High Court of Justiciary and the Sheriff Court. The main branches of the legal profession in Scotland are the judiciary, advocates (members of the Scottish Bar), solicitors (in certain Scottish cities and towns still known as procurators) and notaries.

The Court of Session has been the supreme civil court in Scotland since its establishment, as the College of Justice, in 1532. Its judges are known as the Lords of Session, of whom the most senior are the Lord President and the Lord Justice Clerk. The court is divided into two: the Outer House (responsible for first instance matters that are not within the jurisdiction of the Sheriff Courts) and the Inner House (which deals largely with appeals). Further appeals may be made to the House of Lords. Before 1532, important cases in Scotland were heard by the Lords of the King's Council.

The High Court of Justiciary has been the supreme Scottish criminal court since 1671. The senior judge is the Lord President, who sits with the title Lord Justice-General. The judges preside at trials in Edinburgh and on assize in circuit towns. Most appeals are heard by three judges. Prior to 1671, this court's functions were carried out by the court of the grand justiciar of Scotland (the predecessor of the Lord Justice-General). From the twelfth century, the justiciar dealt with both civil and criminal cases on four circuits (or 'ayers') twice a year. At first there were two justiciars and later five.

The Sheriff Court is the local court, sitting in each main town, hearing both civil and criminal matters. The sheriffs sit as judges and most of them are members of the bar but some are solicitors. Minor criminal matters are heard by magistrates' courts.

Many Scottish courts have disappeared. From medieval times, the barons who held land from the King were entitled to hold barony courts. In some cases, the barons were granted extra powers (a 'holding in regality') which excluded the rights of the king's officers, except in matters of treason. They were entitled to hold regality courts. The barony and regality courts were abolished in the eighteenth century.

Some towns had the right to hold burgh courts, dealing with both civil and criminal matters. After the reformation, secular commissary courts were also established to deal with divorce and probate matters that had previously been dealt with by the church courts.

There were many changes in the nineteenth century. The ancient Admiralty Court of Scotland was abolished in 1825, its jurisdiction being transferred to the other Scottish courts (and the English Admiralty Court). The ancient Court of Exchequer of Scotland was abolished in 1838. Probate work was transferred from the Commissary courts to the Sheriff courts in 1823.

The judges of the superior courts in Scotland and those men appointed as the Scottish law officers, the Lord Advocate and Solicitor-General for Scotland (who have similar functions to the Attorney-General and Solicitor-General in England) are listed in Haydn, *The book of dignities* (noted above).

The Scottish bar consists of advocates who are members of the Faculty of Advocates in Edinburgh (founded in the late sixteenth century). They have the exclusive right of audience before the Court of Session and High Court of Justiciary. Advocates must pass examinations and train for a period with a solicitor. Biographies of advocates are contained in F. Grant, *The Faculty of Advocates in Scotland 1532-1943, with genealogical notes* (Scottish Record Society, 1944). Some of these biographies were expanded in S.P. Walker, *The Faculty of Advocates 1800-1986, a biographical directory of members admitted from 1 January 1800 to 31 December 1986* (Faculty of Advocates, undated), from which a sample entry is:

> *ABEL, Duncan Mearns. Admitted 4 June 1890. Youngest son of Revd John Abel, Minister of the parish of Forgue, Aberdeenshire. Born 21 May 1864. Educated MA (Aberdeen); LL.B (Edinburgh). Married 18 August 1896 Constance Anne (b. 4 August 1870, d. 1 March 1929), dau of John Crombie, woollen manufacturer, Danestone, Aberdeen. Died 4 Jan 1898.*

Further information about the history of the faculty and its members is contained in J.M. Pinkerton, *The minute book of the Faculty of Advocates, vol 1 1661-1712* (The Stair Society, 1976). The minutes refer to the admission of members following their being examined by 'examinators', members being fined for non-attendance at faculty meetings and also to charitable payments being made to relatives of deceased members.

Scottish solicitors are members of the Law Society of Scotland that was established in 1949. Some of them are also members of ancient associations such as the 'Society of Writers to Her Majesty's Signet' (members were indicated by use of the letters W.S.) and the faculties of procurators in Glasgow and other Scottish cities and towns. Confusingly, the procurators in Aberdeen call themselves advocates. Solicitors have rights of audience in many matters before the Sheriff Court.

The Writers to the Signet had their origins in clerks of the king's secretary who prepared documents, mainly private correspondence, to which the king's signet (a seal) was to be applied. By the late nineteenth century, writers practised in the Court of Session, undertook conveyancing and acted as legal advisors or as factors on landed estates. *A history of the Society of Writers to Her Majesty's Signet* (The Society, 1890) includes a list of members (with some biographical details) from 1594 to 1890, lists of office-holders and extracts from the minutes of the commissioners of the society. These minutes record admissions, apprenticeships and disciplinary and financial matters. On 4 January 1671, the minutes record the suspension of John Hamiltoun 'for having been long absent from Edinburgh and not attending his chamber'. The same minutes also recorded the admission of William Innes, who had been apprenticed to three writers in succession:

> *4th January. Admission of Mr William Innes, son of William Innes of Tibbertie, late prentice and servant to the deceased Robert Alexander, and thereafter servant to the deceased William Chalmer, and Mr James Cheyne.*

The minutes of 6 February 1671 recorded that William Innes' new master, James Cheyne, was then under suspension in respect of a complaint made to the commissioners. The biographies of members included in the above work were substantially improved (and further entries added so that it covered 1583 to 1982) for a new list contained in *Register of the Society of Writers to Her Majesty's Signet* (The Society, 1983). A typical entry is:

> *Abercromby, Alexander [admitted] 10 July 1770. Apprentice to John Syme. Son of Alexander Abercromby, merchant in Norway. Married 14 April 1776, Mary (died 10 July 1798), daughter of Charles Ramsay, Surgeon in Edinburgh. Died 9 April 1804.*

A roll of honour for 1914-19 for members of the Society of Writers (and their apprentices) has been published and a copy is held at the SoG.

From 1563, notaries had to be examined and admitted by the Lords of Session (and had their signs registered). NAS also holds many records of notaries (NAS refs: NP1-NP6), including the register of admissions from 1563 to 1873 (with some indexes), rolls of notaries admitted from 1680 to 1903 and warrants of admission since 1579. Some early entries in the register state the notary's age and place of birth. Some entries after 1738 record the name of the notary's father. The notaries kept protocol books in which transfers of property were recorded. Many of these notarial protocol books have been published.

Law lists have been published in Scotland, originally under the title *Index juridicus*, since 1848. They are arranged in similar form to the law lists for England and Wales, and contain details of lawyers and the courts. For example, *The Scottish law list and legal directory for 1957* (Stevens & Sons, 1957) is divided into sections for lawyers in each of Edinburgh, Glasgow, Aberdeen and 'country' (as well as lists of local court officers, accountants, landowners' agents and English and foreign lawyers). The Edinburgh section has lists of the judges and officials of each court, of members of the

Faculty of Advocates, of solicitors and of Writers to the Signet. The Glasgow, Aberdeen and country sections have lists of solicitors and also members of the local societies of solicitors and procurators, such the Royal Faculty of Procurators in Glasgow, the Society of Advocates in Aberdeen, and the Society of Procurators and Solicitors of Forfar. Entries for advocates give an address and year of admission. Entries for solicitors note their firm, address and year of admission.

Scottish directories, to be found in NAS or at the SoG, include lists of lawyers. References to lawyers may also be found in the records of burgesses of Scottish cities and in the records of universities, particularly those of Glasgow, Aberdeen and St Andrews and schools, such as the Edinburgh Academy (for all of which there are published registers).

Many court records are held at NAS. There are 'Books of Sederunt' that include the appointments of judges and court officials and the admission of advocates. The records of the sheriff courts also include many lists of procurators who were authorised to appear in the court. Records of the commissary courts are also at NAS. Information about lawyers can also be found in registers of deeds, registers of sasines and services of heirs, all described in *Tracing your Scottish ancestors* (noted above).

Scottish lawyers before the Reformation
Professional lawyers appeared in Scotland in the late fifteenth century. By 1532, there were advocates, procurators, notaries and 'forespeakers' and a lawyer might act as one or more of these. The work undertaken by procurators was similar to that undertaken by attorneys in England. Until the sixteenth century, a party to an action had to appear personally in court and appoint a procurator to act for him. Records of these appointments survive in some court books held at NAS. J. Finlay, *Men of law in pre-reformation Scotland* (Tuckwell, 2000) is a detailed study of Scottish lawyers and their work in the sixteenth century, with much biographical information.

G. ENGLISH LAWYERS OVERSEAS

The expansion of the British Empire in the eighteenth and nineteenth centuries provided opportunities for young lawyers qualifying in Britain to establish themselves in the colonies. Improved trading conditions also encouraged them to open offices in European countries such as France and Germany. It is not possible in this book to consider all the sources available for these British lawyers. However, the law lists include some information about British lawyers abroad and this is reviewed below. Some records of lawyers in India are also considered because so many English lawyers practised there.

G1. THE LAW LISTS

The first reference in a law list to a lawyer practising abroad is in the *Law list 1820*. At the end of that volume's list of English and Welsh attorneys is an entry for J. E. Manning, solicitor to the British Embassy and Consulate, No. 337 rue St Honoré, Paris. His agent in London was noted as Clarke, Richards & Medcalf, a firm of solicitors with offices at 109 Chancery Lane. Manning's name continued to appear in the law lists until 1825 when it was replaced by an entry for Mills & Ganning, 12 rue du Faubourg St Honoré, Paris. Their agent, William Adair Carter, had offices at 11 Furnival's Inn. The firm Mills & Ganning was also included in the list of London attorneys in this law list (Mills being described as solicitor to the British Embassy in Paris), although both Thomas Mills and Henry Daniel Ganning were noted as practising at the Paris address only. The entry for Mills & Ganning was repeated in the *Law list 1826* but in the *Law list 1827* Thomas Mills appeared on his own, at 12 rue du Faubourg St Honoré, as registrar to the British Embassy and agent to Law Life Assurance. He had a new London agent, named Joseph Bebb, attorney of 15 Bloomsbury Square.

The *Law list 1827* had an entry for another English solicitor in France: William John Carpenter of Belle Vue, St Martin, Boulogne-Suer-Mer [sic]. The *Law list 1825* recorded that Carpenter had been an attorney of the Insolvent Debtors Court, practising at 12 Furnival's Inn and 17 John Street, Bedford Row.

The *Law list 1828* notes two English solicitors in Paris: Thomas Mills and David Elwin Colombine, as well as William Carpenter at Boulogne. David Elwin Colombine had practised briefly in the City of London before setting up as a solicitor in Paris. He first appears in the *Law list 1827* when he had an office at 112 Upper Thames Street. This is confirmed in his entry in the *Law list 1828*, noting that he was 'late of 112 Upper Thames Street'.

The *Law list 1830* contains a heading 'France' at the end of the list of country attorneys (but no heading or entries for any other countries). The only solicitor given under this heading is Thomas Mills, by then at 339 rue St Honoré, Paris and described as solicitor to the British Embassy, registrar to the chaplaincy and agent to Law Life Assurance. His London agents were Joseph Bebb and Henry Daniel Ganning (his former partner in Paris). Mr Colombine had returned to London and taken an office in the West End – at Carlton Chambers, 8 Regent Street. The *Law list 1831* lists three English solicitors in France, all in Paris, Thomas Mills, James Haliday and Robert Stokes Sloper. Both Mills and Sloper, who had offices at different addresses, described themselves as 'solicitor to the British Embassy'.

The *Law list 1832* is the first to mention an English barrister practising overseas. He was C.H. Okey (the law lists in this period frequently omitted Christian names of barristers). He was listed under 'France' and also in the list of barristers, where he was described as 'C.H. Okey, esq., 1 Inner Temple Lane, Special Pleader, Home Circuit and adjoining British Embassy, 35 rue du Faubourg St Honoré, Paris'. Thomas Mills and James Haliday were both noted in this law list (as in 1831) as solicitors in Paris but Robert Sloper was not listed.

The *Law list 1834* notes two solicitors in France: Thomas Mills in Paris and George Morton at Caen; and one barrister: C. H. Okey, counsel to the British Embassy. Joseph Bebb, Mills's London agent, was described in this law list as 'agent for Paris'.[17] The *Law list 1835* also notes the name of William John Carpenter, who had not appeared in a law list since 1827 when he was practising at Boulogne. By 1835 he had an office in Paris and described himself as 'agent for marriages at British Embassy and general agent for law business between Great Britain and France and the Continent'. The *Law list 1836* does not contain his name.

The *Law list 1837* noted Henry Daniel Ganning (whose name had been absent from law lists since 1831, when he was in London) as a solicitor at Boulogne-sur-Mer and as 'agent for Paris and Boulogne'. Thomas Mills of Paris had died and had been succeeded in his practice by Thomas Lawson. The *Law list 1837* also noted a solicitor in Paris named Edgar Smith at '41 Rue Neuve des Mathurins, pre le Madeline'.

The *Law list 1838* is the first to include English solicitors practising overseas in places other than France. In this volume, incongruously still under the heading 'France', are listed, with Ganning at Boulogne and Lawson, Smith and Thomas Outhwaite in Paris, one solicitor (John Cheslyn) in Guernsey and one (John Harrison) in Van Diemen's Land (Tasmania). Harrison is described as 'late of the Temple Chambers, London'. English lawyers who practised overseas continued to appear in law lists under the heading

'France' until 1848. They were practising not only in France, Guernsey and Van Diemen's Land but also in other countries. The *Law list 1843* includes a solicitor practising in Jersey, one who had offices at 'Bathwest' (Bathurst), Gambia in Africa and also Richard Meade, who was a conveyancer at 'Milbourne, Port Phillip, Australia Foelix' (that is to say, Melbourne in Victoria). Subsequent law lists include, under the heading 'France', English lawyers in Hong Kong, Cuba and Belgium.

The *Law list 1849* has a separate heading for each country in which an English lawyer practised: France, Gambia, Australia, Germany, Malta, Italy, Turkey, Burma, China, New Zealand, South Africa, Canada and the United States. The number of solicitors who took out English practising certificates and had offices overseas then increased substantially. The *Law list 1861* included seven such solicitors practising in Paris, including Somerset Maugham's father Robert Ormond Maugham. The *Law list 1891* showed 27 English solicitors (most of them based in London) with offices in Paris.

The inclusion in law lists of the names of English lawyers practising abroad did not mean that all of them were listed. Family historians should therefore consult other sources to obtain information about ancestors who were English lawyers overseas. Some of these sources are described in *Herber's Ancestral trails*.

G2. LAWYERS IN INDIA

British influence in India dates back to the foundation of the East India Company ('EIC') in 1599 by a group of London merchants trading with the East Indies. The EIC was granted a charter in 1600. A new charter granted by Cromwell in 1657 secured its trading monopoly. Subsequent charters ensured sovereign rights for the EIC, the expansion of which was assisted by the decline of the Mogul empire in India. By 1680, the EIC controlled much of India through three administrative areas, known as 'Presidencies', of Bengal, Bombay and Madras. The EIC prospered during the eighteenth century, becoming rich and powerful. However, because of criticism of its activities, the government began to take some control over the EIC and Indian affairs. In 1813 the EIC's monopoly in India was terminated and in 1858 the EIC ceased to exist and its assets were transferred to the Crown. India was then governed by the British government and the Crown's representative, the Viceroy.

A Supreme Court was established in Bengal in 1773, in Madras in 1779 and in Bombay in 1823 (each reconstituted as a High Court of Judicature in 1861), the judges being appointed by the Crown. Law lists of the first half of the nineteenth century did not include British lawyers working in India but later law lists did so. For example, the *Law list 1910* included court officials, barristers who had been called to the English bar and also a few English solicitors in each of the three presidencies. Most of the sources noted in previous sections of this book should also be consulted in respect of a lawyer ancestor who practised in India. Judges who sat in the Supreme Courts (later the High Courts) of Bengal, Madras and Bombay up to the 1880s are listed in Haydn, *The book of dignities* (noted above).

Extensive records of British rule in India between the seventeenth century and 1949 are in the India Office collections at the British Library. I.A. Baxter, *Baxter's guide: biographical sources in the India Office records* (3rd edn. Families in British India Society and the British Library, 2004) is a helpful guide to these records, referring to many that contain information about lawyers. More detailed information about these records is contained in M. Moir, *A general guide to the India Office records* (The British Library, 1988).

The Indian ecclesiastical returns, covering baptisms, marriages and burials, are in three main series for the presidencies of Bengal 1713-1947 (ref: N/1), Madras 1698-1947 (ref: N/2) and Bombay 1709-1947 (ref: N/3). There are also indexes to these records which can be used in conjunction with the births, marriages and deaths listed in Indian directories noted below. An example of this cross-referencing is the entry for the burial of a Madras attorney named Gilbert Ricketts in 1817. After finding him in the index it is easy to consult the directory for that year, which recorded the death on 4 December 1817 of 'Gilbert Ricketts, Esq., Prothonotary and Register of the Supreme Court of Judicature, at this Presidency'. References to lawyers in India may also be found in the records of wills, administrations, inventories and estates for 1618-1725 (ref: G/40/23), 1704-83 (ref: P) and 1780-1948 (ref: L/AG/34/29).

The easiest method of finding a lawyer ancestor in British India is to search directories, many of which can be seen in the British Library and the SoG. *The India calendar 1789* lists judges, advocates and attorneys in Calcutta and *The Bengal calendar* for 1790 and 1792 contains similar lists for Bengal. There are lists of judges, law officers, advocates, attorneys, solicitors and proctors for each of the three presidencies in *The East India register* from 1800 to 1860, *The Indian army and civil service list* from 1861 to 1876 and *The India list* from 1877 to 1895. *The India list* and its successors from 1896 list only judges and law officers but *Thacker's Indian directory* from 1885 contains full lists of lawyers for each of Bengal, Bombay and Madras. Illustration 21 is a page, from the Bombay section of *Thacker's Indian directory 1895*, listing officers of the High Court and advocates, noting the Inns of Court of which they were members and the dates of their call to the (English) bar and admission to the Bombay High Court.

OFFICERS OF THE HIGH COURT & LAW OFFICERS OF GOVERNMENT

Advocate-General, Hon. Basil Lang, 2,200.
Remembrancer of Legal Affairs, H. Batty, M.A., bar.-at-law, J.P., I.C.S., 2,100,
.*Solicitor to Government and Public Prosecutor*, F. A. Little, 2,500.
·*Government Pleader*, R. S. V. Jagannath Kirtikar, 300.
Administrator-General, L. W. G. Rivett-Carnac, bar.-at-law.
Reporter H. C. Kirkpatrick, bar.-at-law, 1,000.
Accountant-General, O. T. Barrow, I.C.S.
Master and Regtr. in Equity and Commsr. for taking accts. and local investigations and taxing offr., G. H. Farran, M.A., 1,700.
Prothonotary, Testamentary and Admiralty Regtr., J. W. Orr, M.A., Dub., bar.-at-law, 2,500.
Asst. Commr. for taking accts. and asst. taxing offr., A. K. Oliver, 700.
First Depy. Regtr. and Commsr. for taking affidavits and clk. to the Chief Justice, L. A. Watkins, 1,005.
Second Depy. Regtr. and Commsr. for taking affidavits, Kaikhasro Framji Modi, 300.
Head asst. to Prothonotary and Commsr. for taking affidavits, Limji Navroji Banaji, bar.-at-law, 800.
Clk. of the Crown, M. H. Starling, B.A., LL.B., bar.-at-law, on depn.; E. B. Raikes, actg., 333.
Official Assignee, C. A. Turner, B.A., L.S.C., bar.-at-law.
.*Sheriff*, Cowasjee Hormusjee, G.G.M.C.
Depy. Sheriff, H. J. Miles. ·
Commsr. for taking affidavits and Judge's Clerk, F. H. de Brito, 400. .

ADVOCATES ACCORDING TO THEIR PRECEDENCE AT THE BAR.

Date of call to the Bar.		Inn.	Names.	Admission to High Court.		Place of Business.
Michaelmas	1852	... I.	Charles J. Mayhew	··	...	Europe.
Easter Term	1863	... I.	M. H. Starling; B.A., LL.B.	.. Mar. 1869	...	Actg. Judge, H. C.
Trinity Term	1864	...	F. H. Lascelles	··	...	Europe.
Trinity Term	1865	...	M. R. M. A. Branson·	... Nov. 1865	...	
Trinity Term	1865	... I.	J. Macpherson, B.A.	··	...	Europe.
Easter Term	1867	... M.	Budrudin Tyabji ·	... Nov. 1867	...	Europe.
Easter Term	1868	... L.	Pheroxshah M. Mehta, M.A.	... 1869	...	
Trinity Term	1869	... M.	Basil Lang	... Nov. 1870	...	Advte.-Genl.
Trinity Term	1869	... L.	H. O. Kirkpatrick, M.A.	... Feb. 1875	...	Reptr., H. Ct.
Easter Term	1870	... I.	J. D. Inverarity, B.A., LL.B.	... Dec. 1870	...	High Court.
Trinity Term	1870	...	Homasji A. Wadia	... Dec. 1870	...	Rajkot.
Hilary Term	1871	... I.	James Jardine, M.A.	... Dec. 1875	...	Europe.
Hilary Term	1871	...	J. Jevanjee Guzdar, M.A;	··	...	Govt. Profr. of Law.
Easter Term	1871	... L.	M. P. Lynch	... Oct. 1873	...	Europe.
Trinity Term	1872	...	E. Mansfield	...	...	Europe.
Michaelmas	1872	... I.	C. W. L. Jackson, B.A.	... Dec. 1873	...	Clk. & Sealer, Insol. Court.
———	1872	...	Jamsetjee Cursetjee Cama	... April 1872	...	5, Bell Lane.
Michaelmas	1872	... M.	Ardesheer B. Kapadia	... Dec. 1872	...	———
Michaelmas	1872	...	Framji Rustamji Vicaji, B.A., LL.B.	... Mar. 1873	...	Actg. Perry Prcfr.
.Michaelmas	1873	...	Alweyne Turner	...	...	N. W. Provinces.
Michaelmas	1874	... I.	R. E. Melsheimer	... Nov. 1891	...	High Court.
Hilary Term	1875	... I.	S. Newcome Fox, B.A.	... May 1875	...	Europe.
·Hilary Term		...· M.	Louis P. Russell, B. A.	... Dec. 1875	...	Europe.
Easter Term	1875	... I.	J. C. Anderson	... Aug. 1878	...	———
Easter Term	1875	... L.	Abbas Shamsoodeen Tayabjee	... June 1875	...	Baroda.
Trinity Term	1875	...	Avetick Aratoon Shircore	... 1875	...	Absent.
———		...	Sadashiv Vishvanath Dhurandhar, B.A., LL.B., Bom.	... Jan. 1876	...	Chief Justice, Indore.
Trinity Term	1876	... M.	Navroji Pestanji Cama	... Aug. 1876	...	———
Hilary Term	1877	... M.	Ganpat Sarvottam Mankar	... Sept. 1877	...	Eldon road.
Trinity Term	1877	... I.	Louis W. G. Rivett-Carnac	... Feb. 1878	..;	Admstr.-Genl. of Bom. & Offl. Trustee, High Court.
Trinity Term	1877	... M.	A. C. Rudra	... Oct. 1880	...	Hyderabad.
Hilary Term	1878	...	Henry H. Massy Bindon	... ———	..	Absent.
Easter Term	1878	...	Nanaji Rastamji Motabhoy	... ———	...	Europe.
Trinity Term	1878	... L.	Sheikh Amiruddin	... Nov. 1878	...	Allahabad.
Michaelmas	1878	...	J.W.C. Fraser, M.A.	...	...	Nagpur.
Hilary Term	1880	...	Allen Cottrel Travis, B.A.	... Feb. 1891	...	Absent.
Hilary Term	1880	...	W. Scott Howell	...	...	Allahabad.
Trinity Term	1880	... M.	Dinsha D. Davar	... July 1880	...	Eldon road.
Easter Term	1882	... M.	Nasarvanji Framji Bhandara	... July 1882	...	Hyderabad.
Trinity Term	1882	...	Anandrao Sheshadri	... ———	...	Absent.
.Trinity Term	1882	... I.	John Sanders Slater, B.A.	... Feb. 1887	...	Europe.
Michaelmas	1882	...	Nunda Lall Ghose	... ———	...	Calcutta.
Hilary Term	1883	... M.	Muncherji Dadabhai Dadysett	... April 1883	...	Surat.
Hilary Term	1884	... I.	Basil Scott, B.A.	... Nov. 1885	...	High Court.
Easter Term	1884	...	Shapurji Kavasji Sanjana	... July 1884	...	9, Eldon road.
Trinity Term	1884	... M,	L. J. Robertson	... Dec. 1885	...	Actg. Profr. of Law.
17th November	1884	... I.	Charles W. Chitty, B.A., Cantab	... Feb. 1886	...	Chief Judge, S C. Ot.
Trinity Term	1884	...	Francis Gibbons	... June 1885	...	Absent.
Michaelmas	1884	...; I.	P. S. Krishnavarama, B.A.	... Jan. 1885	...	Ajmere.

Illustration 21: Officers and advocates of the High Court in Bombay from Thacker's Indian directory 1895.

There are also many directories dealing with a particular EIC presidency up to 1858. *The original Calcutta annual directory and calendar 1813* lists eight advocates, 12 attorneys and six notaries (with dates of admission) practising in the Supreme Court of Bengal. Some entries are more informative. One particularly helpful entry relates to Thomas Stanley. It shows that he was an attorney of the courts of King's Bench and Common Pleas and a solicitor of the Court of Chancery in England, as well as an attorney of the Supreme Court of Bengal. The dates of his admission to each of these courts are given. This directory also notes the official positions held by lawyers. James Taylor, for example, described as 'Attorney to the Honourable Company' (the EIC) is also listed as clerk to Sir William Burroughs, Bt., a judge of the Supreme Court. Richard Cracraft is listed as 'Attorney for Paupers'. In addition, the years when lawyers held official appointments are given. William Hickey, the diarist, is shown to have been deputy sheriff in 1784, 1785, 1801, 1803 and 1805 to 1807. This directory also contains a list of births, marriages and deaths, for example referring to the death on 11 June 1812 at sea of Charles Whalley, Esq., attorney at law.

The Calcutta kalendar and Post Office directory 1821 includes a list of lawyers and officials in the Consistory Court for the Archdeaconry of Calcutta. It lists four chief judges and nine puisne judges with the dates of their appointment. It also lists four proctors who practised in that court. In a section headed 'Detailed List of the Hon'ble Company's Civil Servants on the Bengal Establishment: Senior Merchants' are listed many judges who were in the service of the EIC, information being given about each of them. The entry for William Augustus Brooke, for instance, gives the date of his 'original rank' as 31 May 1769 and describes him as 'Senior Judge of the Provincial Courts of Appeal and Circuit for the Division of Benares, January 30 1804, and Agent to the Governor General at ditto'.

This directory also lists the three judges of the Supreme Court, the eight barristers and the 36 attorneys who practised in it, the three law officers of the EIC and the officers of the court. The dates of admission of 20 of the attorneys are given. Philip Stone, an attorney admitted in 1819, is said to have 'gone to sea for the benefit of his health'. There is also a list of 18 notaries, all of whom were admitted in 1820 and four lawyers (one barrister and three attorneys) who were 'absent with the leave of the Court'. This directory also gives the names of the three judges of the Admiralty Court of Bengal and the officers of that court. After these names there is a note reading 'All the Barristers and Attornies of the Supreme Court are Advocates and Proctors in the Court of Vice Admiralty'.

The third edition of *The new annual Bengal directory and general register* (of 1824) includes a section that lists all the judges, barristers, attorneys and notaries public practising there in that year with their dates of admission. Five of the attorneys are said to be 'in Europe' (probably on leave or business). The lawyers also appear in the section headed 'The British & Foreign Inhabitants of Calcutta and the Upper Provinces of Bengal and its Dependancies with their Residences, Occupation etc. as far as ascertainable'. There is a note with these lists reading:

> *To enable the sheriff of Calcutta, the Coroner and others concerned to distinguish who are liable to serve on Juries, the following distinctive marks have been attached to the names of persons who are not liable to be summoned on that duty, viz * born in India, + Foreigners.*

It is obviously important for any family historian having an ancestor in India to know whether he was or was not born there.

Most of these directories also have a section listing births, marriages and deaths. Family historians with forebears in Bengal should also consult *The Bengal obituary or a record to perpetuate the memory of departed worth, being a compilation of tablets and monumental inscriptions from various parts of the Bengal and Agra presidencies, to which is added biographical sketches and memoirs of such as have pre-eminently distinguished themselves in the history of British India since the formation of the European settlement to the present time* (Holmes & Co, 1848). It lists monumental inscriptions in burial grounds throughout Bengal, including the principal Calcutta cemeteries – the South Park Street Burial Ground (opened in 1767), the North Park Street Burial Ground, the Scotch and Dissenters' Burial Ground and the New Burial Ground. Many of the tombstones relate to lawyers and give a considerable amount of information. For example, Henry Webster died on 13 June 1825, aged 33 years, two months and two days. He was described as 'an attorney of the Court of King's Bench at Westminster and of the Supreme Court of Judicature at Fort William in Bengal'.

Directories of the presidency of Bombay also provide information about lawyers. *The Bombay calendar and register* for 1816 gives the name of the recorder, Sir Alexander Anstruther, of the Recorder's Court in Bombay, that court's officials and the names of the five barristers, six solicitors (or attorneys) and seven notaries who practised in that court. Also listed in this directory are the lawyers (five advocates and five proctors) who practised in the Vice-Admiralty Court of Bombay. The judge of this court is also noted as Sir Alexander Anstruther (who was also the recorder).

The Bombay calendar and general directory 1849 lists lawyers under the heading 'European and East Indian Inhabitants', for example Acton Smee Ayrton, solicitor of the Supreme Court, whose address is given as Church Lane, Fort. This directory, like many others, contains an interesting section of births, marriages and deaths (headed 'Domestic Occurrences') and frequently gives much detail. For example, there is an announcement of a marriage on 29 April 1848 at Bombay of Dugald Bremner of the Oriental Bank to Maria Louisa, the youngest daughter of the late George Ramsey Rodd, of Hampstead, Middlesex, surgeon. She is also noted as the step-daughter of William Brooks, 'Master in Equity of the Supreme Court'.

The Bombay almanac and year book of direction was first published in 1850 by the Bombay Gazette Press. The section for the Supreme Court in the 1850 edition gives the names of the two judges (with the dates of their appointment) and the six barristers (with dates of their admission) practising in the court. Three of the barristers had official positions as, respectively, the Advocate General, the Government Remembrancer for Legal Affairs and the Assessor to the Petty Sessions. Seventeen solicitors, attorneys and proctors are also listed but without dates of admission. Four solicitors are noted as holding official positions. William Brooks, for example, was Master in Equity and Examiner of the Insolvent Court. J.P. Larkins was Registrar of the Diocese, Clerk of the Insolvent Debtors' Court and Attorney for Paupers.

Before the establishment in 1801 of the Supreme Court of Madras, that presidency had a Recorder's Court. *The Madras register* for 1799 lists the civil, military, judicial and medical establishments there as well as the officials of the Recorder's Court and the 13 advocates and attorneys who then practised in Madras. The list does not distinguish the advocates from the attorneys. However, they are also listed under the heading 'European Inhabitants', where more detail is given. Robert Williams, for instance, is described as an advocate and notary in the Court of the Recorder. Subsequent directories also list lawyers who practised in the Vice-Admiralty Court of Madras, which was established in 1808. These directories, like those of Bengal and Bombay, record births, marriages and deaths. For example, the *Madras almanac* of 1855 notes the death on 13 April 1854 'at Colar, en route to the Neilgherries', of 'J. B. Jauncey, esq., aged 47 years'. He was an attorney in Madras. The *Madras almanac* of 1841 lists the advocates practising in the Supreme Court. Their names are printed 'according to seniority at the English Bar, with dates of admission to the Supreme Court' and note the university at which each barrister had been educated. There is also a list of the 16 attorneys, solicitors and notaries and a list of the 16 proctors (with their year of admission) who were then in practice in Madras. All the individuals in the first list also appear in the second.

APPENDIX I: USEFUL ADDRESSES AND WEB SITES

Access to Archives
www.nationalarchives.gov.uk/a2a

Bar Council
289-293 High Holborn, London WC1V 7HZ
www.barcouncil.org.uk

The Borthwick Institute of Historical Research
University of York, Heslington, York YO10 5DD
www.york.ac.uk/inst/bihs

Bristol Record Office
'B' Bond Warehouse, Smeaton Road, Bristol BS1 6XN

The British Library
96 Euston Road, London NW1 2DB
www.bl.uk

The British Library Newspaper Library
Colindale Avenue, London NW9 5HE
www.bl.uk

British Origins
www.britishorigins.com

Business Archives Council
3rd and 4th Floor, 101 Whitechapel High Street, London E1 7RE.

The Council for Licensed Conveyancers
16 Glebe Road, Chelmsford CM1 1QG
www.theclc.gov.uk

Family Records Centre
1 Myddleton Street, London EC1R 1UW
www.familyrecords.gov.uk

Gray's Inn
The Librarian, Gray's Inn Library, South Square, London WC1R 5EU
www.graysinn.org.uk

Guildhall Library
Aldermanbury, London EC2P 2EJ

Inner Temple
The Librarian and Keeper of Manuscripts,
Inner Temple Library, Inner Temple, London EC4Y 7DA
www.innertemple.org.uk

Lambeth Palace Library
Lambeth Palace, London SE1 7JU
www.lambethpalacelibrary.org

The Law Society
The Librarian and Head of Information Services,
The Law Society Library, 113 Chancery Lane, London WC2A 1PL
www.lawsociety.org.uk

The Law Society Regulatory Information Service
Ipsley Court, Berrington Close, Redditch, Worcestershire B98 0TD

The Law Society of Ireland
Blackhall Place, Dublin 7, Ireland
www.lawsociety.ie

Lincoln's Inn
The Librarian, Lincoln's Inn Library, London WC2A 3TN
www.lincolnsinn.org.uk

London Metropolitan Archives
40 Northampton Road, London EC1R 0HB
www.corpoflondon.gov.uk/lma

Middle Temple
The Librarian and Keeper of the Records,
Middle Temple Library, Middle Temple Lane, London EC4Y 9BT
www.middletemple.org.uk

The National Archives
Ruskin Avenue, Kew, Surrey TW9 4DU
www.nationalarchives.gov.uk

National Archives of Ireland
Bishop Street, Dublin 8
www.nationalarchives.ie

National Archives of Scotland
HM General Register House, Edinburg EH1 1EW
www.nas.gov.uk

National Library of Wales
Aberystwyth, Ceredigion, Wales SY23 3BU
www.llgc.org.uk

Public Record Office of Northern Ireland
66 Balmoral Avenue, Belfast BT9 6NY
www.proni.gov.uk

Society of Genealogists
14 Charterhouse Buildings, Goswell Road, London EC1M 7BA
Telephone: (general enquiries) 020 7251 8799 (library) 020 7702 5485
www.sog.org.uk

Society of Writers to Her Majesty's Signet
The Librarian, Signet Library, Parliament Square, Edinburgh EH1 1RF
www.signetlibrary.co.uk

ENDNOTES

1. A detailed explanation of how the dates of the law terms were calculated, and how this varied over time and from court to court, is provided by C.R. Cheney: *Handbook of dates for students of legal history* (Royal Historical Society: 1991).
2. Two volumes of the Principal's accounts (for 1757-85 and 1809-23) were advertised for sale by a bookseller in 1932 but cannot presently be traced.
3. The Public Notaries Act of 1833 extended this area of three miles to 10 miles.
4. By the Public Notaries Act of 1843, persons wishing to become notaries public outside the City of London, Westminster, the borough of Southwark, and a circuit of 10 miles from the Royal Exchange, might be admitted without serving seven years, but they could not practise within this area.
5. Ms. Additional, 6694-6698, 6708-6712 and 6699-6707 respectively.
6. These records were formerly in series CP 9.
7. The catalogue and finding-aids at TNA note these documents as commencing only at Easter 1752 but Brian Brooks found the documents to commence in 1750 when he reviewed them in 1997.
8. These records were formerly in series KB 112.
9. These records were formerly held in series J 9.
10. These records were formerly held in series KB 104 and J 8.
11. The catalogue at TNA states that this series includes one eighteenth-century oath roll for attorneys.
12. A copy of the rolls up to 1858 is also held in the Law Society library on microfilm and CD-ROM.
13. Included in *The manuscripts of the House of Lords, new series vol III* (HMSO, 1965).
14. The Court of Augmentations is not dealt with in this book but it was established by Henry VIII, to administer and sell land taken from the monasteries upon their dissolution, and dissolved in 1554.
15. These records were formerly in series J 10.
16. It could also hear equity cases but most Welsh litigants preferred to use the courts of Chancery and Exchequer at Westminster.
17. Bebb was also noted as 'Registrar of Supreme Court, Sydney, New S. Wales' (amended in the *Law list 1835* to read 'Solicitor to the Registrar of Supreme Court, Sydney'). This is a curious combination.

INDEX

This index is divided into three parts: a general Subject Index, a Sources and Records Index and a Nominal Index. These were all compiled by Nicholas Newington-Irving.

SUBJECT INDEX

Entries marked ** show only the principal entries as there are references on almost every other page.

SOURCES AND RECORDS INDEX

Entries marked ** show only the principal entries as there are references on almost every other page.

NOMINAL INDEX

BANCROFT William   127

BAND Edgar   71

BARBER G.   15

BARBER Melanie   viii

BARDWELL Everett   71

BARKER G. F. R.   72

BARKER Robert   114

BARLOW John   127

BARLOW Samuel Joseph   66

BARLOW Thomas   127

BARLOW William   74

BARLOW William Wycliffe   74

BARNARD Charles   28

BARNARD Christopher   27

BARNEBY Richard   87

BARNES Thomas   27

BARNHAM James   27

BARON Robert   20

BARRETT Peter   45

BARROW G. B.   150

BARROW Michael   133

BARROW O. T.   174

BARRY John   27

BARSTOW Thomas   27

BARTHOLOMEW William   56

BASTIDE Harry   66

BATTIE John   25-26

BATTY H.   174

BATTY John   41

BATTY William   27, 64

BAWDEN Hugh   27

BAXTER I. A.   173

BAXTER Robert   127

BAYLEY (Mr Justice)   130

BAYNES Walter Francis   151

BAYNES (Family)   151

BEAKWITH, DYE & KITTON   71

BEALE John   11

BEALE Richard   11

BEAN Henry   27

BEAN William   27

BEARD Philip Leo (Lieutenant)   21

BEARDER Harold Ingham   66

BEATNIFFE Richard   27

BEAUCLERK John   65

BEAW William (Bishop of Llandaff)   42

BEAW William, junior   42

BEBB Joseph   170-171

BECK John   27

BECKETT Richard   131

BEDDINGHAM P. C.   12

BEDINGFIELD Thomas   138

BELL H. E.   122

BELLOT H. H. L.   17, 34

BENJAMIN Robert Westfield   120

BENNET Mary   131

BENNETT Alexander   116

BENNETT John (Sir)   74

BENNETT (Master)   27

BENNETT: see LEWIS & BENNETT

BENSON Cornelius   149

BENTLEY Frank   66

BERESFORD Edward   27

BEYNON John Fowler   71

BHANDARA Nasarvanji Framji   174

BIGNOLD & FIELD   71

BINDON Henry H. Massy   174

BIRCH John   155

BIRD George Adam   104

BIRD William Frederick Wratislaw   104-105

BIRKETT John   96

BIRKS M.   24, 79

BLACKENBURY Car.   27

BLACKHURST Henry   130

BLAGDEN Thomas   145

BLAKE Francis John   71

BLAKE, KEITH & BLAKE   71

BLAND D. S.   35

BLAND Thomas   149

BLAZEBY James, junior   71

BLENCOWE Henry   20

BLENCOWE John   20

BLENNERHASSETT William   27

BUTLER Edmund	11	CASSON Richard	81
BUTLER Peirce	11	CATCHMAYD William	90
BUTLER Robert	27	CATTERALL Peter	130
BUTLER Thomas	27	CAY Bolt Henry	116
BUTLER Thomas (Sir)	11	CHAD Thomas	81
BUTTERWORTH, legal printers	60	CHADWICK George James	81
BUXTON John	36	CHALMER William	168
BUXTON Jos.	27	CHAMBER John	81
CADLE William	98	CHAMPANTE Robert	135
CAESAR Julius (Sir)	121	CHAMPION William	138
CAISTER John	81	CHANCE: see CLIFFORD CHANCE	
CALCUTT James	26	CHANDLER Samuel Whitty	47
CALDECOTT William	81	CHAPLIN Acton	55
CALLAND Charles	96	CHAPMAN Colin	141
CALTHORPE Henry	122	CHAPMAN & HANSELL	71
CALVERT George	81	CHARLTON Edward	149
CAMA Jamsetjee Cursetjee	174	CHARNOCKE George	14
CAMA Navroji Pestanji	174	CHARNOCKE John	17
CAMERON Duguid & Co	148	CHARNOCKE Pynsent	17
CAMERON John	147-148	CHARNOCKE Roger	14
CAMERON: see THORNELY &		CHARNOCKE Villiers (Sir)	17
CAMERON		CHEESWRIGHT (Mr)	50
CAMPBELL J.	7	CHEESWRIGHTS	51
CAMPION Ellen Wilton	68	CHEESWRIGHT: see GILSON &	
CAMPION Harold Gilmour	68	CHEESWRIGHT	
CAMPION Hubert Wilton	68	CHESLYN John	171
CAMPION Hubert (Admiral)	68	CHEYNE James	168
CAMPION Ivon Hamilton	68	CHIDLAW John	162
CAMPION Marjorie	68	CHILTON James	62, 120
CAMPLIN Charles	70	CHITTY Charles W.	174
CANDY (Mr)	146	CHOMLEY Henry (Sir)	20
CARDINALL Edward	20	CHOMLEY John	20
CARELL (Mr)	121	CHROPER John	81
CARNAC Louis W. G. Rivett-	174	CHURCHILL Else	ix
CARNEGY Wilkes Hawley	87	CHYDLEY Robert	121
CARPENTER William John	170-171	CLAGETT Horatio	155
CARR C.	36	CLARKE Thomas Ambrose	120
CARRICK John	95	CLARKE, legal printers	59
CARRINGTON Caleb (Rev)	10	CLARKE, RICHARDS & MEDCALF	
CARRINGTON Frederick Augustus	10		170
CARTER William Adair	170	CLARKE: see MITCHELL & CLARKE	
CARTER (Mr Baron)	115	CLARKE: see W. CLARKE & Sons	

GOOCH Samuel	71	HALL Edward Marshall (Sir)	150
GOODMAN Fred Touch	66	HALL John	36
GOODMAN Harold Temple	66	HALL John Cressy (Colonel)	146
GOODMAN: see HOMFRAY,		HALL J. R.	66
GOODMAN & MELLOR		HALL Nick Vine	150
GOODRICH Richard	122	HALL Robert	51
GOODRIGE Robert	20	HAMILTON William	96
GOODWIN Jas. & Son	71	HAMILTOUN John	168
GORE, printers	72	HAMPSON G. K.	51
GOULTY William Howard	66	HAMPSON Thomas	20
GRAHAM F. A.	66	HANCE William Lawrence	154
GRAHAM John	95-96	HANDLEY William	91
GRAM Andrew	51, 60	HANHAM John Castleman Swinburne-	
GRAND John	71		147
GRANT F.	167	HANMER Walden Henry	109
GRAVES William	62-63	HANSELL: see CHAPMAN & HANSELL	
GRAY Charles	158	HARBORNE Simon	79
GREEN George	66	HARBY: see HELLIWELL, HARBY & Co	
GREGG William	87	HARDCASTLE (Mr)	158
GREGOR Francis	12	HARDING John	114
GREGORY William	4	HARDING Samuel Suffley	91
GRENHAM J.	163	HARDMAN Edmund	91
GREY William	63	HARDMAN: see SWANN, HARDMAN	
GRICE Nicholas	11	& Co	
GRICE Thomas (Rev)	11	HARDSTAFF R.	151
GRIFFITH George	87	HARDY B. Cozens-	155
GROVE Ernest Harry	66	HARDY Sydney Cozens	148
GRYLLS George William Frederick	120	HARDY Tickner George	63
GULSTON Nathaniel	20	HARE John	122
GURNEY (Mr Baron)	146	HARE & Co	66
GUY J. A.	121	HARGEAVES Thomas, junior	91
GUZDAR J. Jovanjee	174	HARLE Thomas	120
GWINNETT William	90	HARRIS Humphrey	11
GWYN Morgan	38	HARRIS Thomas (Sir)	11
GWYNN William Horatio	71	HARRISON John	171
GWYTHER see: WAKEFORD, MAY,		HARRISON W. E.	48
WOULFE & GWYTHER		HARROD Henry	71
HAGGARD John	43	HART John	42, 82
HAGUE Elisha de	156	HART Sarah	42
HAGUE Elisha de, junior	156	HART Thomas	157
HALES John	20	HART William Henry	62
HALIDAY James	171	HARTLEY William Francis	125

WALKER James	63	WATTS John	63
WALKER S. P.	167	WATTS William	63
WALKER William	63	WEBB Thomas	79
WALL Hawkins	63	WEBB William of the Borough	63
WALL William of Red Lion Square	63	WEBB William of the King's Bench	63
WALL William of West Smithfield	63	WEBBER Robert	149
WALLINGTON Algernon	149	WEBSTER Henry	176
WALLIS Albany	63	WEBSTER John	131
WALLIS John	63	WEBSTER Thomas	63, 107
WALLS: see LEE & WALLS		WEDD Robert	63
WALSH Francis Eldridge	47	WEGENCE Samuel	63
WALSH John Robinson	47	WELDON: see GIBSON & WELDON	
WALTER Edward	63	WESTON George Augustus	66
WALTER Robert	63	WESTON Thomas	126
WALTHAM Francis	11	WHADCOAT John Henry	14
WALTHAM Richard	11	WHADCOAT William Henry	14
WALTON John	63	WHALLEY Charles	175
WALTON Robert	63	WHARTON Humphrey	20
WALTON William	63	WHARTON Thomas	20
WALTONS & Co	68	WHINCOP Robert	56
WARCUP George	123	WHISHAW J.	68
WARD Edward	63	WHITE Arnold	73
WARD Henry	63	WHITE George	57
WARD Joseph	63	WHITE G. S.	158
WARD Towaly	63	WHITE Henry Arthur (Sir)	73
WARDELL Christopher	63	WHITE H. A.	73
WARD: see TOWNLY WARD		WHITE William	70
WARE George	63	WHITEFIELD Charles	100
WARE Titus Hibbert	117	WHITEHEAD John	79
WARMINGTON G. S.	66	WHITMORE J. B.	150
WARMINGTON & EDMONDS	66	WHITTINGHAM J. H.	148
WARRY John	63	WICKENS George	103
WARRY Richard	63	WICKSTEAD John	126
WATERFIELD David	63	WIGHTMAN (Mr)	146
WATERHOUSE & Co	148	WIGLESWORTH & Co	146
WATERLOW, legal printers	60	WILBRAHAM R.	126
WATKINS L. A.	174	WILBRAHAM Thomas	122
WATKINSON William	63	WILDMAN Thomas	100
WATLINGTON George	54	WILKINSON (Captain)	146
WATSON John	63	WILLCOCKS: see BRIDGMAN,	
WATSON Thomas	63	WILLCOCKS & Co	
WATSON William	63	WILLETT William John	103

WILLIAMS E.	39	WOULFE & GWYTHER	
WILLIAMS Griffith	128	WRATISLAW Mar Eugene Townsend	75
WILLIAMS Ivy	5	WREATHCOCK William	31
WILLIAMS John (Sir)	93	WRIGHT Elizabeth	17
WILLIAMS J. R.	160	WRIGHT John	107
WILLIAMS Robert	177	WRIGHT Robert (Sir)	17
WILLIAMS W. R.	160	WRIGHT William	154
WILLIAMS (Mr Attorney General)	146	WRIGHT: see TATHAM v. WRIGHT	
WILLIAMSON John	124	WYCHE Thomas	162
WILLIAMSON J. B.	15, 17	WYCHE (Mr)	158-159
WILLIAMSON, HILL & Co	66	WYNDHAM Hugh	138
WILMOT E. G. Eardley-	148	W. CLARKE & Sons	59
WILMOT & Co	158	YATES James	66
WILSON John	131	YATES (Mr Justice)	32
WILSON Joseph	146	ZOUCHE Francis	42
WILSON William	111	ZOUCHE Richard	42
WILSON & PEELE	60	ZOUCHE Sarah	42
WINDEY Henry George	153-154		
WINDEY Nathan	154		
WINTHROP John	122		
WITHERS John	50		

WITHERS: see COVERDALE, LEE,
    COLLYER-BRISTOW & WITHERS

WITTY Richard Henry	103
WOLSEY Thomas	121
WOOD & WOOTTON	75
WOODHOUSE James Thomas	104
WOODS H. G.	15
WOOLNOUGH Henry	157
WOOTTON Frank Stanley	75

WOOTTON: see WOOD & WOOTTON

WORDEN Alan Fletcher	75
WORDEN Allen Fletcher	76
WORDEN Leonard	75
WORDEN & WORDEN	75-76
WORDSWORTH Thomas Howard	75
WORSFOLD T. C.	39
WORSLEY John Fortescue	75-76
WORTHINGTON Frederick	75
WORTHINGTON Walter	75
WOULFE Gerald Lascelles	75

WOULFE see: WAKEFORD, MAY,